The Rowman & Littlefield Guide for Peer Tutors

Theory & Practice for Peer Tutors and Learning Center Professionals

Series Advisers: Daniel R. Sanford, Bates College,
Michelle Steiner, Marymount University

The series *Theory & Practice for Peer Tutors and Learning Center Professionals* serves the international scholarly and professional communities associated with peer tutoring in higher education. With contributions that address the multiple audiences of learning center professionals, scholars of peer-led learning, and peer educators, the series aims to advance the scholarship and practice of peer-led learning by enriching it with contributions from the broader scholarship of teaching and learning, and by building connections across the many areas of praxis that share the uniquely effective and impactful pedagogy of peer tutoring.

Titles in Series:
The Rowman & Littlefield Guide for Peer Tutors by Daniel R. Sanford

The Rowman & Littlefield Guide for Peer Tutors

Daniel R. Sanford

ROWMAN & LITTLEFIELD
Lanham • Boulder • New York • London

Published by Rowman & Littlefield
An imprint of The Rowman & Littlefield Publishing Group, Inc.
4501 Forbes Boulevard, Suite 200, Lanham, Maryland 20706
www.rowman.com

6 Tinworth Street, London SE11 5AL, United Kingdom

British Library Cataloguing in Publication Information Available

Library of Congress Control Number:2019957514
ISBN 978-1-5381-3551-8 (cloth)
ISBN 978-1-5381-3552-5 (pbk.)
ISBN 978-1-5381-3553-2 (electronic)

To all the tutors.

Contents

Foreword for Learning Center Directors

Learning Center Administration is a field full of people who started out to do something else, and made the happy discovery of learning centers along the way. We were seduced from other career paths, thrown into oversight of new tutoring programs, redirected from other areas of academic support. It's one of the joys of working in the field that learning center professionals represent such an incredibly diverse set of backgrounds, and it's reliably the start of a good story to ask a learning center director how they became a learning center director.

Like just about all of us, I entered the field from other areas. I supervised a writing center before becoming a learning center person more broadly, and I quickly discovered that whereas there are a large number of high-quality introductory texts for writing center tutors and directors, there were no corresponding texts for learning centers (a discovery that planted the seed for this text). I was also surprised, having received my academic training in the area of cognitive linguistics, to see a lot of ideas that no longer hold sway in the cognitive sciences (e.g., the concept of hemisphere dominance or of learning styles) still prevalent in tutor training programs. I found myself in deep agreement with the core pedagogy of learning centers, but unable to deliver these pedagogies to tutors in a way that felt authentic, intellectually rigorous, and in accord with the basic understanding of the mind's architecture for learning that has emerged from brain research. This book reflects the progress that I've made, in conversation with all of the tutors I've supervised, to bring those two fields of knowledge into accord with one another. In writing this book, my goal was to provide a text that can serve as the backbone of a peer tutoring course or training program, across learning centers, writing centers, Supplemental Instruction programs, departmental tutoring programs, language learning centers, mathematics and quantitative literacy centers, TRIO programs, and other programs that use a peer tutoring model. The text is rooted in the active, collaborative pedagogy of peer tutoring that forms the core consensus that all of us in the field operate around. But it approaches these principles in some new ways, grounding them firmly in contemporary cognitive theory and exploring practical implications of this approach for tutors.

PEER TUTORING AND THE BRAIN

The work that we do as educators is fundamentally rooted in the brain, and to do it well requires attentiveness to how the brain works. It is much to our benefit, then, that we are living in the midst of an unbelievable explosion in our understanding of human cognition. Measured against the scope of human history, this explosion has unfolded in only the last blink of an eye. It was only within the last few hundred years that the discussion of human knowledge and thought came to be centered on the brain (indeed, the idea that the brain is where thought takes place is itself a relatively new idea: Aristotle, for example, placed the seat of human intelligence in the heart, positing the brain as a cooling system for it). In the 1800s, people began to understand the role of electrical impulses in the brain and nervous system, and to associate areas of the brain with specific functions. Inexorably and irrevocably, the pace of discovery has snowballed since then, barraged by new sources of empirical data. From the 1960s to the present, as the cognitive sciences have fully come into their own as fields of study, the pace of discovery has been breathless. On the one hand, it's incredible to bear witness to such an unbelievable scale of scientific discovery taking place within such an incredibly short amount of time, and to see in real time humanity's understanding of ourselves as thinking beings expand exponentially. As educators, it's incredible to have available such detailed knowledge of what it is to think.

On the other hand, the incredible pace of all this discovery has not made things easy for those of us who teach. Models of how humans think and learn have thoroughly upended themselves from decade to decade in a way that has often left educators working with theoretical approaches that are no longer accepted by psychologists and neuroscientists. The constant stream of new insights into cognition that emerge in the scholarship—many of which have not yet been incorporated within a coherent model of the mind—can leave people who wish to *do* things with all of this insight struggling to find practical information. However, there are some coherent principles that have emerged in the last several decades that have remained, even as our understanding of the brain has shifted, relatively stable, and which moreover have grown and evolved to encompass our emerging understanding of the mind. These same principles are, fortunately for our purposes, incredibly helpful ones for engaging learners in a way that takes into account the situatedness of learning in the brain.

THE ORGANIZATION OF THIS
BOOK AND HOW TO USE IT

The focus of this book is how the brain works, and how that plays out in tutoring. The core strategy of this text is to first lay out a framework, based on the physical, brain-based reality of learning, for driving the choices that tutors will make in working with learners. These principles are explored in the first few chapters. In subsequent chapters, tutors are guided in thinking through the practical implications of these concepts for working with students. As the text moves into others aspects of peer tutoring (e.g., learning strategies, engaging diversity, critical thinking, online tutoring), the basic concepts established in the first few chapters continue to provide the grounding for more advanced explorations of tutoring pedagogy. It is not the intent of this text to give tutors a set of rules or guidelines for tutoring, but rather to provide them with a grounding in research, theory, and empirical findings that will allow them to be highly intentional in their work with students. At the end of each chapter, "Questions to Drive the Session" highlights for tutors how the principles covered in that chapter apply to the actual work that they will do in engaging with learners.

The first four chapters together comprise a solid pre-semester training for peer tutors. Once tutors have read and engaged with these chapters, and been oriented to the specifics of your program, they should be ready to begin working with students. For subsequent chapters, it's helpful for tutors to have prior experience working with students to draw on. These chapters, particularly chapters 5–9, are ideally suited for in-semester trainings. Chapter 10, while appropriate and relevant reading for any tutor, is especially pertinent to tutors who have accrued an appreciable level of experience working with students, and who are interested in opportunities for further development. For those centers offering (or seeking to offer) tutor training certified through the College Reading & Learning Association's International Tutor Training Program Certification, CRLA training topics have been identified in the index in bold face.

To build out robust cognitive models for interactive ways of facilitating learning, students need to see these approaches in action. If we want our tutors to view learning as an active, collaborative process, then that's an approach that we need to be modeling in training. To put a finer point on it: tutors are smart, and they smell hypocrisy a mile away. If we're telling them to listen more than they talk, to treat knowledge as constructed rather than received, to view learning as a social process, and to present themselves to students as co-learners rather than experts, then we need to practice what we preach. With this is mind, at the end of each section of the book are a set of questions and exercises ("Ways to Engage") that are provided to give tutors the means to actively and collaboratively engage with the content of the chapter. These sections provide activities that can be used in tutor trainings, courses, and meetings. "Questions for Discussion" encourage tutors to reflect on, and inquire further into, what they learned. "Activities" provide ways for tutors to practice and apply the principles discussed in the reading. "Questions for Reflection" encourage an ongoing habit of relating theory to practice. They are suggested prompts for tutors who are creating a journal, portfolio, or other piece of writing that documents and reflects their growth as peer educators. Generally, these sections offer more discussion questions and activities than could reasonably be handled in a one-hour training. The intent is for facilitators to choose among them according to their timeframe and needs, and to have sufficient materials to return to the same topic multiple times with new activities as tutors return for successive terms and become more experienced in their work.

A NOTE TO WRITING CENTER DIRECTORS

Writing centers and learning centers have different (if related) histories, and it can be the case that we run in different circles despite the fact that the work we do is very similar. Please be assured: this book is for you, too. The line between writing tutoring and content tutoring is far blurrier than it is often presented. Frequently, content tutoring is mediated through writing tutoring, with tutors engaging with students' incomplete understanding of prerequisite concepts while engaging with their writing (many areas of the humanities and social sciences, such as philosophy, history, and sociology, aren't generally even supported in learning centers, precisely because content learning in these disciplines is nearly always developed, demonstrated, and assessed through writing). Many real-world tutoring sessions fall in a gray area between writing and content, rather than exemplifying one extreme or the other. Is a session in which a peer tutor meets with a student to help clarify the student's understanding of core concepts in an academic discipline acting as a writing tutor, or a content tutor? What if the discipline is biology? What if it's gender studies? What if it's for a research paper? What if it's for an essay exam? What if the student is working on a paper in a foreign language course? The answers to these questions inevitably have more to do with the solutions that individual institutions have arrived at for dividing the work of ensuring every student receives support, and with intensely local histories

of how academic support emerged on campus, than with any actual difference in the work that tutors do. Moreover, writing is itself a powerful way
to facilitate learning. The two areas can't possibly be understood as separate
from one another, despite the fact that they often occur in different places
on campus. While writing and content appointments can and do play out in
different ways, they are better understood as ends of a continuum, with any
one particular session falling at some intermediate point, than as exclusive
categories. The approach that this book takes applies to tutors working at
any point on that continuum. Writing tutors will find the concepts, strategies,
and examples offered in this text relevant to the work that they do. They will
also, after completing this book, be extremely well prepared for sessions that
approach the more content-oriented end of the continuum, engaging learners
over their understanding of ideas and concepts.

ON TUTOR TRAINING

When we hire and train peer tutors, we don't just staff our programs, we
make a commitment to the professional development of the students who
do the work that a learning center does. That's a responsibility that must be
taken incredibly seriously. We can do so by providing students who have
self-elected to the role of helping their peers excel with a venue to learn about
research-based principles that can guide their work, practice new approaches
before they try them with students, and reflect on the work that they do as
educators.

   We also, in hiring and training tutors, take a lot of very smart students and
put them in a room together. Rising to the occasion requires trainings to be
intellectually engaging. They should challenge preconceptions, intrigue the
curious mind, and invite students deeper in to the scholarship of teaching and
learning. I hope that this text provides some helpful tools and guidance for
you, as you strive to create trainings that do so.

Acknowledgments

The concepts that are presented in this book are the result of years of hashing out ideas and workshopping trainings with tutors. I'd like to extend my sincere thanks to every peer tutor I've had the pleasure of working with over the years at the University of New Mexico and at Bates College, each of whom has in some way affected this book and the ideas in it. Thank you to all of my coworkers at the Academic Resource Commons at Bates College, who besides being amazing friends and colleagues, have been invaluable in providing feedback on this book and the ideas in it. In particular, I'd like to voice my appreciation for Dr. Stephanie Wade, whose passion for reflective writing as a tool for learning can be found as an influence throughout these pages. Thank you to my editor Mark Kerr at Rowman & Littlefield, for being so very supportive of the vision for this book (and of the series of books of which this is the first). Thank you to the incredibly supportive, welcoming community of academic support professionals who make this such a great field to work in. And above all, thank you to my wonderful family: to my kids who have been so incredibly tolerant of dad being tired and crabby after staying up late writing, and to my friend and partner Celeste, without whom none of this would have been possible.

Chapter 1

Introduction to Peer Tutoring

Welcome to Peer Tutoring! It's reliably challenging. It's often frustrating. It's indescribably rewarding. It offers endless opportunities for growth, as a scholar, as an educator, and as a person. It will force you to look at the things you've learned as a student in new ways and to reevaluate what it is to have knowledge. Your time doing it will change not only the way that you think about concepts in your field but also what it is to learn and what it is to educate. Peer tutors provide learners with the support that they need to succeed independently in the work that they do as students. The goal of this text is to provide the same support for you in your growth as an educator, giving you the support that you need to succeed in your work as a peer tutor.

Know that learning center theory is a field of learning unto itself. The scholarship of learning centers has its roots in several fields (e.g., education, psychology, composition, and others), together comprising a family of ideas, theories, and research-based principles that form a constantly evolving, but generally coherent body of knowledge that motivates the work that we do with learners. As with any domain of inquiry, it contains within itself varying (and often competing) schools of thought: at academic conferences, in books, and in scholarly journals, researchers debate the role of learning centers within institutions, question long-held assumptions, and bring new ideas to the field. Learning center theory is a field that can provide structure and tools for your work with students. At the same time, there is space for you to bring your own unique strengths and personal style to your identity as a peer tutor.

Learning centers are also places where many different fields intersect. Each of the fields of study that exist in the academy has its own way of knowing and its own way of constructing knowledge. Mathematicians come to knowledge through the application of formal rules, while natural scientists come to knowledge through a cycle of observing, theorizing, hypothesizing, and experimentation. Literary scholars approach theories as lenses for understanding authorial intent and the collective literature of a group of people; social scientists determine the value of a theory based on how well it accounts for empirical facts. The historian studies the past through critical inquiry of the written records of human societies, while the archaeologist studies the past through careful analysis of its material remains. Philosophers come to knowledge through logic, and also use logic to inquire into the nature of knowledge. Artists ask us to question what we know, and our very stances toward knowledge, with work that challenges our preconceptions about ourselves and the world around us. Different academic fields don't just study different things; they have their own way of approaching the world and the very enterprise of studying something. Each employs tools for inquiry that are unique to the field, and also traditions that have been cultivated within that field for passing along knowledge to new generations of scholars. As a peer tutor, you're a practitioner, but you're also a student yourself. You bring with you, to your work in the center, your grounding in another field (or fields) of study, and your familiarity with the tools and pedagogies of that field. You may be a student of anthropology, bringing a familiarity with the use of ethnography, giving you particular insight into how the learning center operates as a cultural space. You may be an emerging engineer, accustomed to learning through problem-solving. You may be a creative writer, with insight into the methodology of peer critique that artists use to develop an understanding of how work is received by an audience, or a student of the medical field, versed in job shadowing as a way of passing along situational expertise. Whatever you study, and whatever you're a tutor of, you not only have the knowledge of the skills and content of that field that made you a good candidate to be a tutor, you also have, as a student of that field, a unique lens on the work of peer tutoring. I encourage you, as you read this book and as you gain experience working with students, to think about the unique perspective that you have to offer on peer-led learning and on learning centers, based on your academic background. What connections can you draw between the concepts in this text and the concepts that you're learning about in your classes? Where do you see opportunities for the field of learning center studies to be enriched by a concept from your field, applied in a new way? I also encourage you to learn as much as possible from your fellow tutors. One of the many joys of learning centers is that it brings people together from many different fields, putting these various ways of knowing in conversation with one another. Through ongoing dialogue about our work, we all have the opportunity to continually improve our practice with new ideas and perspectives from across the academy.

Know that peer tutoring works. It's an incredibly effective model for increasing student success. Students who participate in peer tutoring are likelier to persist and excel in college. They do better in their courses, receiving higher scores than their peers. They are likelier to remain in college past the critical first year and ultimately to graduate. Through peer tutoring, students develop self-direction and self-awareness. They experience a greater sense of belonging and academic confidence and a greater feeling of control and ownership over their own education. These outcomes are real, and they make a real difference in people's lives. In a world in which the outcomes of a college education are integral to professional and academic success, and in which a college degree is an important determiner of social mobility, the work that you'll do as a tutor *matters*.

Know that peer tutoring will also help *you*. As a tutor, you'll engage deeply with the curriculum, applying knowledge in different venues, making connections between your identity as a student and your identity as a professional, and assuming a leadership role in your institution. There is a strong academic benefit to tutoring. Peer tutors are constantly refreshing their understanding of the material that they tutor, deepening and enriching their knowledge of concepts as they return to them in the role of educator. Tutors draw connections between the introductory concepts that they tutor and the more advanced ideas that they are studying in their own courses, developing robust, well-articulated knowledge structures and deep awareness of tools and resources for success that serve them well as they advance in their studies. Peer tutors don't only, by their experience as tutors, improve their grades; they also increase their intercultural awareness, interpersonal relationships, and connections to faculty mentors.

A SAMPLE OF RESEARCH FINDINGS ON THE BENEFITS OF PEER TUTORING

For Students Receiving Tutoring

- In a study that analyzed factors affecting student success in a community college setting, **Kostecki & Bers (2008)** found that students who utilize peer tutoring enjoy higher grades for the course in which they receive tutoring, higher overall GPA, and higher likelihood to persist in college from the fall to spring semesters. The authors found that this effect held even when other predictors of academic success (such as high school GPA and college entrance exam scores) were taken into account.
- **Cooper (2010)** found that students utilizing drop-in tutoring during their first year of college were more likely than their peers to persist to the second year. Students utilizing drop-in tutoring ten times or more per term had a significantly higher GPA than their peers, controlling for other factors in predicting academic success.

- In a study of economically and educationally disadvantaged students at a large public university, **Reinheimer et al. (2010)** found that peer tutoring had a significant, positive effect on performance, retention, and graduation.
- **Grillo & Leist (2014)** found, in a study utilizing six years of data from a large public university, that the cumulative number of hours that students spend accessing peer tutoring during their undergraduate careers correlates positively and significantly with both GPA and likelihood to graduate.
- In a study of students in an introductory mathematics courses at a large public university, **Xu et al. (2014)** found that utilization of peer tutoring correlates with higher final exam scores, even when other factors for academic success are taken into account.
- In an experimental study of civil engineering, chemical engineering, economics, and pharmacy students, **Arco-Tirado, Fernández-Martín, & Fernández-Balboa (2011)** found that students who participated in ten 90-minute tutoring sessions over the course of a single academic term demonstrated significantly more acquisition of beneficial learning strategies and metacognitive skills than those who did not.

For Students Who Serve as Peer Tutors

- **Beasley (1997)** found that students who participated in a robust tutor training program and served for two semesters as peer tutors reported improved subject matter knowledge and communications skills.
- **Jones and Kolko (2002)** found that serving as a mentor in peer-led learning relationships has a beneficial effect on students, leading to greater leadership skills, academic improvement, and significant development of value systems.
- Based on a survey of fifty-five institutions of higher education in the UK, **Keenan (2014)** reported that students serving as peer tutors gain "a range of personal and professional skills, deeper subject learning, increased inter-cultural awareness and enhanced employability skills" (p. 8).
- **Colvin (2007)** found that students serving as peer tutors gain experience and skill at navigating social dynamics, become more adept at impression management and overcoming interpersonal conflict to accomplish learning outcomes.
- **Arco-Tirado, Fernández-Martín, & Hervás Torres (2011)** found that peer tutoring positively affected the cognitive strategies and social skills of tutors. They also found that tutors enjoyed greater confidence in communication and presentation, and more effective curriculum vitaes and job interviews.

These benefits are as important for career development as they are for academics. Peer tutoring is phenomenal preparation for any role as an educator, whether that be as a TA, professor, or K-12 teacher. Tutors develop experience breaking concepts down in ways that make them easier to apprehend, and fluency with tools for making learning active and collaborative that carry over well to the classroom. They develop ways of relating challenging concepts, and an intuitive ability to see where the pitfalls are in the material. As a teacher, it's easy to lecture to the nodding heads in the front row, taking their feedback as encouragement that one is doing a good job. As a former tutor, it's impossible to do this: you think reflexively of the student who isn't following along, and are able to respond to their concerns based on long experience engaging learners individually and in small groups. These skills and others that you'll develop and practice as a tutor—leadership, interpersonal communication, presentations, group facilitation—go well beyond education, providing useful experience for any number of careers. As a tutor, you're gaining directly relevant professional experience in your field, an incredibly valuable thing for a recent graduate to have on their resume (and something which you'll want to be sure to highlight in all of your future applications for employment).

Know that peer tutoring is a commitment. As a peer tutor, you're both a student and an educator. These two roles reinforce and enrich one another, in many ways. Through your work as a tutor, you'll develop a deeper, more complex understanding of the core concepts in your field, and you'll also accrue a wealth of experience that will help you to bridge your identity as a student to your identity as a professional. There are other situations in which these roles can come into tension with one another. The times when the center is busy and students are stressed tend to be the very times that you, in your own life as a student, may be feeling stretched thin. It can be a challenge, when this is the case, to find the reserves of compassion and patience within yourself to bring your best self to your work with students. On the other hand, the work of doing so is perhaps the most valuable opportunity for growth that you have access to through peer tutoring.

Know, finally, that tutoring is a personal challenge. Engaging in tutoring interactions in the way that will ultimately be of the most benefit to learners isn't generally the same as the approach that may feel the most intuitive or comfortable. Doing it well requires personal growth. This growth will require you to set aside your preconceptions about how to educate, and your attachment to your own expertise. It will place new demands on you as a listener and as an empathetic individual. It will require that you develop new skills for engaging with learners, having difficult conversations, managing groups, simplifying ideas, asking productive questions, and many other things. All of the skills that you'll gain as a tutor will help you in life beyond the academy, whatever you do. In facing these challenges, you're not alone. In your growth as a tutor, you have the support of your fellow tutors, the professional staff who oversee your program, and a highly supportive national community of learning center scholars and professionals.

1.1 WHAT IS PEER TUTORING?

It's helpful, to avoid confusion right off the bat, to distinguish *peer tutoring* from *tutoring*. Tutoring can mean many different things, but generally a tutor is someone privately hired to teach in a venue outside of schools and classroom, usually individually or for a small group of students. Often, a tutor is hired with a very specific goal: to help a student to pass a class, prepare for a standardized test, or maintain a certain GPA. Private tutors generally have a more advanced level of education than the students they are working with, and are very frequently adults working with children. Tutors may be advanced learners, even experts, in their fields, with many even holding doctorates or other terminal degrees. The major qualifying criterion of a tutor is their knowledge of the subject area.

Peer tutoring is something else. In peer tutoring, students act as academic guides to other students. The "peer" in peer tutor refers to the fact that peer tutors are at a similar level of educational achievement as the students who they are working with. Peer tutors are generally a little bit further along in their studies than the students being tutored, but it's a key part of the model that they're participating in the same curriculum (e.g., courses for the biology major at the same university). Peer tutors were recently at the same point in the learning process that the students receiving tutoring are currently, and because of this they are able to act as mentors, providing insight based on their own hard-won experience on how to succeed and excel in a course. Peer tutors may well be excellent students, but the most important qualification to be a peer tutor isn't one's grades or mastery of the material. It is rather one's ability to empathize with learners, communicate well, ask questions that help students arrive at answers themselves, and offer support for students in their own path toward mastery.

From the perspective of a student being tutored, the most important thing that a peer tutor provides is not answers, or instruction, but mentorship. Tutors are role models. The tutor is the kind of student that the student can reasonably aspire to be, with some hard work and attention to their own habits as a student. Excellent peer tutors are relatable, so that students using tutoring can see aspects of themselves and their own journey in their tutors. They are open about their struggles as students, so that learners are able to internalize that it's okay to struggle. They model the strategies that they've applied to ultimately overcome these struggles, and to be successful students.

Peer tutors are not experts. Every student, at every college and university, has more than enough access to PhDs talking at them. Peer tutors provide something different. Imagine the journey toward a degree, or toward acquisition of a concept, as a climb up a steep mountain. You, as the peer tutor, aren't the sage at the top of the mountain who lives in the clouds, breathing the rarified air of mastery. You're the climber just up the trail. You were just there, in the location that the student is now, and are able to offer advice based on your recent experience: Mind that rock! Careful where the trail splits! Watch for that loose handhold! You provide a hand up, using your experience to help your fellow climber get to where you are.

WHAT IF I DON'T KNOW THE ANSWER?

For many new tutors, this question is a point of anxiety: What if a student who I'm working with asks me a question, and I don't know the answer? Will it undermine my credibility as a tutor if I'm revealed as someone who doesn't know a concept in my field—whether it is an aspect of MLA citation, the steps of cell division, the process for calculating molarity, the formula for binomial expansion, the difference between opportunity cost and differential cost, the Italian future subjunctive, or anything else of relevance to the session?

Questions from students are a defining aspect of the dynamic of tutoring sessions. Many sessions will begin with a driving question, and the path of most sessions will be defined by the successive questions that students pose as they think concepts and problems through. Generally, when a student asks you a question about how to solve a problem, the least productive thing you can do is to answer it. When a student asks you how to solve a problem, or what the answer is, or how to do something, and you tell them, it reinforces your status as an expert. Our goal, however, is not to empower ourselves, but to empower learners. We want the students who we work with to see themselves not as passive recipients of knowledge, but as having agency in their own process for learning.

This is all to say: if you don't know the answer to a question, that's fantastic, because you won't have to wrestle with the temptation to answer it. What can you do instead? You could make the student aware of resources they have at their disposal, by guiding them toward a helpful online guide, or by showing them how to use the index in their textbook and waiting as they look up a definition for themselves. You could ask the student to pull out their notebook, encouraging them to return back to their notes after lectures as they are solving problems. You could gather several students working on the same problem together, fostering collaborative learning by asking them to put their heads together and try to arrive at an answer together. All of these strategies will serve to lessen, rather than increase, their dependence on you: an important outcome for every session.

Perhaps the absolute best thing you can do when you don't know the answer to a question? Ask a fellow tutor. When the students who you work with see you asking another tutor on your team for help, it relieves any stress that they may be feeling over a potential stigma associated with seeking out assistance, and it models for them that successful learners are successful precisely because they work in groups and take advantage of the resources at their disposal. Most importantly, it demonstrates to them that *it's okay not to know*. Good students are good students because of, not in spite of, the fact they identify gaps in their own knowledge and seek to address them.

1.2 WHAT IS A LEARNING CENTER?

Generally, peer tutoring is situated with a learning center. There is enormous individual variation in learning centers, and much of this variation has to do with the complex history of peer-led learning. *Peer tutoring* is a broad term, encompassing a number of types of academic support that, while they share the defining feature of students helping students, each have their own unique approach to working with students. Writing centers, Supplemental Instruction programs, language learning centers, and mathematics and quantitative reasoning programs are all movements within their own right, each with their own unique (if overlapping) history, ways of engaging students, and guiding philosophy. Individual learning centers may encompass some, all, or none of these elements. They may serve as a physical space where tutors from different academic support programs can collaborate. They range from employing just a handful of tutors to employing hundreds. Learning centers are all located within the wholly unique context of their own institution. Each emerges from its own local, idiosyncratic history, serves a different student body, and contributes to the overarching mission of its own institution.

Despite all of this, learning centers have more in common than they do things that separate them. Learning centers are sites for peer tutoring. They are where students go to do the work of being a student—to study, to write papers, to do homework, to prepare for exams, to review their notes—and to do so in the presence of other students working on the same things, and among tutors who can offer support as needed. They are places to talk about the shared challenges of being a student, to reflect on learning itself and to build awareness of one's own process for learning. They are learning communities, where students at all levels of achievement are united by the shared goal of personal academic growth. They are places that don't approach students as classes or cohorts, but as individuals, each motivated by their own unique goals and concerns, and each at a unique point in their own journey as learners.

Learning centers exist, as the name implies, at the center. They span all of the various departments, areas of study, and student constituencies that comprise the institution, residing at the very heart of the experience of being a student. At the same time, learning centers exist apart. Most aspects of educational institutions (classes, testing, grades) are designed to hold students to the demands of a curriculum. Institutions of learning set objective criteria, and hold students to them. But learning centers don't exist to serve institutions, and they don't exist to support instructors. Learning centers support learners. Generally, this goal is aligned with the needs of faculty and with the needs of institutions. But whenever they do come in to tension, educators within learning centers make decisions based on the needs and goals of students.

PEER TUTORING AND STUDENTS' RIGHT TO PRIVACY

One of the most important ways that learning centers advocate for students is by protecting their privacy. Students' rights to privacy are guaranteed in the United States by the Federal Educational Rights and Privacy Act (or FERPA, 34 CFR §99.31) and in Canada by the Freedom of Information and Protection of Privacy Act (or FIPPA, R.S.O. 1990, c. F.31). Under FERPA and FIPPA, an adult student is the sole owner of their educational records (e.g., their course grades), and the institution that the student attends is merely a custodian of these records. Information on students' utilization of support services, such as peer tutoring, is also protected by FERPA and FIPPA. As a peer tutor, you are privy to legally protected information, and you have the legal and ethical responsibility to keep it private. You are only legally able to share information on students' use of tutoring with individuals who work for the college, and who have a legitimate educational interest in a student (e.g., advisors, professors, financial aid officers). Should a fellow student, the student's parents, a friend, or anyone else not covered by FERPA or FIPPA seek information from you on a students' utilization of tutoring, it's absolutely essential for you to politely decline.

Beyond these legal requirements, individual learning centers set their own policies on protecting student information, and you should seek guidance from the professional staff of your center on those policies. Broadly, however, learning centers, as advocates for students, tend to err on the side of giving students power over their own information, only sharing information on students' visits to the center (whether or not they visited, how often they did so, what was discussed in sessions) with explicit permission from the student. Support to succeed is a right, and an important part of the college experience for every student. But so is privacy, and a students' information on their utilization of tutoring is theirs to share or not, as they see fit. All requests for information on a student's use of tutoring, even within the institution (e.g., a faculty member asking you whether one of their students came to see you) should be referred to the professional staff of your center. One situation in which it is important *not* to maintain students' privacy is any tutoring scenario that comes under the purview of Title IX of the Education Amendments Act of 1972 (2019), a law designed to prohibit gender-based discrimination in institutions of education that receive federal funding. For tutors in the U.S.: as an employee of the institution you work at, you are required by federal law to report any instances of sexual harassment or assault that students disclose to you to your institution's Title IX coordinator (who is trained to handle such reports with all due privacy, sensitivity, and expedience).

The work of a learning center is the work accomplished by the peer tutors who work within it. Every other aspect of a center—the physical space, the training program, the professional staff—is peripheral, designed to support students in engaging their peers. The interactions that you'll engage in with learners are at the very heart of every learning center's mission. As a peer tutor, you have enormous power over how students perceive your center, which in turn will have an effect on whether and how they use it. Obviously, the way that sessions unfold is a central part of students' experience of using the center. Most of this book will be dedicated to the topic of doing that work as well and mindfully as possible. But there are other important ways that you have an impact on students' impression of the learning center as a space, as a program, and as a learning environment. The decorations on the walls, the ways that you greet students when they enter, the way that you interact with your coworkers in front of student users, the advertising for the center that students see around campus—all of these things shape how students think of their relationship to the center, and all of these things are, to at least some extent, under your influence (if it's not immediately apparent how, I encourage you to talk to your center director about ways that you can engage with the look and feel of the center).

One thing that's incredibly important about learning centers is that they have to feel open and welcoming. Learning centers are, as much as anything else, fun places to work, and it's both common and good for a sense of cohort and shared purpose to emerge among a group of tutors. It's important to be vigilant, however, against ever presenting (however unintentionally) as a "club" that feels closed to newcomers. The students who most need your help are often the ones who are most reticent, fearful, or intimidated about using the center. Always be mindful of the student who may be entering the center for the first time, feeling apprehensive and ready at any moment to turn back around and leave. How can you make that student feel not just welcome but explicitly invited into the learning center? How can you help them to connect to the support that exists in the center, but that they don't yet know how to access? In peer tutoring, being friendly and responsive to students as they enter the center is far more than just customer service. It's absolutely necessary to the mission of the center.

CONCLUSION

Students place incredible trust in tutors. They'll share with you their greatest vulnerabilities, and their deepest fears, about themselves as students—for most people, the most important identity that they have while at college. The way that you as a tutor can reciprocate this trust is to do your work as well as possible. That means proceeding with the greatest possible mindfulness toward learning science, pedagogy, the relative strengths of different approaches to tutoring, the unique needs of different groups of students, and the best ways to respond to various types of situations. In the chapters ahead, we'll explore principles that you can use to drive the choices that you'll make in your work engaging learners as a peer tutor.

QUESTIONS TO DRIVE THE SESSION

Within a learning interaction, we are always confronted with the question "How can I help this student?" Based on the concepts in this chapter, these are questions that you can ask yourself, in the moment, to drive the decisions that you make as a peer educator.

- How can I show vulnerability about the ways that I struggled when I was learning this material?
- How can I model the attitudes, behaviors, and strategies that make me a successful student?

- How can I help this student feel welcome in the center?
- How can I help this student to feel invited to work with me?
- How can I help this student to understand how this center works?

WAYS TO ENGAGE

Questions for Discussion

1. Think of a moment of crisis in your academic career. What were the factors involved? What help did you receive? What help do you wish you had received?
2. Why is your learning center important, on your campus?
3. Imagine that you're in class, and your professor (who knows that you're a tutor) approaches you asking whether a student in one of their intro classes came to see you in the center. What would you do?

Activities

1. Take a few moments to write out your answers to the following questions, then take turns sharing them with a partner:
   a. Who are you, and what do you tutor?
   b. What do you feel are your strengths as a thinker? How do you think that these strengths will apply in tutoring?

Partners should then share out to the larger group, introducing their partner to the group based on the answers provided above.

2. Working in a small group, create a conceptual map of your learning center on a large piece of paper, or on a whiteboard/chalkboard. Your map can take any form that your group decides best articulates the points that you want to make. You might consider the following questions:
   a. Within the overall center, are there teams of tutors with specializations? What are they? Do they align with the format, or content of tutoring (or both)?
   b. What does each team contribute to the overall center?
   c. Who are the various groups of stakeholders in the work of the center, and what is their relationship to the center?
3. In groups of three to five, tutors should take turns acting out the scenarios below. Decide in advance who will play each role, practice it once or twice, and then perform it for the large group. Everyone who is not performing should stand in a circle around the performers, observing.

a. A student enters the center looking for support. They have not used the center before, and are feeling some trepidation. The tutors in the center, who know and like each other, are having an animated conversation about a book that they all enjoy, and do not immediately notice the student entering. The student has to try to break into the conversation in order to get support.

b. A student enters the center looking for support. They have not used the center before, and are feeling some trepidation. The tutors are all sitting with their backs toward the door of the center, working intently on something. The tutors have headphones in.

c. A student enters the center looking for support. They have not used the center before, and are feeling some trepidation. The tutors are facing the door of the center, and see the student enter. They welcome the student, and ask how they can help.

After each activity, discuss in large group how the scenario felt for the student entering the center.

Questions for Reflection

1. Looking ahead to your work as a peer tutor, what are you excited about? What are your concerns? What do you think you'll be like, as a tutor?

Chapter 2

Learning and the Brain

There are many ways to think about what we do when we tutor, but there is also one literal truth that it all boils down to: when we tutor, we are helping students to learn. When we talk about learning, we are talking about the mind, and at the most basic level, about the physical processes whereby information is stored and processed in the brain. The human mind is incredibly powerful, but everything that it does is predicated on a few principles and processes that together form our basic cognitive architecture. Both learning and education are most effective when these principles are taken into account.

As a peer educator, you'll be supporting learners as they master concepts, memorize information, solve problems, write papers, take notes, study, and otherwise engage in the work of being a student. On the surface, these are all discrete types of tasks, which moreover play out in different ways in different courses and disciplines. In a deeper sense, however, they are all manifestations of the same fundamental processes for learning: creating operational systems for accomplishing cognitive tasks, developing a robust understanding of concepts, and using what we already know as platforms for further growth. Understanding the basic nature of these processes is the foundation of all effective peer tutoring, allowing you to make informed choices on how to empower learners in accomplishing the work that they bring to the center, and to guide and mentor students in cultivating a critical awareness of their own processes for learning.

2.1 COGNITIVE SCHEMAS

Human brains contain inconceivable amounts of information. We all walk around containing vast, untold volumes of memories, facts, skills, and countless other things that we, in some form, know. The information in our brains is not free-floating. It does not exist in discrete, independent units, like a collection of books scattered on a table. Neither is it neatly organized in tables, rows, or directories, like files in a computer, because human minds aren't things that were purpose-built for a specific function. Rather, knowledge in human brains is structured in a way that builds on the basic cognitive architecture that humans share with other animals, and that arises from our need to *use* what we know to navigate our environments.

The way that knowledge is structured in human brains is a schema. A schema is everything you know about something, and all of the connections among that knowledge.

Think about cars. Think about absolutely everything you know about cars. You can imagine a typical example of a car. You can conjure more peripheral examples of cars (trucks, for example, or types of cars designed for specialized uses). You have knowledge of the mechanical operations of cars, which is more or less detailed depending on how much need and/or interest you've had in learning about and working on them. You're aware of current issues around cars and environmental policy. You have linguistic information on cars, including synonyms and words for closely related concepts. You have cultural associations with cars—ideas about which cars are cool, boring, or innovative. You can recall books and movies in which cars have appeared, and probably have associations between specific types of car and those books and films. You may have emotional associations with cars you or your loved ones have owned. If you drive, you have highly detailed operational knowledge of driving: operating its controls, the rules of the road (and knowledge of which rules of those rules are contextual), and customs around socially acceptable behavior for drivers.

You've probably never taken mental stock of everything you know about cars, because it's just such a basic concept. It's probably not information you're using to impress people at parties, and you'll likely never have to take a test on cars. It's just information you've accrued over the course of your life, and you use it to navigate the world. Taken together, however, it's an incredible amount of information. Moreover, it's information that's linked. All of the information described here, and much more, together form your entire, complete understanding of cars, their role in the world, and their relationship to you. This is your schema for cars, and it's enormous. And yet, it's just one of countless topics that you have this kind of incredibly detailed, complex, multilayered knowledge of. Chairs, dogs, walking—each of these concepts and countless others is a schema unto itself, containing endless rabbit holes of knowledge and countless individual memories of experienced examples, all available for you to access at any moment. They nest, with

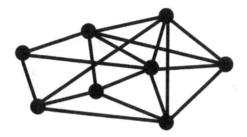

Figure 2.1   **Simple cognitive schema**. *Dan Sanford.*

some schemas acting as sub-schemas that comprise parts of larger schemas (which can in turn participate in larger schemas still). They overlap and inter-relate, such that one memory, idea, or concept can be a part of more than one schema. Schemas structure conceptual structures, but they also structure physical processes, spatial awareness, strategies for solving problems, and everything else you do with your mind. In purely physical terms, a schema is an activation pattern, among neurons in your brain, which has become to some extent automatic due to repetition.

Schemas can be more or less complex, depending on how much experience and knowledge an individual has about a concept. If a concept or domain of knowledge is something you've been exposed to, but have no detailed knowledge of, then your schema for that topic is relatively simple (figure 2.1).

You can probably think of any number of concepts that, for you, exist in this state: you know them well enough to have some functioning knowledge of them. When they come up in conversation, you easily follow what everyone is saying. You navigate the concept in appropriate ways when it comes up in your everyday life. But because they're not things you've had a lot of experience with, or have studied intensively, your knowledge has limits. You wouldn't be able to explain, in any detail, the concept to others, and if you came across a situation in which you had to perform a complex task based on the concept, you'd probably want to seek out the services and knowledge of someone with more expertise.

On the other hand, for concepts that you know well, have detailed knowledge of, and are called upon to utilize often, your schemas are far more complex, incorporating more ideas and more connections between those ideas (figure 2.2). Such concepts, for you, are those things that you can easily explain to others. You confidently face new situations, making informed choices, engaging in complex tasks, and performing tasks that would be daunting to someone less experienced and informed than yourself, because you've engaged with and thought about that concept a lot.

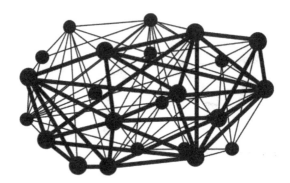

Figure 2.2   Complex cognitive schema. *Dan Sanford.*

Schemas develop naturally, emerging in people's minds as they are repeat-edly exposed to ideas, memories, facts, and experiences, and as they form connections between them and generalizations over them. We use schemas to understand ideas, solve problems, navigate our environments, place new information in context, process the information we receive from our senses, use language, guide our bodies in performing complex series of move-ments—just about every mental operation we perform, we accomplish by taking advantage of a schema or schemas that can be brought to bear on the task at hand.

Schemas are not always active. They are dormant when they are not being used, existing outside of your conscious processing where they don't make demands on the processing power of your brain. To be used, they have to first be activated. This activation is completely automatic, happening in the instant you are exposed to an idea that exists within the complex activation network of the schema. When you read the word "car" a few paragraphs ago, it initiated a cascade of neuronal activity in your brain. Everything you know about cars was primed: the schema was activated, and all of the information it links leapt to the fore, ready to be used—in this case, to provide context for the information that you were reading, and to give you a framework for making inferences. By activating the appropriate schemas, you bring all of your relevant experience to hand as you navigate the situation in front of you.

Every time a schema is activated, it becomes stronger. It becomes more persistent, likelier to be remembered as time goes by. It becomes more likely to be used as a way for understanding new, or difficult to understand, ideas and concepts. It also becomes easier and faster to bring them to bear on pro-cessing tasks. As schemas are activated again and again, the route to their activation becomes streamlined.

Schemas that, through repeated activation, take on these properties are said to be entrenched. The more deeply entrenched a schema is, the easier and faster it is for us to use and apply. Schemas can become so deeply entrenched that we're barely, if at all, consciously aware of them. One example of this comes from the domain of physical activity. What we often speak of as "muscle memory"—our ability to perform a motion (a runner's stride, a free throw, riding a bicycle, a basic element of choreography) without having to apply any thought to it whatsoever—is a function of schemas governing complex sequences of muscular gestures, each originating as a series of neurons firing in the brain, practiced so often that the schema has become deeply entrenched. You may have noticed the same thing happening for you with any number of different tasks that, for whatever reason, you've performed with great frequency in your life. Something that you at one time, when you were first learning how to do it, had to devote a lot of conscious thought to—operating a cash register, starting a car, putting a diaper on an infant—may have become, depending on your life experiences, a task that you can easily perform while also easily keeping up your end of a conversation with a friend. You may even find yourself performing complex tasks such as these without having a clear memory afterward of doing them, the schema for accomplishing the task having become so deeply entrenched that it barely intrudes on your conscious thought. This is a function of schemas becoming highly routinized with repeated activation.

2.2 SCHEMAS, ACADEMIC LEARNING, AND TUTORING

All learning is a process of adding complexity to a schema. As a student in a course of study, you have schemas in place for all of the concepts and skills that people in your field study. As you progress in your studies, and as you encounter new facts, examples, and complexities, your schemas for those concepts become more full, robust, and intricate.

The schemas that you've developed as a student have depended on your interests and course of study. An individual with no particular interest in American politics, for example, is likely to have a fairly sparse schema for how laws are created in the United States, incorporating a few key ideas (e.g., the house, the senate, voting, checks and balances, Republicans, Democrats), sufficient to navigating these ideas as they arise in everyday life, but without a great deal of nuance. On the other hand, a student majoring in political science will have a far more detailed, complex schema, incorporating all of the information about the U.S. government that they have been exposed to over the course of their studies.

One way, then, that schemas play out in how we learn in an academic setting is that we develop, as we progress in our studies, more and more complex schemas around core concepts in our field. Students in introductory courses are exposed to new concepts, or concepts of which they have at first only a limited knowledge: atomic structure; post-colonialism; cell division; the Roman Empire, etc. As they progress through a curriculum—a course of study in chemistry, or literary theory, or biology, or classical history—their schemas become increasingly complex, incorporating much more information and making possible much more sophisticated inferences and analyses. As students approach mastery of a topic, they are able to use and apply their knowledge of a concept in highly developed ways to solve multifaceted problems and to create wholly new insights in the field.

The other important way that schemas come into play in an academic environment is in helping us to quickly perform tasks and solve problems. Humans are highly intelligent, and when we encounter a new kind of problem, we're able to use our intelligence to reason the problem through. The first time you encounter a new kind of problem in your studies (e.g., solving a complex polynomial equation, using the Spanish subjunctive to form an expression of doubt, writing an abstract for a scientific paper, calculating molarity, establishing whether the results of a t-test are statistically significant), you apply the processing power of your mind to the problem and you figure it out. You have relevant schemas (your knowledge of the topic, and schemas for solving similar types of problems) that you can apply, and you probably have a set of steps that you are told to follow. But it's a slow process, because you have to reason it through, and it takes all of your conscious attention to do so. The second time, it becomes a little easier, because you're able to apply and draw on your experience from doing it the first time. As you repeat the task, doing it again and again, a streamlined cognitive pathway—a schema—begins to form for the pattern of neuronal activity that you use to solve that type of problem. With further repetition, the schema becomes more and more deeply entrenched, becoming increasingly routine and automatic. With enough practice, you've effectively formed an alternate processing route, allowing you to solve that type of problem rapidly, efficiently, and without making large demands on the processing power of your mind.

TUTORING AND THE "A-HA MOMENT"

A common mistake that students make when they are studying is to pass over information that they feel like they understand, or to stop studying once they feel like they "get" a concept or type of problem. The problem is that at the stage of just coming to understanding of a concept, a schema has just been formed or added to in some significant way. The student has, by devoting cognitive resources, arrived at an understanding of the topic, but that schema is not in any way routinized. To be retained in memory and easily available for later use, schemas have to be repeatedly activated so that they become entrenched. To be able to quickly and accurately solve a certain type of problem for the purposes of academic assessments such as exams, students must develop operational schemas for solving that type of problem and make those schemas as automatic as possible through repetition. Practice, in other words, makes perfect.

This idea has a very clear correlate for peer tutors: in tutoring sessions, it's a common experience to bear witness to an "a-ha moment"—the instant when the puzzle pieces click in to place, and a concept that a student had previously been struggling with, and which had been impeding their comprehension of more advanced concepts, suddenly becomes clear.

These moments can be incredibly rewarding for peer tutors. Participating in them by helping students to see concepts in new ways is not only an important part of what a tutor does, it's also why peer tutoring is such immensely gratifying work: it's an amazing gift to be able to share such moments of insight with learners. The schema-based view of learning, however, reminds us of the importance of pushing the student one step further, past the "a-ha moment" in which a student intellectually grasps a concept, and toward practicing using it (first with help, and then independently) to solve problems.

These ideas lead us to two important ways of construing the work that a peer tutor does: Peer tutors help learners to develop complex schemas for important concepts in their fields and peer tutors encourage learners to develop routinized schemas for efficiently performing the tasks, and solving the problems, that students must be able to do/solve in order to advance toward mastery and toward their desired degree. It also helps us to understand one of the most important, and also most frequently overlooked, aspects of peer tutoring: the effect of peer tutoring on tutors themselves. When you tutor, you are constantly accessing your schemas for foundational concepts in your field of study. As you apply these schemas in your work with students, you develop new connections between related ideas and make your internal cognitive representations for these concepts more complex. As you return again and again to foundational concepts that are common stumbling blocks for students, these schemas become deeply entrenched through repeated activation. And as you progress in your studies to more advanced coursework, these complex, entrenched schemas provide a strong basis for apprehending new ideas and for more sophisticated types of problem-solving.

2.3 WORKING MEMORY AND LONG-TERM MEMORY

Within your mind, you have two distinct cognitive systems that work together to accomplish everything that you need to do: working memory and long-term memory. Working memory is short. Unless you do something to actively retain a bit of information in working memory, it's forgotten or passed along to long-term memory within about 10 to 15 seconds. Long-term memory is, of course, long. Information in long-term memory can be retained for days, years, or decades. One thing that this two-part system provides you with is a way to determine what information is important enough to store, and to then store it in such a way that it can be later recalled when it's needed. We are receiving a constant flow of information about our environment, a stream that is only interrupted when we sleep. Most of that information simply isn't important enough to store. When we involve that information in a thought process, however, we effectively "flag" that information as being significant enough to be retained. We involve it in a schema, which effectively makes it a part of the knowledge that we carry with us across time.

Working memory and long-term memory have often been compared to a glass bottle, with a narrow neck at the top and a large reservoir on the bottom. The large inside of the bottle corresponds to our long-term memory, comprising all of our existing knowledge, structured in schemas. The neck of the bottle is our working memory, a narrow gateway through which information from our world must pass in order to be stored in long-term memory (figure 2.3). This metaphor captures one very important aspect of working and long-term memory: working memory is a gateway through which all information must pass before it can be retained in long-term memory. Working memory and long-term memory are far more, however, than a filing system for retaining information. Together, these two systems allow you to do everything that you do to function as a thinking, reasoning being, and to draw on past experience in doing so.

Working memory is, for all intents and purposes, where you live. It is where the constant streams of information that you gather from your senses is integrated into the movie that is your experience of being conscious. It is also where you apply the processing power of your mind to the tasks that you face in the world, whether that be totaling a series of numbers, talking to a friend, or stepping down off a curb to the street below. Working memory is capable of doing a lot, but it's small and limited. Its resources are easily overwhelmed, and as we've seen, information does not persist in it for long. Long-term memory, on the other hand, is not limited. It's vast—so vast, in fact, that its upper limits are not well understood. An enormous amount of information, a

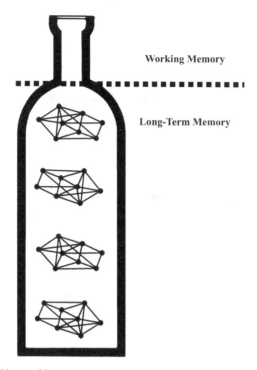

Figure 2.3 **Working and long-term memory as a bottle.** *Dan Sanford.*

library beyond measure, exists in even a child's long-term memory. But long-term memory is only a repository. To be used, information has to be pulled into working memory, where it can be manipulated and applied.

To take a different analogy, imagine a pilot flying a plane. The pilot experiences the outside environment through the windshield, and navigates the plane using the controls in the cockpit. Watching the sky outside the plane windshield and the ground below, checking the instruments for information, and making the plane respond appropriately are the pilot's experience of flying a plane, and these correspond to how working memory operates for you as you operate the machine of your organism (figure 2.4). Working memory is our interface with the world. It comprises transitory information (visual, verbal, auditory), as it comes in and as it's processed and manipulated in the moment: integrations, processing, and problem-solving. Everything else—all of the technical details and mechanical operations of the plane that are outside of the pilot's active awareness—are like long-term memory. They determine what the plane is capable of, and what the pilot can make the plane do. But they are outside of the pilot's direct experience of flying the plane.

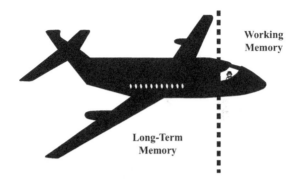

Figure 2.4   Working and long-term memory as an airplane. *Dan Sanford.*

New information is processed through working memory, but our existing knowledge structures, into which new information has to be integrated for learning to take place, is in long-term memory. For meaningful learning to take place, information has to make it through working memory. Working memory is a threshold through which information has to pass, in order to be placed in long-term memory. But working memory isn't just a gateway. It has an active role to play in the process of learning, in that it's also where that integration takes place. It's essential, in that it's where new knowledge is integrated with existing schemas.

2.4 WORKING MEMORY, LONG-TERM MEMORY, AND PEER TUTORING

Schemas, as we've seen, don't just store information; they routinize processing of that information. Schemas effectively expand an individual's processing power, because when a schema is recruited into working memory for solving a problem, fewer resources need to be devoted to it. The difference between an expert and a novice is that novices are hashing through new tasks and new information in working memory, while experts have those knowledge structures and processes routinized in schemas in their long-term memory. In an academic setting, as students progress in a curriculum, they encounter new concepts and new problems. At first, as they seek to understand, engage with, and apply these ideas, they have to devote considerable resources from working memory to do so. If it is the students' first exposure to a new kind of problem, then no relevant schemas can be recruited. The student is forced to use a "brute strength" approach, muscling through the problem using the processing power of working memory. The capacity of working memory is limited. If a problem is sufficiently large and/or unfamiliar, it can easily overwhelm the online resources at the student's cognitive disposal.

The problem, of course, is that college students encounter large, unfamiliar problems constantly. Learning centers, as a result, are full of students who are feeling overwhelmed. As a peer tutor, you'll quickly learn to recognize the look of a student who has reached the limits of their available processing power and is, in a word, stuck. The student would like very much to solve the problem that is keeping them from completing their homework, or to have the relevant idea or concept safely stored in their long-term memory where they then use it for the exam they have coming up, but a bottleneck has formed where that idea, concept, or problem-solving strategy encounters the narrow gateway of working memory.

One important way that tutors can assist students in managing the limitations of working memory is to help learners to see ways in which larger problems can be broken up into smaller ones, which will fit through the narrow neck of the bottle in ways that the larger concept will not. This strategy is so powerful because whereas a student may not have a schema in place for solving the entire problem in front of them, they probably have schemas for solving simpler, related problems.

Consider the student who brings to their math tutor the issue that that they are stuck on this problem:

$$\sqrt{\frac{5}{x}} = 25$$

The relative difficulty of the problem doesn't matter—like any problem, it's easy if you know how to do it and hard if you don't. In this case, the student is stymied by the fact that they don't have a schema for solving equations that involve both a square root and a fraction. If they've been following along in the class so far, however, then they probably do have entrenched schemas for solving these types of equations:

$$\sqrt{x} = 16 \qquad \frac{16}{x} = 4$$

If the student can be guided to see how the first problem can be broken up into problems that take the same form as the second two, then they will likely be able to solve the problem on their own. In the process they will create a new schema, involving the two sub-schemas, for solving this new, more complex kind of problem.

Alternately, we could think about a sociology student who has been asked to write a short essay on how hyperreality can help create ideological control in modern American society. The complexity of these concepts, as well as the unfamiliar terminology, can make this prompt completely impenetrable for a panicked student in their first course in the major. But with some time spent aiding the student in developing schemas for postmodernism (the theoretical framework that hyperreality comes from) and for Marxism (the framework that provides the idea of ideological control), the overall task becomes approachable. Both examples amount to breaking large problems up into smaller ones—one of the most important and fundamental tools in the tutors' toolkit.

Working memory is finite. Whenever a learner's processing power is split, they end up with less to apply to the task at hand. Another important strategy that tutors can apply, then, is to help learners overcome the limitations of working memory by reducing extraneous demands on the learner' attention. Such demands may come from the learning center itself, and it's often helpful to think about ways to minimize auditory and visual distractions—anything that stands out from the general, ambient background buzz of a healthy learning environment—in the immediate tutoring environment (a Spanish tutoring session taking place directly adjacent to an Italian tutoring session, for example, or a colorful, prose-filled table-top sign). Distractions can also come from other aspects of the learners' life. Encouraging a student to turn off social media notifications on their phone while studying, or to close all windows and tabs on their computer except for the one they're currently working in, can be a valuable piece of mentoring. Distractions can also, however, be inherent to educational materials. A poorly designed diagram that forces students to refer to a legend for interpreting symbols, an essay prompt that buries the main task in confusing questions, a textbook containing terms the student doesn't know—all of these can introduce unnecessary complexity to a task. As a tutor, you can help students to devote cognitive resources to the inherent difficulty of a concept or problem by aiding them in creating a single, integrated, clear source of information (e.g., by making a new and more clear version of the diagram in their notes, by rewriting the prompt in a way that highlights the central goal, by rewording a textbook definition in language the student understands).

Another important, and related, aspect of working memory is that working memory isn't just one undifferentiated channel: we have a certain amount of capacity for audio information, and a certain amount of capacity available for visual information. If too much information is presented in one channel or the other, the learner's attention is split and the capacity for that channel can be overwhelmed. If, on the other hand, information is presented in both auditory and visual channels (as happens, for example, in a documentary film with narration), learners can take advantage of the full bandwidth of working memory. As tutors, then, another way that you can help students to navigate the limitations of working memory is to ensure that you engage with the learner using both auditory and visual means (e.g., by pairing an explanation with an illustrative drawing), and that they engage with the task at hand using both auditory and visual means (e.g., by restating an idea in their own words, and also sketching out a diagram that represents the concept graphically).

COGNITIVE LOAD THEORY

Cognitive load theory, developed by educational psychologist John Sweller (1988), is a full treatment of the limits of working memory in solving problems. This theory asserts that, for any given cognitive task, there are three relevant sets of demands on working memory:

Intrinsic Cognitive Load is the inherent difficulty of the task.

Extraneous Cognitive Load are factors that increase the processing power required, without actually helping with the task—poorly designed instructional materials, distractions in the environment, or anything else that forces learners to split their attention such that they are less focused on the immediate task.

Germane Cognitive Load is the formation and automation of schemas that takes place during processing. It's helpful to long-term learning.

Cognitive load theory suggests that to help learners solve problems, we should help them to reduce the extraneous load associated with a task so that they can apply all of the resources of their working memory to the inherent difficulty of the problem. To help learners develop lasting schemas in long-term memory, we should support them in developing and practicing problem-solving strategies. Tutors can also help learners to manage the constraints of working memory by taking advantage of the way that working memory is structured. In the working memory/long-term memory model of cognition, working memory has both a verbal-auditory and a visual-spatial component. Cognitive load theory construes these as "channels" in working memory, each with a separate capacity that can be individually overwhelmed. When both are utilized, more of a learner's attention can be devoted to a problem.

You may have heard of the concept of learning styles, the idea that there are learners of different types (e.g., auditory, visual, kinaesthetic) that roughly correspond to the human senses and that we can improve student learning by fitting teaching to a learner's style. The idea of learning styles is no longer accepted in educational psychology or any other cognitive science, because studies have failed to demonstrate that customizing learning materials for learners of different styles results in better attainment of learning outcomes—much like the idea of hemisphere dominance (the notion that there are right- and left-brained learners, with thinkers of different types displaying dominance in one hemisphere or the other) learning styles is an idea that has long been scientifically discredited but remains in widespread circulation. Cognitive load theory's concept of discrete channels in working memory is in some ways related, in that it encourages us to be attentive to different modes of learning. It has very different implications, however. What cognitive load theory suggests educators do is not to focus on specific modes for different students, but rather to take advantage of both auditory-verbal and visual-spatial modes in working with every learner.

Another important implication of working and long-term memory for academic learning comes from the fact that in long-term memory, there are no free-floating items. To learn something is to have stored it in long-term memory, which means integrating it with a schema. A fundamental part of academic learning is integrating new information with old information, so that it can be contextualized and therefore retained.

As a tutor, there are several ways that you can take advantage of this fact. The first is to find ways to connect new information to old information. This often means helping students to see how new ideas fit within a broader context. For example, many new students of Latin struggle to understand when and how to mark nouns as nominative, genitive, dative, vocative, ablative, or accusative. For a native speaker of English, or any other language that doesn't use a grammatical case system, the concept of using case rather than word order or prepositions to show the relationships of words in sentences will be unfamiliar. Beginning with a discussion of how the students' native language shows information about how nouns in sentences relate to one another will help a student to ground the new concept they are learning in things they already know. This will allow them to take advantage of their existing schemas to interpret the new information, and therefore also to incorporate the new information within an existing schema in long-term memory (where it can then be used to muddle through Ovid).

Another tool that emerges from the same principle is using metaphor to make concepts more clear. In metaphor, we overlay one schema against another, forming a new set of connections between them. In a cognitive sense, we use the terminology and inferences of the first schema to think and talk about the second, bringing new insight into our understanding of the concept being described in metaphorical terms. As a tutor, you can use this to take advantage of a students' existing, well-entrenched schemas for easy-to-understand concepts in order to bring clarity and understanding to areas that are new and unfamiliar to them. In many cases, these metaphors are so helpful that they become fundamental ways of talking and thinking about basic concepts in a field—the use of trees, for example, as a way for biologists to talk about the way that species diverge from one another through evolution, or flowing water as a way to describe electricity. In such cases, exploring the implications of a metaphor can be helpful for students. In others, creating a new metaphor and encouraging students to explore the implications of it can be productive (e.g., how might it help a student creating an in-class presentation on the ecological impact of disappearing wetlands to think of wetlands as filters for pollutants?).

CONCEPTUAL METAPHOR THEORY

Conceptual metaphor theory, developed by cognitive linguist George Lakoff and Philosopher Mark Johnson (Lakoff & Johnson, 1980), reconceived metaphor—traditionally viewed as a serving a primarily poetic function—as a fundamental element of the human conceptual system. According to the view of metaphor articulated in this theory, metaphor is a cognitive mechanism whereby we apply the systematicity of one "domain" of thought (a schema, or set of schemas, that structure our understanding of a topic) to another domain of thought. For example, a large number of English utterances are predicated on a mapping of the physical directions "up" and "down" onto the emotions of happiness and sadness (e.g., "I'm feeling a little down," "that gave me a boost," "he's in low spirits," "thanks for lifting my mood"). Generally, we apply the understanding of more concrete, easily understood domains of thought (e.g., physical space, directions, motion) to more abstract, less easily understood concepts (e.g., emotions, time, relationships). The domain that supplies the terminology structure is the source. The domain to which this structure is applied is the target (figure 2.5).

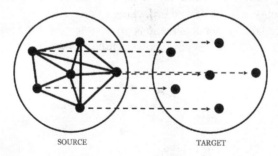

SOURCE   TARGET

Figure 2.5 Metaphor as a mapping between cognitive domains. *Dan Sanford.*

Many metaphors draw on our most basic, literal experiences of inhabiting a human body (such as standing upright, as in the metaphors above). Metaphor pervades languages so deeply, evidencing the patterns of mappings of schemas that we use to structure our basic understanding of the world, that we are often unaware we are even using it. The insight of conceptual metaphor theory is that metaphor is not a linguistic phenomenon, but rather an underlying feature of human cognition that is instantiated in language as well as in other areas.

Another strategy is to prime schemas by having a student call to mind everything they already know about a topic before introducing new information. This provides the student with a frame of reference for understanding the new information. It brings to conscious awareness those concepts that can provide a context for understanding the new information. And it sets up the process of learning, facilitating the connection of the new information to the appropriate schema(s), where the information will be stored and the schema(s) will be made more complex.

One way for you to do this is, in a tutoring session, to simply ask the student to tell you everything that they know so far about a topic (this could begin by asking the student to define or summarize the topic). You can then keep following up with questions, to draw out more of, and in greater detail, the knowledge that the student is entering the session with. Another way to do this is to set aside a few moments for the student to write out what they know and what they've learned about a topic so far. This could be in their own notebook or on a whiteboard; it can be in prose, a bulleted list, or a concept map; and it can be an individual exercise or something a few students work together on. Regardless of the method, devoting time to this step guides the student in their learning, building toward mastery by using new information to build on and enrich what they already know. It also provides you with valuable diagnostic information on where a student's understanding of prerequisite concepts may be flawed or lacking (figure 2.6).

We've been talking about situations in which new information cleanly builds on what a student already knows. Often, however, the story is more

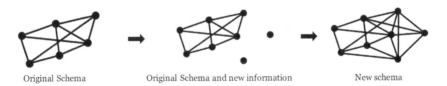

Original Schema   Original Schema and new information   New schema

Figure 2.6   Integrating new information with an existing schema. *Dan Sanford.*

complicated. As a student is working to integrate new information with their existing knowledge structures, they may encounter places where there is tension between new information and old information. The new ideas and concepts can't be smoothly integrated with an existing schema, because the schema governing a student's understanding of the idea is overly simplistic, predicated on a misconception, or in some other way incompatible with the new information. (What does it do, for example, to your schema for the history of life on earth to contemplate that more time passed between Stegosaurus and Tyrannosaurus Rex than between T. Rex and modern humans, or for the schema for your timeline of human history to consider that more time existed between the building of the Great Pyramid at Giza and the birth of the Roman Empire than has passed between the birth of the Roman Empire and the present?) When new information can't be accommodated within our existing schemas, schemas must be reorganized to accommodate the new information. In the process, they become more complex, forming a better basis for future learning.

Another tool that you can employ, then, as a tutor, is to exploit these moments of contradiction between old and new information to prompt students to reanalyze their existing schemas in such a way that the new ideas they are being presented with can be added to them. A learner with an understanding of the seasons built around the false (but very common) idea that the seasons are determined by earth's distance from the sun will have a difficult time progressing to a more advanced understanding of many concepts in earth science, because so much is predicated on the idea that seasonal variation is caused by changes to the angle of earth's axis of rotation and resulting changes in the angle of sunlight relative to the atmosphere. But if the student can be prompted to see the tension between their existing schema and the observation that the sun follows a different arc in the sky in different seasons, a reorganization of the schema that allows for a whole new set of insights (e.g., why the earth is warmer at the equator than the poles, or why the Northern and Southern hemispheres are always in different seasons) can ensue.

CONCLUSION

These tools provide specific, concrete, and implementable ways that you can help learners to accomplish the goals and outcomes that they have as students: to retain information so that they can reproduce it later, to arrive at a deeper understanding of concepts, to become fluent, to be able to solve problems quickly and accurately, to write papers, and much more. Understanding the theory behind them can help you to make informed choices about how, in the moment, you can best guide students toward getting over their immediate hurdles in the learning process.

Ultimately, however, the point is not for you to help the student to do these things. The point is for the student, through working with you and your fellow tutors, to begin to internalize and apply these principles themselves. This awareness of one's own processes for learning is known as metacognition, and it's the key to learning more effectively, being a better student, and getting more from your education. The work of being a student—taking notes, reading textbooks, writing papers, taking exams, and doing all the other things that students do in their academic lives—is mental work, accomplished with the brain. Helping students to approach this work with general cognizance of how the brain works, and how to get the most out of it, is an essential aspect of what a tutor does.

QUESTIONS TO DRIVE THE SESSION

Within a learning interaction, we are always confronted with the question "How can I help this student?" Based on the concepts in this chapter, these are questions that you can ask yourself, in the moment, to drive the decisions that you make as a peer educator.

- How can I guide this student in developing a more complex, robust schema for this concept, process, or problem-solving strategy?
- How can I facilitate the entrenchment of this students' schema for the relevant concept, process, or problem-solving strategy?
- How can I help this student to connect the new information they are grappling with to their existing schemas?
- How can I help this student to break this large problem into smaller ones that can be managed within the constraints of their working memory?
- How can I direct this student's awareness toward areas of tension between the existing schema they are using to understand this topic and the new information they are receiving?
- How can I utilize metaphor to make this complex concept easier for this student to understand?
- How can I use multiple sensory channels in my interactions with the student(s), in order to take advantage of the full bandwidth of working memory?

WAYS TO ENGAGE

Questions for Discussion

1. What was a concept that you used to have only a fuzzy notion of that you now understand well?

    a. What were some of the key moments in the process of coming to a more full understanding of it?

    b. What were the misconceptions that you had, and how did you move past them?

2. When you study for exams, what are some of the strategies that you use to retain information? How might you explain the effectiveness of these tools, in terms of schemas, working memory, and long-term memory?

3. Think of a professor that you think uses multiple sensory modes effectively in their teaching. What's an example of the professor using this approach? Do/did you find it effective?

Activities

1. Working individually or in small groups, identify a critical concept in your field. This concept should be something that students learn about in introductory courses, but that their understanding of becomes more complex as they move through subsequent courses. It should be a challenging concept that many students struggle to understand.

    a. As students progress toward greater mastery of the concept, are there stages that they tend to go through? What are they? How might these relate to the complexity of students' schemas for the concept?

    b. Thinking about the curriculum at your institution, what is some of the extraneous cognitive load that students encounter as they attempt to make progress in their understanding of the concept?

    c. What are some of the critical pieces of information that, when students learn them, challenge their previous understanding of the concept and force them to develop a more complex schema?

2. Working in a small group, identify some of the key metaphors that are used to teach and conceptualize key concepts in your field.

    a. What order does each metaphor impose on the idea?

    b. How does it affect learners' understanding of the concept?

Questions for Reflection

In your work as a peer educator, how do you plan to take into account the cognitive processes that underlie learning?

Chapter 3

Learning Center Pedagogy

Pedagogy is the study of teaching and learning. It's a practical discipline. Even when pedagogs are at their most theoretical, the discussion is grounded in concerns of what educators should *do*. The concern of pedagogy is educating effectively, which always means educating in a way that takes into account how learning works. This is particularly true in learning centers, where the focus is explicitly on learners. Peer tutors, because they are generally working with students one-to-one or in small groups, are uniquely positioned to take into account the particular needs of individual learners.

One way to conceive of learning (and, in fact, the dominant way to think about learning, both for most of history and in many educational sites today) is to think about learning as a process of transfer. Educators have knowledge; students seek knowledge. Students' minds are empty vessels, and educators teach by filling their cups, relaying their expertise to students in speech and writing. Within higher education, to be a teacher is to be a *professor*—one who professes. To be a student, then, is to be professed at—to be a receptacle for the knowledge being transferred.

CRITICAL PEDAGOGY

Critical pedagogy, developed in the 1960s by Brazilian educator and philosopher Paolo Freire (1920–1997), represented a crucial break between older, traditional models of education and more contemporary, learning-based approaches. Freire was particularly attentive to metaphors for education, and was an outspoken critic of what he called the banking model of education, which conceives of education as a transfer of knowledge from teachers to learners, and of learners as passive recipients of knowledge whose role is to receive and repeat it. Critical pedagogy takes the stance that because such an educational model passes down knowledge intact from generation to generation, it maintains systems of knowledge and values that serve to oppress some members of society based on race, gender, and class, and even to indoctrinate some members of society to participate in their own oppression.

Critical pedagogy centers the role of the learner in education, focusing on how learners use reflection and evaluation to develop by continually unlearning, learning, and relearning what they know. Critical pedagogy is focused on education as a means to empower students to draw connections between larger social concepts and their own lived experience, to connect knowledge to power, and to take action to effect positive change toward greater freedom in society.

One of the problems with this model is that, as we've seen in the previous chapter, the cognitive schemas that contain knowledge can't be transferred or copied from one mind to another. Like a ship in a bottle, they have to be painstakingly created anew in every learner's mind, slowly built up piece by piece, in a process of new information building on existing schemas. For this kind of learning (the only kind of learning that human minds are capable of) to take place, students have to be active in the process of learning. When students *do* things with new information—talk about it, use it to solve problems, evaluate it—they put that information in the context of what they already know. In integrating new information with old information, students develop their knowledge structures, helping them to grow toward mastery of a concept. This view of learning, even when it's not reflected in what classes often look like, is in deep alignment with the mission of education. There is no discipline for which the ultimate goal is to be able to recite facts. Medical professionals treat patients. Literary theorists create analyses of works of literature. Physicists account for the physical phenomena of force and matter. Artists create art. In every field, the goal isn't just to have information but to have deep understanding of how that information interconnects, and to *use* that information to accomplish things. As students progress through a curriculum in a field or discipline, they become able to solve progressively more advanced problems, predicated on progressively more complex information. At the same time, they are integrating what they learn with their own lived experiences, adopting a critical stance toward it and using it to advance toward personal goals.

3.1 LEARNING AS GROWTH, AND THE
ZONE OF PROXIMAL DEVELOPMENT

Learning is a process of continuous development. Students enter academic disciplines as novices, learning basic terminology and beginning to build a base of knowledge. At the same time, they are exposed for the first time to the concepts, methods, and problem-solving strategies of the field. In subsequent courses, students build on this base, solving problems that help them to develop a framework for addressing challenges in the field and beginning to develop the habits of mind and ways of looking at the world that people in the field use to engage in academic research or professional practice. As learners develop mastery, they are able to *use* critical concepts in the field to accomplish the work that people in the field do. As they progress along this path, learners are able to solve increasingly more advanced and complex types of problems. Behind them are tasks that they have learned and practiced, and are comfortably able to perform independently: doing so does not represent any challenge, and does not offer any opportunity for further growth. Ahead of them are wholly new kinds of problems, tasks they simply are not able to accomplish, because they don't have the prerequisite skills and information. Even with assistance, the problem is beyond the abilities of the student, because they have not advanced enough in their development to have relevant schemas that can be applied to the problem. They are missing too many foundational concepts to be able to find a handhold on the problem.

Growth takes place at the threshold between these two types of problems, at what educators refer to as the zone of proximal development (ZPD). In working to solve problems just beyond (i.e., proximate to) the limits of their current abilities, learners are able to develop in their skills and abilities. The growth opportunity that such a problem represents is most ideally realized when the learner has the opportunity to engage with someone more knowledgeable than themselves (either an instructor or peer) who can provide support for the student in navigating the problem. As the student internalizes the guidance they receive, the new kind of task becomes a problem that they are able to solve independently, and the student is able to move on to still more advanced problems as opportunities for further growth. Over time, more information becomes part of the learners' structures for knowledge, and more (and more advanced) kinds of problems come within the domain of what the learner is able to accomplish independently. With continuous exposure to progressively more difficult problems and to more advanced learners, learners develop continually toward mastery.

THE ZONE OF PROXIMAL DEVELOPMENT

The concept of the ZPD, of learning as progression toward the ability to independently complete tasks, and of educators' role as providing scaffolding, comes from Soviet Psychologist Lev Vygotsky (1896–1934). Vygotsky used the basic model of learning described in this section as a way to describe how children develop mastery of complex concepts, but his views have since became influential in education more broadly. Educational approaches influenced by Vygotsky are often described as constructivist, because they focus on the way that learners use input to construct knowledge for themselves.

Vygotsky viewed education in terms of learning, focusing on learners and on their independent development rather than on teachers and their imposition of objective standards. He was guided by the insight that students learning a skill are generally first able to perform it in a group, before moving on to the ability to complete it on their own. In his view, as learners develop, they progress from being unable to perform a skill to being able to accomplish it independently. The intermediate stage is the ZPD, which is critical for learning (figure 3.1).

For a skill existing within a student's ZPD, the student is able to develop through assistance from an instructor or from a more advanced peer. Educators facilitate students in their development by providing support

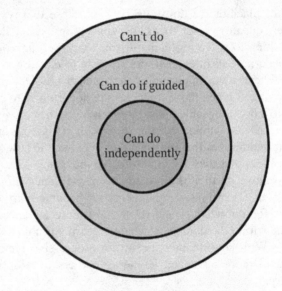

Figure 3.1   **The zone of proximal development.** *Dan Sanford.*

(scaffolding) that allows students to accomplish tasks that they would otherwise not be capable of.

With time and practice, these become skills that students can perform independently, in any setting. Teaching approaches grounded in the ZPD are focused on continually challenging students' abilities through interactions with more advanced learners, on attentiveness to individual learners' stage in development, and on student assessment as a way to guide instruction rather than to impose adherence to a standard.

The guidance and support that allows students to operate within their ZPD, solving problems slightly beyond their current abilities, is known as *scaffolding* (a term which introduces yet another metaphor for education—the idea that educators provide support for students as they develop in the same way scaffolding provides a literal structure for construction workers to work continually on a structure as it grows upward). Scaffolding is responsive, in that the level of support is constantly being adjusted in response to the learner's needs. Scaffolding is applied to help students through moments in which progress slows to a stop, and is reduced as students are able to move forward independently. All of the tools that were discussed in the previous chapter for helping students to manage the constraints of working memory and to attach new information to existing schemas—breaking larger problems apart into smaller ones, linking new information to things they already know, utilizing metaphor to make concepts more intuitive—are forms of scaffolding that help students to grow by operating at or beyond the limits of their abilities. Scaffolding can also take the form of hints, promptings, cues, or questions that help the student to find a way forward through a difficult problem. The most important aspect of scaffolding, however, is modeling. The core way that students grow, within the ZPD, is by observing and emulating the strategies that more advanced learners use. Through exposure to the ways that more advanced learners approach the kind of problem that they are currently struggling with, whether it be solving an equation with more than one variable, writing a research paper, calculating vectors, evaluating online sources, or anything else, they are able to fill in gaps in their own understanding and in their own processes for approaching the problem. In doing so, they further their own development.

This is the absolute most central concept in peer tutoring, existing at the very heart of what a learning center is: learning centers provide a space (both physically and in ways pertaining to emotions, feelings, and attitudes) for productive learning interactions between learners and their more advanced peers. Within the center, students have the scaffolding to operate within their ZPD, to engage with problems just beyond the upper limit of their problem-solving ability, and to internalize the problem-solving approaches being modeled by more advanced learners. In some cases, peer tutors may themselves serve as the more advanced learner. In others, tutors may act as facilitators of fruitful interactions between students who are at slightly different levels of advancement within the same curriculum. The learning center is a space that fosters the cooperative, collaborative dialogues within which these critical learning interactions can take place.

For peer tutors, the most important implication from this view of learning is that the ZPD, containing problems that are just beyond a students' current abilities, is the arena within which there is an opportunity for growth. That makes the absolute first task of any learning interaction to ascertain where, for that learner, their ZPD lies. Diagnostic questions help you to figure out where the edge of the students' current abilities with the material lies. Doing this allows you to ascertain where a students' ZPD lies, so that you can center the session within it and provide appropriate scaffolding.

DIAGNOSTIC QUESTIONS

The phrase "diagnostic question" sounds clinical, but with a bit of practice is very natural to utilize—they double, in fact, as good ways to break the ice at the start of a session. Any of the questions below could make a good starting point; keep asking follow-up questions to drill down further into how the student understands the task in front of them.

- How is this class going?
- How are you feeling about this assignment?
- Can you tell me how you would go about solving this?
- How did the last paper go? What went well, and where are you hoping to improve?
- What do your notes say about this?
- Where did you start finding your professor's explanation confusing?
- At what point in trying to work this out did you get confused?
- I'm noticing this issue in your work. Could you tell me what your thought process was here?
- How about these previous problems? Can I see the answer you got for those?

This view of learning is also important in framing the ultimate goal of the work that you, as a peer tutor, do with students: to create independent learners. Within the learning center, students have the scaffolding to operate within their ZPD. The center also provides a safe and low-stakes environment for doing so: failure means only an opportunity to try again, and the opportunity to learn from the mistake. Within this environment, students develop and practice skills which can then be repeated in other, higher-stakes environments such as classrooms, labs, and testing venues. The supportive, social, and highly scaffolded environment of the learning center is vital to their role in students' learning, but it isn't an end in itself. The goal is for students, having developed a skill within the learning center, to transfer it to other arenas where they can perform it independently. As learners grow and develop, new kinds of problems—problems that at one time were completely beyond their reach, even with help—enter their ZPD. As they engage with them, problems continually pass through the ZPD to become tasks that the learner can accomplish independently. This goal, to help students to learn independently, is at all times the objective of our work. Scaffolding is how we accomplish it.

3.2 ACTIVE LEARNING

We've seen that scaffolding is a way for students to be exposed to the processes that more advanced learners use to solve problems and engage with concepts. It may appear, then, that the most effective way for learning to take place is for you to demonstrate your own problem-solving strategies, and explain your own understanding of concepts. This approach, in addition to being intuitive, also has the advantage of being comfortable. Peer tutors generally hold the position of tutors because they know their stuff. They are good students, who were often recommended and selected for the position of tutor because they have a good understanding of concepts in the field, and have demonstrated success in accomplishing discipline-specific tasks. As such a student, it is likely very easy for you to open your mouth and let your knowledge of the topic come out, or to grab a pencil and show the student how to solve the problem. This is not, however, an effective strategy.

Learning, as we've seen, takes place when new information is integrated with existing schemas. Approached from a cognitive standpoint, the process that a student undergoes as they develop mastery in a field is a process of developing progressively more complex schemas for solving problems, encompassing a wider array of information and linked to a deeper and more robust understanding of the relevant concepts. For a problem within a student's ZPD, it's not enough for a student to receive the information that will allow them to solve the problem. It's very likely, in fact, that the student has already been exposed to this information in their textbook or in class. The problem is that the new information has not been integrated within their existing schemas for solving problems in the field. For this to happen, they have to bring their stored schemas from long-term memory to working memory, where new information can be integrated. In order to do this, students have to *use* their schemas in processing tasks that utilize both their existing schemas and new information. As both are activated simultaneously, new neural connections form, the new information is integrated, and the schema increases in complexity in a way that licenses a new level of problem-solving. In order to be able to accomplish the new kind of task independently, the learner must grapple with it themselves. In order to learn, students must be active in their own process for learning. In active learning environments, students *do* things with concepts. They write. They explain things. They draw diagrams. They act things out. They solve problems. They analyze ideas. They synthesize information. They evaluate arguments. In the process, they recognize ways that their internal knowledge structures are lacking, and identify areas of dissonance or incoherence in their beliefs. They fill out and entrench their existing schemas, relating new knowledge to existing knowledge.

Consider, for example, a student in an art history class. The course is a large lecture, in which students look at images of art works and listen to the professor of the class talk about their significance. The students enjoy the class, which is about a topic that they love, and the professor, who they find funny and engaging. But they have the final exam coming up, and are feeling overwhelmed. For the exam, they will have to identify the date, artist, and artistic movement for a series of works of art that span from ancient times to the present. They've come to the learning center because they have been struggling to memorize this information. When the tutor sits down with the student and starts asking diagnostic questions, they learn that the student is also having trouble keeping straight the various art movements they have been learning about.

It's natural for the learner, in this situation, to seek support that lines up with the tasks they have been struggling with: explanations of strategies for memorization, and of art movements, are likely what the learner is expecting from a tutor. For the tutor, these strategies aren't necessarily, however, what will be most successful in creating an independent learner, because they place the learner in a passive role. They won't help the learner to attach new information to schemas, which is what will help them to retain it in long-term memory where it can be used for the test and also as a foundation for more advanced learning in subsequent courses. What if, instead, the tutor asked the student to create a timeline, to place all of the works of art they had studied along it, and to label stretches of the timeline according to art movements? What if they asked the student to sketch a painting typical of abstract impressionism, or to take the point of view in a mock argument that Baroque painting is superior to neoclassical painting? Any of these ways forward, much as they may seem on the surface like a distraction from the task at hand, will place the learner in an active role in the session. The learner, in actively engaging in these tasks, develops their internal representations for knowledge. In doing so they not only develop toward mastery of the concepts covered in the course, they also develop a cognitive framework that the contextless facts they have been trying to memorize can be attached to. Through strategies like these, the memorization task doesn't just become easier, it becomes moot, because the student can answer questions based on a robust, well-developed understanding of the material.

ACTIVE LEARNING STRATEGIES

If you've ever had the common experience of having to write a paper or give a presentation on a topic, and afterward found yourself with a much clearer understanding of the concept, you've experienced the benefit of active learning. In tutoring sessions, creating an active learning environment is as simple as making sure that the majority of the time, the student is the one doing the talking, writing, moving, drawing, etc.: they should be the ones doing the work. Here are some sample prompts for shifting the dynamic of a session toward a more active role for the learner:

• Can you draw a diagram of this concept for me, in your notebook?
• Could you come up to the whiteboard and show me what you mean?
• Okay, imagine I'm someone who isn't familiar with this issue. Can you explain it to me?
• Could a few of you come up and write your definitions on the board?
• Could you sum up for me what the point of your paper is?
• Let's map this out, so we can keep all this straight. What would that look like?
• Before we jump into that, could you take a few minutes to write about everything you know about this topic?
• Let's work together to act this out. Your role is _____, and your role is _____. Go!

Even in passive learning environments (sitting in a lecture, reading a book, watching a film), it's possible to be active. Learning to approach venues like these as active learners (e.g., by entering them with questions you are hoping to get answered or by organizing the material thematically as you take notes) is a valuable academic skill, and one that it's often productive to offer coaching on. Learning centers, however, aren't just spaces that make active learning possible. They are spaces *optimized* for active learning. One of tutors' most important roles is to create this active learning space on campus, by facilitating learners' active engagement with course material.

This is important work, because very often, educational institutions aren't terribly active places. Students sitting in a lecture hall watching a professor speak, or quietly reading, are some of the most salient mental images associated with colleges and universities. Often, the students who excel in the academy are students who perform well in environments like this (a pattern that becomes self-reinforcing when students who did well in college go on to graduate school, get PhDs, become professors, and design their own courses based on what worked for them when they were in college). Learning centers level the playing field, ensuring that every learner has the opportunity to engage actively with the curriculum.

3.3 COLLABORATIVE LEARNING

Collaborative learning refers to learning venues in which students work together toward a common goal. Whether studying for an exam, solving a problem, resolving a debate, settling a question, writing a paper, presenting a project, or discussing an idea, learners who work together are able to realize some very tangible educational benefits. In engaging their peers within a group, learners are exposed to diverse points of view. Learning becomes a shared endeavor, with each individual learner benefiting from the collective knowledge of the group. Collaborative learning is also enjoyable. Study groups, one of the most common and organic forms of collaborative learning, don't owe their existence to any of the positive outcomes above so much as they do to the fact that it's much easier to face the challenge of a long, dedicated study session in a group than individually. Humans are social animals, naturally dwelling within small groups. We are more at ease, and more productive, when we work toward goals alongside others in a social group than when we do so alone.

One way to think about collaborative learning is as a subset of active learning. Within a group environment, it's never the case that everyone is in full agreement: everyone brings their own point of view, their own approach, and their own set of knowledge structures. A group faced with the challenge of working in concert toward a shared goal must arrive at some kind of agreement (on the answer, on the way forward, on the best strategy) in order to do so, which involves negotiation through dialogue. In articulating and defending their own positions, learners have to synthesize their existing knowledge and beliefs. In considering the arguments of their peers, students apply their own knowledge structures to evaluating others' positions. Both of these are critical active learning tasks, involving the recruitment of existing schemas into short-term memory to be applied to the task at hand. In the process, the schema becomes more complex as new information (drawn from the perspectives of others in the group) is incorporated, and more entrenched as it is repeatedly activated. Consider a student asked to create a definition for a concept within their field (e.g., *culture, life, art, justice*). Doing so individually is absolutely an active learning task, requiring them to activate their existing knowledge structures in working toward an outcome. Making it a collaborative learning task however (e.g., by asking a group of three students to collaborate on a single, shared definition) adds in layers upon layers of active learning, requiring them to collect, justify, and argue for their own ideas, and to compare, analyze, and appraise the ideas of others.

COLLABORATIVE LEARNING TECHNIQUES

Collaborative learning techniques (Angelo, Major, & Cross, 2001; Barkley, Major, & Cross, 2014; Luzzatto & DiMarco, 2010) are time-tested tools for educators to create structured, active, collaborative learning environments. They work well both as a way to pre-plan an interactive component in a workshop or other group session, and to use improvisationally to create more interaction in moments where energy has ebbed and students are becoming isolated or passive. There are many collaborative learning techniques; these are a few (adapted from Barkley, Major, & Cross, 2014) that are of particular use to peer tutors. Each offers different benefits, optimal for different goals and conditions. They all can and should be modified according to the needs of the situation.

Write/Pair/Share

Give students a short amount of time to independently reflect, writing about a topic in response to a prompt that you give them (e.g., "How have you experienced prejudice in your life?"). Then pair students off, giving them time to share what they wrote with their partner. Finally, ask for volunteers to share their own or their partners' ideas with the larger group.

> *Write/Pair/Share gives people an opportunity to develop and vet ideas before sharing them with a group. It makes discussions more active, and structures things in a way so that everyone engages with the material.*

Group/Share

Separate learners out into groups of three to six. Within each group, have students work together for a set amount of time to arrive at an answer to a question or solution to a problem. Have groups work together to present their answer to the larger group (perhaps by creating a visual representation of it).

In group/share, students first develop their ideas within their groups before sharing them out to the larger group. Group/share works well when a large group is all working on the same problem. Within groups, students have to come to a consensus, which forces learners to evaluate their own positions.

Jigsaw

Separate students out into groups of three to six. In the first round, each group works on a different topic (e.g., "Summarize the basic principle of economic theory outlined in this short reading"). Like in Group/Share, each group has to come to consensus within itself. Next, redistribute the groups so that the new groups all have one member each from the old groups. Give the groups a new prompt (e.g., "How should we solve income inequality in the United States?"), and have each person in the group contribute based on the topic they explored in the previous group.

In Jigsaw discussions, participants have the opportunity to develop a sense of ownership and expertise in a topic as they explore it in a first group, then teach it to a new group. It's a great tool for quickly exposing a group to a large number of concepts.

Peer Review

Place students in pairs or small groups to look at and comment on one another's work. Provide specific guidance to students on what they should be paying attention to, being as specific as possible. Have students take turns reading/reviewing their co-learners' work. Students should be prompted to both provide feedback for improvement to the author of the work and to consider ways that they can use the model provided to improve their own work.

Peer Review allows students to benefit from feedback from their peers. Just as importantly, being exposed to other students' ways of achieving the same task allows them to develop an internal model, and to develop a critical eye that can then be applied to their own work.

Round Robin

Appoint one student as a leader, who poses an open-ended question or states a point of view. This student then leads the group in taking quick turns offering their own answer or point of view. Repeat until every student has served as leader.

Round Robin discussions ensure equitability, and guarantee univer-
sal participation. They work well in ensuring that everyone takes
part, that everyone has the chance to lead, and that everyone has
multiple opportunities to have the floor while speaking.

Speed Dating

To set up a speed dating conversation, first have each learner decide on an
open-ended question that they would like to ask others in the group (e.g.,
"Do you think humans should use geoengineering to solve global warming?"). Then, divide the group into two equal groups and have them sit in
lines opposite one another, creating pairs of students sitting opposite one
another. Give students a few moments, in their pairing, to ask and answer
one another's questions. Then, have one row of students shift down one
chair to create new pairing, and do another round. Repeat until everyone
has met with everyone else.

Speed dating creates the opportunity to hear lots of different stu-
dents' perspectives on a question or issue, providing new insights
and highlighting the many ways that intelligent people can disagree.
It also works well as an icebreaker for new groups.

Practice in Pairs

To implement practice in pairs, have students break out into groups of
two to practice a skill or role-play a scenario that was just discussed in
the larger group (e.g., "Take turns pretending to place your order at a
Spanish-speaking restaurant, using the subjunctive"). Once everyone has
had the chance to practice the new skill (a few minutes at most), return to
the larger group.

In Practice in Pairs, students move concepts from a theoretical to an
applied understanding by acting out an application of the concept.
The practice routinizes the skill, making it faster and easier for them
to do it again in the future. It's a good way to punctuate less active
sessions with interaction, and to insert collaboration when there is
not a great deal of time to do so.

Fishbowl

First, have students work in pairs or small groups to develop scenarios
based on concepts the group has been discussing (e.g., "perform a short
debate on how to live to a good life, in which each of you represents a
different moral philosopher"). Then, have everyone form a circle around

a central area. Have the smaller group take turns acting out their scenario
for the larger group. After each round, the larger group can weigh in with
their observations, comments, and questions.

Have the students in the group form a circle, sitting around a central
area.

*In a fishbowl, student take turns performing the concept being
learned in small groups, while the rest of the group watches. It
encourages students to internalize concepts by applying them, while
keeping the entire group engaged in the exercise.*

A social environment is also critical to the benefit that students receive from
operating within the ZPD. Solving problems beyond the limits of their current abilities requires students to be able to benefit from modeling from more
advanced learners: they observe how other, more advanced learners approach
the problem, and they integrate these strategies with their own in order to
internalize a method that they can then apply independently. This can only
take place in a collaborative, social learning environment that allows for
an exchange of ideas, and for students to observe the ways that their peers
approach the same challenges that they are facing.

Collaborative learning is a more accurate reflection than individual
learning of how knowledge operates in the world: knowledge is situated in
human minds, and one way to think of collaborative learning is as a way
to facilitate that. Just as important, however, is the fact that knowledge is
socially constructed. Knowledge is created through a social process. Within
a culture, we arrive at knowledge through social interactions, mutual inquiry,
and the competition of ideas. Within the sciences, ideas are vetted through
peer review. In interactions among friends and family members, individuals
engage in dialogues about values and beliefs. In the popular press, narratives
for construing nature, politics, and international relations compete against one
another. Through all of these venues, and in thousands of other social forums,
knowledge is negotiated and forged to become the shared assumptions that
structure our views of the world. When we participate in social learning
environments, we don't just learn more effectively, we also engage in a more
authentic manner with the way that knowledge is developed and embedded
within social structures.

For tutors, sometime the collaborative aspects of peer-led learning emerge
through one-to-one interactions in which the tutor encourages a student user
of the center, through dialogue, to engage more critically with their own
ideas. In other cases, tutors may serve as facilitators of interactions between
students at the same curricular level, structuring their interactions and

scaffolding the process of working collaboratively toward a shared goal. In either case, the tutor supports the role of the learning centers as communities of learners, within which students at different levels of academic achievement unite over shared challenges.

CONCLUSION

Active learning and collaborative learning are the foundations of learning center theory and the touchstones of all tutoring interactions. There are many types of learners, many types of learning interactions, and many choices to make in the service of helping a student to learn more effectively. There are many theoretical approaches to the work of peer tutoring, some of which we have touched on already, some of which will come up in later chapters, and many of which are beyond the scope of this book. Active learning and collaborative learning both precede and cut across all of these. In working with students, and in seeking to support individual learners as effectively as possible, there are no strategies more effective in accomplishing a broad range of pedagogical goals than making the session as active and collaborative as possible.

QUESTIONS TO DRIVE THE SESSION

Within a learning interaction, we are always confronted with the question "How can I help this student?" Based on the concepts in this chapter, these are questions that you can ask yourself, in the moment, to drive the decisions that you make as a peer educator.

- How can I encourage this student to adopt an active, critical mental stance toward their studies?
- What types of tasks are within this student's ZPD?
- What is the appropriate scaffolding to help this student to operate just beyond their current abilities?
- How can I model the strategies that I use to accomplish this kind of task?
- How can I make this learner more active in this learning interaction? What activity would help them to engage more deeply with the relevant concepts?
- How can I make this session more of a collaboration between the learner and myself?
- How can I facilitate collaboration between learners working on the same or similar concepts? What activities would help to structure the interaction?

WAYS TO ENGAGE

Questions for Discussion

1. Consider your own educational experiences.
   a. In which courses have you mostly read and attended lectures?
   b. In which courses have you engaged with the material actively and collaboratively?
   c. How did this affect your learning?
   d. In courses that used active and collaborative approaches, what form did this take? Did you find it helpful? Why, or why not?
   e. What strategies did you use to learn effectively in courses that placed students in a more passive role?
2. Think of a time in your academic, personal, or professional level that you were operating within your ZPD. In what ways was the task beyond your current abilities? What scaffolding helped you to be able to accomplish it? How did you grow as a result?
3. Imagine a student who comes to see you in the center who has been offered extra credit by their instructor for meeting with a tutor. How might the fact that the student's motivation for visiting the center does not come from within themselves affect the dynamic of the session? How would you seek to make the student an active learner within it?

Activities

1. Working in a pair or small group with another tutor, think of a course in the area that you tutor. It should be a course that you've taken, it should be a required course (either as a general education requirement or for majors in that discipline), and it should be a course that many students find challenging. Look over the questions below, and choose a course (e.g., Algebra I, Microeconomics, Medieval History, Composition II, Introduction to Biology) for which you can answer all of the following questions. For the course you've selected, answer all of the following questions:
   a. Make a map of the major concepts covered in the course, starting at the beginning of the course and moving to the end. You can represent this however it makes the most sense to for the course you've selected, but your map should include all of the major ideas and concepts that are involved in the course, as well as how these build on one another.
   b. For each major concept, indicate the following:
      i. What are students required to do with the information (e.g., solve a certain type of problem, write a paper, deliver an oral presentation)?

  ii. What are some of the common pitfalls, points of confusion, mis-conceptions, and other difficulties that students encounter for this type of task?
  iii. What forms of scaffolding might be appropriate for students at this stage in their growth as learners?
c. Join with another group, and take turns sharing the strategies you've developed for providing scaffolding to students as they progress through the concepts covered in the course.

Questions for Reflection

1. What makes active and collaborative learning effective? What role does/will active and collaborative approaches to learning play in your own approach to working with students?

Chapter 4

Applying What We Know
Working with Students

All peer tutoring is driven by the same fundamental questions: How can I help this student to develop complex, well-entrenched schemas for the concepts and skills that they need to excel as students? How can I help them to navigate the constraints of working memory, devoting as much as possible of their finite processing power to tasks that will help them learn? How can I help this learner to retain information in long-term memory, and to integrate new information to existing schemas, through active and collaborative approaches? How can I help this student to practice this skill, so that it becomes automated for them and they can perform it again in the future, quickly and accurately? Peer tutoring is flexible enough to respond to these questions while taking fully into account the needs of individual students as unique learners. The signature pedagogies of learning centers, active and collaborative approaches to learning, provide opportunities for students to engage in deep learning, using existing schemas to navigate new information and making their knowledge structures more robust as they are applied in new ways. Helping students to operate within their ZPD, tutors provide scaffolding for students to grow and develop, thus becoming independent learners who will be able to do on their own tomorrow the task they need a tutors' help to do today.

The actual forms that peer tutoring can take, however, are quite diverse. Some formats for peer tutoring correspond to formal models (such as Supplemental Instruction), whereas some are preferred modes of delivery that have developed within disciplinary areas (such as individual consultations in writing centers). Others are local models that have emerged out of an institution's specific history and the needs of its students. Smaller centers may offer all services within a single format, while larger programs may offer several formats of tutoring for the same class, with students able to select among them according to their needs. Peer tutoring can present in very different ways in different tutoring formats, and individual learning centers can look and feel very different depending on the formats of tutoring that are favored within them. Many tutors have preferences for working in one format over another, and many students find it easier to get their needs met in some tutoring formats than in others. Nonetheless, there are far more similarities than differences across these different modes of working with learners. Across all formats for peer tutoring, there is a basic pedagogy and set of driving principles, expressed in different ways in different kinds of interactions. Understanding the differences between these formats, and understanding the strengths and potential weaknesses of each, can help you to understand your own center, excel at all of the formats of tutoring that occur within it, participate in the development of new programming, and to make informed choices in referring students to the appropriate service for them.

This chapter provides specific guidance for three of the most common formats of tutoring: individual appointments, drop-in labs, and group learning venues. There are many formats others than these, and each category itself contains internal complexity. However, most formats of tutoring can be understood as a hybrid of or middle ground between these three (e.g., study groups can be thought of as a midpoint between drop-in labs and group learning, and drop-in appointments as individual appointments with a few elements of drop-in labs). Because each represents a unique style of working with learners, a comparison of the three is helpful in understanding how the core pedagogy of peer tutoring can play out in different environments.

PRIORITIZING YOUR TIME

It's the nature of learning center work that it tends to come in waves, so slow at some times that it's hard to know how to be productive, and so busy at others that it can be challenging to know what students to focus on. In addition, as a peer tutor, you're both an educator and a student yourself. Within the learning center, how do you manage these fluctuating demands on your time, and these different identities? These priorities can help you to make these decisions, in the moment.

1. The Student Actively Seeking Out Your Help

Your first priority, as a peer tutor, is always the student who is identifying themselves to you as someone seeking support. Nothing takes priority over the student sitting across from you in an individual appointment, the student raising their hand in a drop-in lab, or the student attending your workshop. Job one is always to make sure that students who are seeking support from you receive it.

2. The Student Who Could Use Your Help, but Isn't Actively Seeking It Out

Your second priority, after attending to the students who are being proactive in seeking your assistance, is to yourself be proactive in reaching out to students who could use your help but who for any number of reasons (because they don't know how to, because they are intimidated, because they are shy, because they aren't aware help exists) aren't seeking it out. Who in the drop-in lab could use a tap on the shoulder, to ask what they are working on and if there's any way you could help out? What students in the workshop you're leading may be quiet because they're confused, and how can you bring them in to the discussion? What classes could use a visit, so that the students know about the support that you offer? Often the students who most need the support that tutors have to offer are the ones least likely to have the self-advocacy to seek it out. As a tutor, you have the opportunity to make sure that every student has the support to succeed and excel.

3. Other Work for the Center

The next priority for your time is other projects for the center, beyond your work with students. Are there any resources that are in need of development for the center (handouts, online tutorials, advertisement)? Is it a good time to check in with faculty or TAs who teach courses that you support to coordinate services? To observe other tutors? Are there things to read, to refresh your knowledge of courses you support? If there are any other aspects of your position other than direct engagement with students, or anything to attend to with respect to your center's tutor training program, now is the time.

4. Your Own Work

In many centers, it's okay for tutors to attend to their own studies if there is down time. If this is the case in your center, and if all of the priorities above have been satisfied, it may be a good time for you to write, study, do your homework, or anything else you need to do. Make absolutely certain, however, to remain visible and accessible to students, and to maintain a welcoming tone toward anyone who enters the center seeking support.

4.1 INDIVIDUAL APPOINTMENTS

In individual appointment, tutors meet one-to-one with learners for a pre-
determined amount of time. The format of individual tutoring, in which a
learner has the undivided attention of the tutor for a set amount of time,
makes them ideal for students to work carefully through concepts that they
have been experiencing as a barrier to forward progress. Tutors have the time
and space to explore the students' understanding of the material, to assess
factors that may be at play in affecting the students' engagement with it, and
then to implement a plan. Because the tutor is working with only one student, they are able to tailor the session completely around the needs of that
individual as a unique learner. A plan well-suited to the unique opportunities
that an individual appointment affords is to assess the state of a student's
understanding of a topic, and then to work with the learner toward developing
a robust, complex schema for the concept that encompasses all of the material that they have been grappling with. The scaffolding that tutors provide in
one-to-one sessions is very often highly dialogic. Tutors ask questions that
encourage students to think of a problem in new ways, and they provide alternative explanations or ways of viewing the material. They invite the student
to share their understanding of a concept, in the process calling the student's
awareness to areas in which their knowledge structures may be incomplete,
incoherent, or misaligned with the way that more advanced learners tend to
conceptualize it.

The planfulness that individual appointments allow can extend to multiple
sessions. Over a series of appointments, a learner is able to build up a level
of comfort with a tutor who they can then seek out for repeated appointments,
while the tutor can get to know the student as a learner, and the two can collaborate to develop a longer-term strategy. The highly personal, one-to-one
interactions that take place within individual appointments also create an intimacy that is well-suited to addressing the emotional aspects of peer tutoring.
Students feeling insecurity about their place in the academy or in their major,
or even shame over accessing academic support, may feel comforted by the
privacy of individual appointments.

There are significant disadvantages to the format as well. Within a
one-to-one session, it is easy for a tutor and student to fall into the comfortable roles of expert and learner: the expert speaks from their greater experience and knowledge, while the learner adopts the role of nonexpert—the
one who is there to listen and to receive knowledge. This dynamic has a
tendency to place the student in a passive stance within the learning interaction. This is in direct opposition to one of the core goals of peer tutoring,
which is to bring all of the students' previous knowledge into the session,

and to a core principle of learning centers, which is that students should be active in their own processes for learning. It's important for you to be aware of this, and to take every opportunity to encourage learners to be active in the session. One of the most straightforward ways to accomplish this is to keep sessions focused on tasks (solving problems, drafting, revising, explaining, analyzing) and by making sure that whatever work there is to be done, the learner is the one doing it. The benefits of active learning should accrue primarily to the student using the center, not to the tutor, which means that learners should be the ones doing the bulk of the writing, speaking, and problem-solving. One simple red flag to watch for, a sign that the dynamic of the session may be off, is that you are talking more than the student. Another is that whatever the immediate order of business is (e.g., making a diagram, taking notes, writing down a plan, drafting a statement of thesis), the pen is in your hand, and you're the one doing the work. Table 4.1 provides a template for approaching individual appointments with learners.

"CAN YOU LOOK OVER MY PAPER/ HOMEWORK/PROJECT?"

Very often, one of the most critical moments for establishing productive tutor–tutee roles arrives at the very beginning of the session. Frequently, students make appointments because they have work (a draft of a paper, a homework problem that they got stuck on, a project that they aren't happy with) that they would like to have reviewed by a tutor. In this situation, students will often place their work in front of you to read. When you oblige by picking it up and reading it to yourself, it forces a situation in which the student is quietly, passively waiting, and in which the students' work is literally in your hands rather than in their own. Because this occurs at the very beginning of the session, it can set a pattern that it's difficult to then change.

In this moment, instead of spending time reading over the students' work, assuming the role of editor, it's important for you to seize the opportunity to nudge the learner into a more active role by pushing the homework/paper/review sheet/project/prompt back across the table, and by having them read it aloud, answer questions about it, or otherwise assume an active role in whatever way is most appropriate to the session. The benefits to doing so will persist throughout the session, in that it sets up the tutoring session as a space in which the student learns by doing.

Table 4.1   A Basic Framework for Individual Appointments

Beginning the Session (the first 5 minutes)

Welcome the student(s) to the center and introduce yourself.	*Use this time to set the student at ease, establish a conversational tone, and establish rapport. If it's their first visit to the center, let them know what to expect and how it works.*
Ask diagnostic questions.	*Asking questions establishes an active role for the learners, and gives you the information that you need to establish where the students' zone of proximal development lies, as well as what other factors may be at play (e.g., stress, study skills, lack of prerequisite coursework).*
Work with the student to develop a plan for the session, considering the following: • What is it most important for this student to learn, in this session? • What skill/knowledge will facilitate their being able to work independently after this session? • What can be realistically accomplished, within the time available?	*A plan that establishes clear goals for the session maximizes what can be accomplished within the time available, while negotiating it with the learner helps to manage their expectations for the session (e.g., they shouldn't expect to leave having mastered several complex concepts). If the learner has the plan for the session written down in their notes, it provides them with a blueprint for how to proceed in their own studying if there isn't time to complete it.*

During the Session

Implement the plan for the session.	*Give the student active tasks to accomplish, providing as much scaffolding as they need to accomplish them. Try to maintain a roughly even balance of who is doing the talking. Continue to ask diagnostic questions, and to redirect questions back to the student.* *Try not to worry about how much you cover — students remember more when they do more, even if it means less content is covered.*

Ending the Session (the last 5 minutes)

Ask the student to explain back to you their takeaways from the session.	*This encourages learners to label and internalize what they learned, which helps them to transfer the newly acquired skills and knowledge to other venues.*
Have the student write down their plan for the paper/homework/exam/project etc., after they leave the center.	*This critical step gives students a framework to continue working independently, without feeling adrift.*
Thank them for coming in, and help them plan future use of the center.	*Make sure that students realize they can come back to see you, and also let them know of other help available in the center (other tutors, workshops, etc.) that they may find helpful.*

4.2 DROP-IN LABS

In drop-in labs, students do the work of being a student—doing homework, writing papers, studying for exams, etc.—in a supported space where they are able to be around other students working on the same task, and tutors who can offer help and guidance as needed. Generally, there are no time constraints on students' use of drop-in labs. A student could stop by to ask a quick question, or stay for hours to complete an entire project. Tutors in drop-in labs circulate throughout the space, responding to raised hands and checking in on students as they work. If the goal of individual appointments is to work intensively, in a process of dialogue, through a difficult concept, then the goal of drop-in labs is to provide just enough targeted support for students to continue to make progress within their ZPD. Scaffolding, within a drop-in lab, may take the form of hints, alternate explanations, worked examples, sample problems, suggested problem-solving strategies, or any number of other succinct interventions that provide students with the immediate guidance that they need to move forward.

Drop-in labs are incredible venues for fostering active learning. The format makes it easy for tutors to provide guidance, and then give the learners space to implement it (e.g., "This is looking good so far! One thing I'm noticing is that your statement of thesis is something no one would really disagree with. Often, a strong thesis will make a claim that it's possible for intelligent people to disagree on. I'm going to keep moving—could you try rewriting this? I'll be back in a bit to check back in on you." Or "This symbol stands for a factorial—you solve these by multiplying every whole number between zero and the number. So 3! Is $1 \times 2 \times 3$. Why don't you try doing a factorial for 10? I see a hand over there, but I'll be back in a few minutes." Drop-in labs also give tutors opportunities to observe students as they work to accomplish learning tasks, which allows them to engage with the processes that students use for doing so. A tutor may observe, for example, that a student is taking notes by attempting to copy nearly every word from their textbook, beginning to write without first developing a plan, or trying to reason out a word problem without first making sure they understand all the terms within it. This gives tutors the opportunity to engage with a student not only over the material of the course but the strategies that the student applies across *all* of their courses.

One potential drawback of drop-in labs is that they can be intimidating environments for student users. Individual learning centers all have their own unique systems for organizing and managing learning interactions. Students may sign in at a log-in station, or with a tutor. They may signal that they need help with a raised hand, with some kind of flag, or verbally. Tutors may wear name tags, shirts, vests, or some other kind of identifier. The space of the center may be organized using signage or dividers, according to class, discipline, or tutoring format. There are as many systems for organizing tutoring as there are learning centers, each entirely suited to the needs of the program and the students it serves. Such systems, as intuitive and helpful as they may be for students who are accustomed to them, can be opaque and intimidating to a student who has never used the center before—and no one enjoys looking like they don't know what they're doing in front of an audience. For tutors, making the process of logging in, getting to work, and getting help as transparent and welcoming as possible for students (and especially first-time users of the center) is an important first step in setting up an inviting, healthy, well-functioning learning environment in which students can relax and focus their full attention on their own goals for learning. You can also ensure that students who may feel hesitant to seek out help for themselves, or who dislike calling attention to themselves in front of a group, receive the support they need by being sure to check in not only with those students who are actively signaling for help but also those who may appear, on the surface, to be quietly and self-sufficiently working. Table 4.2 provides a general approach to tutoring within a drop-in lab environment.

RUSHES OF STUDENTS

It's a common experience, in learning centers, for tutors to encounter rushes of students. This often happens because a large class has an assignment due, or an exam coming up, in the near future. This can be a stressful situation, as the ratio of students to tutors creeps up beyond your previous experience and beyond your comfort zone. In a drop-in lab setting, the problem comes with its own solution, in that many of the students (because they are facing the same due dates) will be working on the same papers, problems, and issues. Drop-in labs provide the tools and flexibility to capitalize on the educational opportunity that such a scenario represents, by providing opportunities for you to work with students in groups that can function as small learning communities, or to become a facilitator of interactions between peers. When drop-in labs become busy, seek opportunities to put students working on the same assignment, writing the same paper, solving the same problem, studying for the same test, and/or grappling with the same concept together. Ask students to move into groups, and to introduce themselves to one another. Move furniture as needed to accommodate student interactions. Then focus on engaging with students in groups (incorporating strategies, as needed, from the next section, on group learning) and on setting up interactions between students that will

Table 4.2   A Basic Framework for Drop-In Labs

As Students Enter the Center

As students enter the center, welcome them. If possible, let them know that they can get to work, and that they can raise their hand if they'd like you to come around.

It's important for students to feel invited and oriented to the space, and also for them to know that they don't need to wait for a tutor in order to start their projects.

During the Session: Four Strategies for Drop-In Labs

Microinterventions

- Use observations and diagnostic questions to ascertain what factors may be preventing a student from making progress.
- Provide the learner with the support that they need in order to be able to continue making progress.
- Move on, giving the learner time to practice and integrate their new understanding of the material.

Microinterventions provide the minimum necessary scaffolding for learners to operate within the zone of proximal development, performing tasks at the limits of their abilities.

Mini Workshops

- Seat students who are grappling with the same issue together.
- Engage the students as a group, providing the support that they need in order to be able to continue making progress.
- Move on to other students, giving the students the option to continue working together.

Mini workshops, like microinterventions, provide students with the support that they need to continue making progress. By addressing your interventions to groups rather than to individuals (e.g., by pulling three students together for an explanation, using a whiteboard, of a challenging concept), you can make more economical use of your time. More importantly, you create support networks of learners helping one another, which may persist even after students leave the center.

Peer Review

- Seat students who are working on the same task, and who are at similar levels of progress, together in small groups of two to four.
- Give the learners specific guidance on what they should pay attention to in their peers' work.
- Have students exchange homework/ papers/projects, giving them a set amount of time to look it over and provide feedback according to the criteria the group agreed on. Within a group, everyone should review and comment on everyone else's work.
- Give the group time to discuss their feedback, ask clarifying questions about feedback they received, and discuss what they observed in others' work that they can apply in their own work.

Peer review is an appropriate intervention when students have work at some stage of completion, in a form that can be shared. Peer review provides students with the benefit of multiple sets of eyes on their work, providing them with feedback that they can use to correct errors, add further complexity, and otherwise make improvements. Just as importantly, students are able to see how other learners approach the same prompt. In being exposed to diverse approaches and points of view, students expand and make more complex their own knowledge structures, while also having modeled for them problem-solving strategies used by others.

(Continued)

Table 4.2   A Basic Framework for Drop-In Labs (*Continued*)

Group Work	Group work provides less advanced learners
• Seat students who are working on the same task, and who are at similar levels of progress, work together in small groups of two to four. • Have the group work together, in dialogue with one another, on the problem. • Check in on the group periodically to address any questions, concerns, or misconceptions that may arise.	*the opportunity to receive the benefit of modeling from more advanced learners, while less advanced learners experience the benefit of developing and entrenching their own schemas in applying them to the task of explaining their understanding of the topic to others.*

allow less advanced learners to benefit from more advanced learners, and more advanced learners to accrue the educational benefits of applying what they know in explaining it to others. With intentionality, and a bit of practice, busy drop-in labs become ideal opportunities to capitalize on the active and collaborative nature of the format.

Within a drop-in lab, the core strategy is to keep moving. Tutors in drop-in labs circulate among the students in the center checking in on everyone, on the lookout for students actively seeking assistance (often signaling this with a raised hand, or eye contact), but also being sure to check in on everyone working in the space. In working with students, the tutors' goal is to provide the minimum scaffolding that will allow students to get over their immediate hurdle and keep working independently or within a group of co-learners, and then to keep moving, giving students time to apply and integrate the new information. When there is more than one tutor in the lab, they are able to work as a team to cover the whole lab, provide different insights, pool their collective knowledge, and together consider approaches that may be helpful for learners in the space. When multiple students are working on the same thing, tutors can get them working together. When multiple students are facing the same hurdle, scaffolding can be provided for the group rather than individually.

4.3 GROUP LEARNING

Group learning environments are venues that are optimized for collaborative learning. They can include workshops, Supplemental Instruction sessions, exam reviews, or any other format for tutoring in which large groups of students are brought together for sessions covering a set topic, facilitated by a peer tutor. The goal of a group learning session is to give learners the opportunity to engage with course material in a different, generally more active and collaborative and active, way than they may have the opportunity in class. Group learning is an opportunity for students to work together toward a common goal. Scaffolding in group learning environments can take many of the same forms as it often does in individual appointments and drop-in labs, but the focus should be on collaboration. Group learning environments are a good venue for handling topics, concepts, and skills that come up repeatedly for students within a curriculum (e.g., drafting strategies for writers, solving story problems in mathematics, understanding cell division in biology, memorization skills for premed students, developing a business plan for business students).

Generally, group learning environments are scheduled events, offered at a specific time and for a specific duration. This makes it possible for tutors to plan in advance for group sessions, in a way that isn't often possible for other tutoring formats. It's a very good idea for tutors to enter group learning session with a clearly articulated plan of what topics will be covered, the goals for the session, how much time will be spent on each topic, and what activities will be used to structure the session. On the other hand, it's important for such plans to be reactive to the needs of the students in the room. There should be plenty of time built in for addressing unexpected concerns and questions. It's always desirable to cover less material well, rather than more material poorly. As with all tutoring, students will ultimately learn more when they have the chance to engage with the material actively and in a variety of ways, even if it means less material is covered. A good way to begin a collaborative learning session is by talking about the planned agenda, agreeing on it and modifying it as needed, as a group. Table 4.3 provides a suggested framework for approaching the planning and delivery of workshops, SI sessions, and other group venues.

RESPONDING TO QUESTIONS

Because learning centers are driven by learners' needs, students' questions will be at the center of peer tutoring interactions, moving them forward and directing your attention and your planning. How you respond to those questions is essential to the dynamic of the session. Simply providing direct answers to students' questions can place the learner in a passive role, putting the focus on your knowledge rather than on empowering the student as an independent learner. In some cases, when a student simply does not have enough knowledge to build on, an explanation (one that presents the information in a new way, that gives an alternate means to

Table 4.3   A Basic Framework for Group Learning

Before the Session

Articulate the goals for the session.	*After the session, what will students have learned? What will they be able to do?*
Develop activities for the session.	*What activities will support the goals above? How will students' schemas be made more complex, and how will they be routinized? How will students benefit from their peers? How can students engage with the material in a different, more active way than they do in class? Refer to the sample collaborative learning techniques in chapter 3.*

Beginning the Session (the First 10 Minutes)

Establish shared goals for the session.	*Engage the group in a dialogue around the goals for the session, setting expectations for the session and altering the plan you entered with as needed to accommodate learners' goals.*
Get everyone ready to learn with an opening activity.	*The main goals for opening activities are to break the ice, and to get everyone in a mental space for learning. Consider activities in which students both introduced themselves to the group and prime their existing knowledge about a topic.*

During the Session

Implement the plan for the session.	*In the main body of the session, your role as a facilitator is to frame the activities, setting up collaborative learning interactions. Try to restrict the comments you make to the group to briefly laying a principle or piece of information, before giving the group an opportunity to work together to share knowledge, apply information in new ways, and collaborate toward solutions.*

Ending the Session (the Last 10 Minutes)

Have the group collaborate in an activity that fosters awareness of ways in which individuals' knowledge structures have developed.	*The main goal for closing activities is to for students to develop awareness of what they learned, which will help them to retain it. Consider closing activities in which student label and articulate their takeaways from the session.*

understand the material than they received in class, and that connects the new information to what they already know) is the best way forward. Usually, however, it's preferable to have answers come from learners, rather than from you. Here are a few strategies that you can use, when students ask you questions about the material:

- Redirect the question to the student, having them tell you about what they know so far.

  "Tell me where you're at. Could you tell me about your understanding of supply and demand? How does it work?"

- Redirect the question toward other learners.

"A-ha! Michael has identified a really good question to help us think about this. What do we think? What would happen if the fluid in the water bottle rocket was replaced with something that weighed less, like alcohol?"

- Ask questions that guide the student toward ideas that will help them to solve the problem.

"Before we try to answer that question, it might help to think about what it actually means. What is atomic weight, exactly? How would you define it?"

- Give the students hints that will help them to arrive at the answer themselves.

"Remember that Japanese doesn't make questions by changing word order, like English does, it does it by adding the question particle '-ka.' Knowing that, how would you go about turning this into a question?"

- Show the student resources to which they have access in order to answer the question themselves (e.g., an online resource, their textbook). Show the student how to use it, and have them look up the answer.

"The definition of a microclimate will definitely be in your textbook, we just have to find it. Can you flip to the index, in the back? This is alphabetical, so you'll want to look under 'm.' If it's not there, you could look under 'climate' and then see if there are sub-entries for 'micro' and 'macro.' Okay, can you head to that page number, and we'll see what the book says?"

- Have the student refer back to their own notes, to seek any relevant information.

"Did your professor cover this in lecture? Maybe it would help if we looked back at your notes, to see what you got down there, and then we can build on that. Can you pull out your notebook?"

- Invite the students to draw a diagram, create a mindmap, or do a free-write to articulate their understanding of the concept/problem/process.

"I'm not sure where your essay should go next. Maybe if you drew a diagram that showed its overall structure, it would help you to decide. Do you want to try that out?"

- Provide the answer to a different-but-related question, and then pose the original question back to the student.

"So that's my process for solving a problem about these functions that have an asymptotic curve. Could you try that same process out, for the one you were asking me about?"

- Use a metaphor or an example to try to frame the question in a new way, and then redirect it back to the student.

"The way that languages split from each other is a lot like how species split from each other. What happens to a species if it's divided for long enough, and the populations can't interbreed? Okay, so what do you think happens to languages when speakers in different groups go long enough without talking to one another?"

Group learning sessions often take place in classrooms, and on the surface they can look a lot like classes. But group learning sessions are not classes, and tutors are not teachers. Every student, at every college and university, has adequate opportunities to sit in a room and be talked at. Group learning sessions provide an opportunity for learners to engage with the material in a different way (or, ideally, in a variety of different ways) than they do in class. In group learning sessions, as in all learning center interactions, the goal for tutors is to guide and facilitate student learning, not to act as an expert. Every opportunity that tutors can take to deflect the role of teacher (by moving furniture around to avoid the room having an audience/presenter setup, by walking around rather than standing at the front of the room, by avoiding lecturing) and the role of expert (by redirecting questions back to the group, by having learners write on the board rather them doing it themselves, by introducing oneself as a fellow student) is an opportunity to give students a more deep, complex, and entrenched view of the concepts covered in their courses and of the work of being a student.

One of the most significant advantages of group learning venues is that their highly social nature helps to mitigate any sense of stigma that may be associated, by some students, with utilizing academic support. Well-attended events that students can attend in groups, bringing along friends, tend to invite a broad cross-section of a college or university's student body. And because support is attached to challenging courses, concepts, or skills, rather to individual students, students may attend who would otherwise feel uncomfortable identifying themselves as students in need of support. The disadvantages of group learning venues follow, as well, from their highly social and interactive nature. Like drop-in labs, group learning sessions can be intimidating, or even off-putting, environments for more reserved, introspective, shy, or reticent students. It's important for you, in facilitating group learning environments, to ensure that the conversation isn't dominated by more extroverted and outgoing students. In addition, it's a good idea to be cautious about taking a quiet student's lack of questions as a signal that they are fully comfortable with the material.

CONCLUSION

In this chapter, we've looked at suggestions intended to help in working with students, in the form of tools, useful questions, and guidelines. They are intended to serve as useful templates, a good starting point for any tutoring session. It's important to remember, though, that there are no rules in tutoring, only guiding principles. Much of the point of peer tutoring is to be responsive to the unique needs of individual students. At times, your intuition and experience will point you in a direction that deviates from these defaults. The concepts covered in chapters 2 and 3 can serve as touchstones for improvisation. In further chapters, we will cover additional lenses for understanding the work of peer tutoring, the unique needs of various kinds of students, more things to consider in working with learners, and other types of tutoring scenarios. All of it builds on the foundation that you've built in these chapters, and on the experience and skill that you'll accrue as you begin to develop your tutoring practice, applying these principles in action and developing your own unique style as a tutor.

QUESTIONS TO DRIVE THE SESSION

Within a learning interaction, we are always confronted with the question "How can I help this student?" Based on the concepts in this chapter, these are questions that you can ask yourself, in the moment, to drive the decisions that you make as a peer educator.

- How can I make sure that this student is accessing the form of support that is most appropriate and relevant to them?
- How can I make sure that this student has clear, realistic expectations for what will take place during this session?
- How can I conclude this session in a way that will help the learner to continue working, and that will allow them to leave with a clear sense of what they accomplished?
- How can I respond to this learners' question in way that gives the student agency in finding the answer?

WAYS TO ENGAGE

Questions for Discussion

1. How do these formats line up with your program? Does your center do individual appointments? Drop-in labs? What are group learning environments that take place in your center (Workshops? Study groups? SI sessions? Exam reviews?). How would the templates above need to be altered to fit the way that your center operates? Are there other formats for tutoring that your center uses that aren't covered here? Are there any tools here that can offer guidance for structuring them? Are any of the formats listed above not attested in your center?
2. What are situations in which you would refer a learner to individual appointments? To drop-in labs? To group learning venues?

Activities

1. Practice Individual Appointments: Pair off. In groups of two, take turns being the tutor and the tutee, practicing the steps above. For tutoring content, tutees should select from one of the following (with tutees feigning total ignorance on the topic): (a) changing a bicycle inner tube, (b) getting a ride through a ride sharing app, (c) changing the oil in a car, or (d) selecting a good restaurant to eat at when visiting an unfamiliar city.
2. Practice Drop-In Labs: Separate into groups of three. In groups, the tutors take turns being the tutor and the tutee, practicing the strategies above. For tutoring content, tutees should select from one of the following (with tutees feigning total ignorance on the topic): (a) making a peanut butter and jelly sandwich, (b) making macaroni and cheese, (c) making a grilled cheese sandwich, or (d) making a smoothie.
3. Imagine that you've been approached by an area high school that is interested in developing a peer tutoring program. You've been asked, based on your experience with college/university learning centers, to provide a two-hour training workshop for the group of 10 students who have been selected as tutors for the program. This group has received no previous training or orientation aside from being notified that they were selected for the program. Following their session with you, the group will be asked to organize services and begin meeting with students. Using the guidelines for Group Learning Venues provided in this chapter, and drawing on all of the content that we've covered in the previous chapters, develop an outline for your training workshop.
4. Based on this chapter, develop a list of useful strategies, and things to avoid, in tutoring sessions (e.g., *do* make sure that the student is doing

most of the talking, *do not* respond to student questions by providing the answer). Design this document as a poster that can be placed on the wall of the learning center, or another location where tutors can refer to it.

Questions for Reflection

1. In your work as a peer tutor, which of these formats of tutoring do you expect to be working within the most? Are there any areas of particular concern or anxiety that you have about meeting with students? Are there any strategies provided here that could be helpful in addressing your concerns?

    If you've already been working with students, are there ways that the templates provided here depart from the pattern that you've established so far? Are there tools that you think you may find helpful in addressing issues that have emerged in your sessions to date?

Chapter 5

Peer Tutoring and the Affective Domain

Up to this point, we've been discussing students' knowledge: what they know, how they learn, and how new information is incorporated within their existing knowledge structures. In this chapter, we turn our attention to students' attitudes, values, emotions, and motivations. Learners' emotional states—the way that they feel about themselves, their lives, the things they are studying, and their place within the college or university at which they are pursuing their degree—are deeply important aspects of learning, which have an effect both on other aspects of cognition, and on student's overall likelihood to attain their academic goals.

The traditional view of how humans think (the enduring legacy of Descartes, who beginning with the famous words "I think therefore I am" argued that the mind and body are fundamentally different entities, and that our true identity as thinking beings lies with our minds) is that our capacity to reason is separate from our physical bodies. This view, which was reinforced and strengthened by the advent of computing and the use of computers as a metaphor for understanding ourselves, looks at the mind as a general system for storing mental representations and performing mental operations upon them: while it exists in the physical organ of the brain and is informed by the body's senses, it exists apart and can be understood independently of the body. More recent views of cognition have challenged this distinction, focusing on the ways that our mental processes are shaped, informed, and ultimately inseparable from the complete organism within which our minds are situated.

EMBODIED COGNITION

Embodied cognition is the point of view that our minds are fundamentally shaped by and grounded in our basic experience of inhabiting human bodies. A deeper and more far-reaching claim than the simple assertion that our minds are grounded in the physical processes of the brain, scholars who have advanced views of embodied cognition have argued that cognitive processes interact at every level with our physiology and physical environments (Barsalou, Niedenthal, Barbey, & Ruppert, 2003; Chemero, 2009; Clark, 1997; Gibbs, 2006; Shapiro, 2011; Smith & Semin, 2007; Varela, Thompson, & Rosch, 1991). Two of the concepts that we've covered in previous chapters, working memory and long-term memory, make particularly excellent examples of embodied cognition. The system of working memory and long-term memory arose in response to the evolutionary pressures of our environment, enabling us to draw on our experience in rapidly performing tasks and making decisions in the moment. The organization of our working memory into separate channels to correspond to our major avenues of sensory input again shows how our cognitive systems are shaped by the bodies we inhabit, as does the way that much of the information stored in our long-term memory is rich with sensory experience (sights, sounds, and smells). The way that we use physical concepts such as "up" and "down" (rooted in the physical experience of inhabiting a body that exists in a gravitational field) to metaphorically structure our basic understanding of abstract concepts such as quantities and emotions is another good example of embodied cognition.

For peer tutors, the implication of embodied cognition is that students are not thinking machines, and their capacities as learners can't be separated from other aspects of their identity. In order to engage with students as learners, it's necessary for us to consider the entire organism: mind, body, and emotions.

Attention to the affective domain, and to the physiological states associated with emotions, is one of the most important ways that you, as a peer tutor, can attend to the way that learning is a process that is situated within human bodies. It's also one of the most important ways that you can be present for the students you work with. People become peer tutors for a lot of reasons. You may have decided to join your learning center because you were interested in engaging with course material in a different way, because you were seeking an opportunity for student leadership, or because you wanted to start building professional experience in your field. The most important and dependable reason, however, that people become tutors is that they are caring, empathetic people who want to help. Engaging students over their feelings doesn't just help them to learn more effectively; it also helps them to feel heard and valued within their social and academic communities.

THE AFFECTIVE DOMAIN AND BLOOM'S TAXONOMY

The term *affective domain* comes from Bloom's Taxonomy. Covered in more detail in chapter 8, Bloom's Taxonomy separates learning into three domains: the cognitive (our representations of knowledge), the affective (the way they affect us), and the psychomotor (relating to our coordination of physical movement) (Bloom, 1956). Within the affective domain, Bloom's Taxonomy organizes learning into levels, ranging from the simplest to the most complex (Krathwohl, Bloom, & Masia, 1973): (figure 5.1).

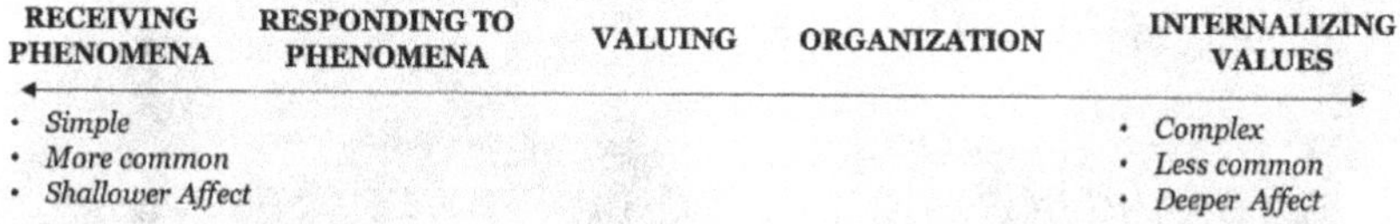

RECEIVING PHENOMENA	RESPONDING TO PHENOMENA	VALUING	ORGANIZATION	INTERNALIZING VALUES
• Simple • More common • Shallower Affect				• Complex • Less common • Deeper Affect

Figure 5.1   Levels of learning in the affective domain. *Dan Sanford.*

As students develop in their mastery of a topic (and as they grow as learners), the ways in which knowledge affects them changes and develops. They progress from the emotional capacity to being able to passively receive information (e.g., respectfully listening), to actively engaging with it (e.g., participating in discussions), to integrating it with their beliefs and values (e.g., developing a respect for cultural diversity), to organizing values into a system that compares, relates, and synthesizes different values (e.g., appreciating how the personal freedom interacts with social responsibility), and ultimately to incorporating values within their personal character (e.g., developing a sense of ethics that drives day-to-day decision-making).

In reflecting on your own experiences as a college student engaging over time with a curriculum of study, you may have observed a slow progression within yourself from passively reading and listening to the information presented in introductory classes, to the incorporation of values, beliefs, and ethical systems that define the academic community with which you've aligned yourself. Bloom's Taxonomy, and it's articulation of the affective domain, reminds us to be attentive to the emotional journey that college students undergo, and mindful of the role that we can play in shepherding them, especially by personal example, toward a deeper, more meaningful integration of disciplinary content and values with their own systems of belief.

5.1 THE PREFRONTAL CORTEX, STRESS, AND THE ROLE OF NEUROTRANSMITTERS IN LEARNING

The traditional view of "thinking" and "feeling" treats these two activities as completely separate from one another, reflecting distinct aspects of our psychology. A large and growing body of contemporary cognitive research challenges the view that our capacity to think and reason exists independently of our affective states, demonstrating how our feelings infuse all aspects of our cognition. Our emotions are physiological, affecting our physical being in complex ways, and our cognition is rooted in our physical bodies. It is simply not possible to fully attend to an individual as a learner and thinker without also attending to the ways that they feel.

A SAMPLING OF RESEARCH IN THE COGNITIVE SCIENCES ON THE AFFECTIVE DOMAIN

Contemporary research in the cognitive sciences indicates that affective states (mood, stress, motivation), once considered totally separate from the storage and processing of information, play an important role in thought.

- **Arnsten (2009)**, based on a wide-ranging survey of the literature on the ways that stress affects the cognitive operations associated with the prefrontal cortex, makes the case that stress has an extremely significant negative impact on the operation of working memory.
- **Estrada, Isen, & Young (1987)** found that positive affect has a highly beneficial effect on college students' performance of creative problem-solving tasks. The authors interpret their results to show that positive affect has an effect on cognitive organization, facilitating learners' ability to see connections among disparate elements.
- **Ashby, Isen, & Turken (1999)** collect findings from a large number of studies indicating that positive affect has a significant effect on cognitive processing, affecting individuals' recall, decision-making, and problem-solving. They argue that these findings are due to the effect of the moderately increased amounts of dopamine that accompany positive aspect on neuropsychological function.

- **Gray, Braver, & Raichle (2002)**, in an MRI study looking at patterns of neural activity during subjects' performance of complex cognitive tasks, found that emotion and cognition are functionally integrated, contributing equally to controlling thought and behavior in tasks that make large demands on working memory.
- **Duncan & Barrett (2007)**, based on a large and wide-ranging review of medical, animal, psychological, and neurological studies, argue that the distinction between cognition and affect lies in the way that we experience them rather than in any true distinction in our neurology or psychology.

In chapter 2, we examined the brain at a functional level—what it does and the basic mechanisms that it uses to do it. In order to consider the ways that affective states bear on our thinking, we must turn our attention to the brain in a more physical sense: *how* our brains do what they do, in accomplishing the acts of cognition that represent our experience of the world.

Our brains are composed of neurons and synapses, and all our thoughts, memories, and cognitive processes correspond to patterns of activation among neural networks in our brains. Connections between neurons, via synapses, is what makes these networks possible. While electrical impulses are an important part of brain activity, there is a strong chemical component to our thinking as well. Connections between neurons across synapses, tiny gaps in the connections between neurons, take place via chemicals that are released at the terminal end of one neuron and taken up by corresponding receptors on the adjoining neuron. These simple chemicals, known as neurotransmitters, are manufactured within our bodies and released by our synapses as needed to facilitate neuronal connections, making cognition possible. They also make our thinking vastly more sophisticated than it would be in a simple mechanical structure of electrical connections between synapses: the ability for synapses to release specific neurotransmitters means that the state of a connection between neurons is not simply "on" or "off" but can be defined by a large number of states corresponding to the specific neurotransmitters involved (figure 5.2).

Our cognition, then, is dependent on, and strongly influenced by, neurotransmitters. The higher cognitive functions that we associate with more complex forms of learning, and specifically with the operations of working memory, are rooted in the prefrontal cortex (the forwardmost, and outermost, section of your brain, located directly behind your forehead). The efficiency of our cognitive functioning—our ability to store memories, solve problems, accomplish tasks, and retrieve stored information—corresponds directly to the levels of certain neurotransmitters in the prefrontal cortex. For example,

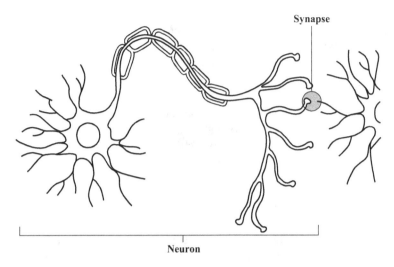

Figure 5.2 Neuron and synapse. *Dan Sanford.*

the operation of working memory is most efficient in the presence of moderate levels of the neurotransmitters dopamine and serotonin. These precise neurotransmitters are also strongly associated with specific emotional states. Serotonin is associated with happiness (and depression with the absence of it). Dopamine is associated with the pleasure of achievement, or of having a desire satisfied. In a very real physical sense, our brains are optimized for learning by positive emotional affect.

Stress, on the other hand, has a powerful depressing effect on learning. Stress causes the release of cortisol and adrenaline, both of which inhibit dopamine, serotonin, and other neurotransmitters that are associated with the effective operation of working memory and decision-making in the prefrontal cortex. This has the effect of pushing decision-making away from the prefrontal cortex, toward more central parts of the brain that are more strongly associated with emotion and instinct than with higher-order cognition. This system evolved for a clear purpose, and remains helpful in many of the situations that we encounter in our lives: in urgent, dangerous scenarios, the role of our prefrontal cortex in executive function and higher cognition is inhibited, allowing us to react as quickly as possible using instinctive, emotional reactions (e.g., jumping out of the way of a falling object) rather than slower processes of reasoning (e.g., thinking carefully though the possible options at hand to avoid danger). However, the fact that the part of the brain most involved in working memory and higher-order thinking is also the part of our brain most negatively impacted by stress can be problematic for us. Environments which require the effective operation of working memory, but which also involve high levels of stress, create severe challenges for us. This tension often comes into play for college students, who are called upon constantly to make decisions, perform cognitive tasks, and retain information while operating under stressful conditions.

MINDFULNESS

Mindfulness is the process of bringing one's full attention to the present, rather than to the past or future. Derived from Buddhist meditative traditions, mindfulness is a highly effective tool for reducing stress. When we focus on the past (through regret, for example) or the future (through worrying or anxiousness), we introduce stress and distraction to the present without creating any corresponding benefits: worrying about the past and future doesn't solve problems; it only reduces our ability to be fully present within our immediate surroundings. In an educational setting, mindfulness allows us to direct our full attention to the current moment, bringing our full cognitive faculties to bear on it.

Mindfulness has its origins in meditative practice, but it doesn't necessarily take meditation to reap its benefits for reducing stress. Peer tutors can introduce mindfulness to their sessions with students through any number of methods that encourage learners to direct their full attention to the immediate task at hand, applying their full faculties to it doing it to the best of their abilities before moving on to the next task:

- Taking a few moments from the session to write a to-do list, so that the learner can set aside their anxieties about the future in order to focus on the goal of the session.
- Starting the session with an engaging discussion about a concept covered in the class, helping them to disregard other concerns and immerse themselves fully in the course.
- Helping students to develop the practice of dedicating blocks of time to particular courses, rather than trying to accomplish everything at once.
- Focusing learners' attention on the next step in solving a problem or accomplishing a task, rather than on the problem/task overall.

Planning is deeply important. Worrying, however, is not. For learners, devoting one's full attention to the present and to the task at hand optimizes working memory both by reducing extraneous load and by reducing stress.

5.2 ATTENDING TO THE AFFECTIVE
DOMAIN IN TUTORING

Learning—the development of progressively more complex cognitive schemas—is completely dependent on the effective operation of working
memory, where the integration of new information with existing schemas
takes place. Learner's affective states have a large impact on the operation of
working memory, and on their ability to learn and to make effective decisions
for themselves. As an educator, one of the most effective ways that you can
support students as learners is to attend to their affective states. Peer tutors
are in a particularly good position to engage with learners as emotional beings
because the formats of education that tutors operate within tend to provide
more time and space to engage with learners' affective states.

One way you can do this is by participating in making sure that your center
is as comfortable and welcoming as possible. Stress is a powerful inhibitor
of learning, and college students all face levels of stress in their daily lives
(from class obligations, interpersonal relationships, financial concerns, and
the competing demands that the many different aspects of college life make
on their time and attention) that make effective learning extremely challenging. Learning centers should strive to support learners in doing the work of
being a student, without themselves introducing any new sources of stress.
Confusion about how tutoring works, time pressure, fear of disappointing
one's tutor, pressure to succeed, or feelings of being unwelcome are all
potential sources of stress that should be minimized as much as possible in
order to create a respite from stress within the center. Moreover, consider the
ways that you and your fellow tutors can create a learning environment that
supports learners in feeling positive—relaxed, engaged, focused, and intellectually curious—about their studies. Every aspect of the center, from the
decorations to the furniture to the way people are greeted when they walk in
the door, contributes to the culture of the space. A space that fosters positive
attitudes toward learning is a space that supports the mission of the center to
support students as learners.

The same is true of your individual consultations with learners, in every
format for tutoring: stress and negative affective states make learning more
challenging, while positive affective states streamline the functioning of
working memory and make learning more efficient. Within a session, you
can help learners to reduce stress by working with them to set a realistic
agenda for the session, and encouraging them to focus on one aspect (or a
few aspects) of the overall task or problem rather than on the entire endeavor.
Treating large, daunting problems as a series of small, attainable tasks is
both an important tool for reducing stress within a session and an important
habit of mind to support students in developing as an overall strategy for

approaching their studies. It also allows students to experience the reward (and accompanying release of dopamine, which in turn facilitates and encourages further learning) of completing objectives. As a peer tutor, you have an enormous influence over how learning interactions *feel* for students. Praise, encouragement, and comfort all help learners to approach their work from a positive affective state that will not only make their visit to the center more productive but also influence the way that they approach their studies overall. Modeling the positive affective states that you bring to your own studies (your enthusiasm for the discipline you tutor, your pride in being a good student, the joy you take in applying your mind to problems in the field you chose to study) is of incalculable value in helping learners to approach their own studies in a frame of mind that will help them to learn well, both within and beyond the session.

You can also accomplish this by attending to the whole person. Stress, sleep, diet, and exercise are all factors that contribute to the presence of beneficial neurotransmitters for learning, and to an overall physiological state that optimizes learners to succeed. Diagnostic questions that inquire into how students *feel* about their studies as well as about their overall well-being (e.g., "How do you feel about this class?" "What do you do to relax?" "Are you getting much sleep these days?") can both help you to gather useful information on factors that may be affecting the operating capacity of students' working memory, and create a more comfortable environment that fosters positive emotional states that prime the brain for learning. At the same time, you demonstrate that you care, making students more likely to share their vulnerabilities and insecurities with you about their studies. There is nothing more important and effective that you can do to make your sessions with learners more comfortable and more conducive to learning than making time for their emotions. Engaging with the attitudes, feelings, and motivations with which students enter the center is an essential part of approaching every user of the center as a unique learner, and of attending to learners as full, complete individuals.

STUDENT MOTIVATION, BELONGING, AND PERSISTENCE

Students' motivation to complete their studies is an important factor in whether or not students persist in their studies, ultimately completing their intended degree. A higher education degree in any course of study is a major undertaking, full of challenges, and requiring a massive investment in time and effort. Inevitably, there are times in the course of every student's path to degree completion when the challenges seem insurmountable, or the investment in time and effort does not seem worth the potential benefit. It is students' motivation—their sense of purposefulness in attaining goals that they have set out for themselves—that allow them to pass through these crises and continue on toward graduation.

Students' sense of belonging is their feeling that they are members of a community to which they belong, within which they perceive themselves to be valued, and toward which they feel a sense of investment. Whether to the overall institution or to a program or department within it, students who feel a sense of belonging feel embedded within a community of faculty, staff, and their fellow students, and this sense of belonging makes an enormous difference in students' motivation, and in the likelihood of their persisting to the eventual completion of their intended programs of study (Bean & Eaton, 2000; Bergen & Milem, 1999; Kuh, Kinzie, Schuh, & Whitt, 2005; Strayhorn, 2012; Tinto, 2015).

Students often enter learning centers feeling not only frustrated but also disaffected and alienated. As a peer tutor, you have an incredible opportunity to help students, through your interactions with them and through your work facilitating their connections to other learners, to feel connected to a larger community within which they matter. In embedding students within groups of learners, in acting as a guide and mentor to the discipline(s) you tutor, and in the simple act of demonstrating that you care and value their success, you help students to feel a sense of belonging to a community larger than themselves. This feeling of connection bolsters students' commitment to the community, motivation to engage within it, and ability to persist in pursuit of their goals.

5.3 ACTIVE LISTENING

Within our daily lives, we listen for a variety of reasons and in a variety of different ways. As a student, you've likely cultivated a form of critical listening, in which you attend carefully to the words of your instructors and fellow students, scanning for important information and for claims that you either disagree with or have questions about. In some cases we listen passively, receiving input as a form of entertainment or relaxation. In many other venues we listen with an eye toward framing our own participation, as when we engage in a back-and-forth conversation with friends. Active listening is separate from all of these. In active listening, the goal is to make the speaker feel heard, devoting one's full attention to the task of listening and responding in ways that signal to the speaker your attention and interest. Active, empathetic listening is the most effective method at your disposal for supporting learners as affective beings, signaling with your full, undivided attention your respect for the student across the table from you as an individual, as a member of the learning community defined by the center, and as a full (if novice) participant in the academic discipline you represent.

The core principle of active listening is empathy: through active listening, you are seeking to fully understand the feelings, ideas, and point of view of the person speaking to you. It's important to distinguish empathy from sympathy. Empathy is centered on the person speaking. In empathic listening, your role is to understand, as much as possible, the speaker's point of view: to fully grasp, and to comprehend from the inside out, the way that they are experiencing the world. The responses that you make as an empathetic listener have the function of signaling to the speaker that you hear and understand their words, providing them with the security of knowing that you are listening, and that you appreciate and comprehend what they are saying (e.g., "I hear you—that sounds like such a challenging experience"). Sympathy, on the other hand, is about the listener. In a sympathetic approach to listening, the focus isn't on the speaker or the meaning that they are conveying, but on the emotional response that it elicits in the listener ("I feel so bad for you!"). Sympathy is compassionate, and in many life situations it's an appropriate response. But in active listening, an empathetic approach—seeking to fully grasp the speaker's point of view, and to reflect this understanding back to them—is the goal.

Listening is not judgment. The goal of listening is to understand the speaker, and help them to feel heard and understood. Nothing is more toxic to the feeling of security created by being listened to and appreciated than to have the response take the form of a judgment of the speaker or of something they said. Consider a student who is sharing with you, during a tutoring session, a difficult experience that has caused them to question their own abilities (an exam that went poorly, for example, or a paper on which the student received a much lower grade than expected). The student may be feeling a sense of disappointment in themselves, shame over what they perceive as an embarrassing failure, alienation from their peer group, or any of a number of other negative emotional responses. Their affective state is creating, in addition to emotional pain, a barrier to learning within the session, because physiologically it hinders the operation of the prefrontal cortex in implementing higher-order cognition to solve the problem at hand, restrategizing their approach so the experience does not repeat itself. It is likely also affecting their motivation, weakening their ability to persist to graduation by inserting doubt as to whether or not they have the resources to do, and a sense of isolation from peers who they may be perceiving as more capable or intelligent than themselves. You, as an experienced student, are likely to have a clear sense of how the learner's lack of success resulted from their choices (how they chose to manage their time, for example, or the method that they used to prepare) rather than from any innate flaw in themselves as a person or as a learner. Responses to the student's emotional pain that involve advice ("next time, you should devote a lot more time to studying") or criticism ("that was a pretty ineffective way to tackle this assignment") are almost certain to be experienced by a student in an emotionally vulnerable state as a judgment upon themselves, damaging the sense of warmth, security, and trust that is essential to an effective relationship with you, and an optimal affective state for learning.

Listening is also not rescuing. As a caring person, you are likely to feel within yourself, listening to a student articulating their emotional pain, an urge to help. Often, a response emerging from this impulse will take the form of attempting to argue the student out of what they are feeling ("don't feel bad! This was a really hard test!" or "it's not a big deal—this is only 5% of your grade"). The urge to rescue students from what they are feeling, while it comes from a good place, is ultimately at odds with the goals of listening. Rescuing, rather than affirming students in their feelings and signaling your understanding of it, diminishes their feelings. It sends the implicit message that they way that they feel is not an appropriate response, and that they should feel a different way from the way that they do. Like judgment, trying to rescue someone from their feelings has the opposite of the intended effect: rather than helping the learner to grow from their feelings, it encourages them to move on to learning without having released or resolved them. Devoting your time and attention to fully attending to their affective state, using listening and empathy, is what will lay a foundation within the session for learning to take place, and for learners to feel a sense of belonging to the community that will support them in attaining their goals. Table 5.1 provides a basic framework for approaching tutoring sessions as an active, engaged, empathetic listener.

MOTIVATIONAL INTERVIEWING

Motivational Interviewing is a therapeutic approach that was outlined by Clinical Psychologists William Miller and Stephen Rollnick (1991). Designed as a tool for working with clients with addictive behaviors, the approach is relevant wherever practitioners work with clients who are acting in ways that undercut their ability to achieve their own goals, and it has been applied widely outside of clinical settings. Motivational interviewing can be understood as a form of active listening, but it is also itself highly dependent on active listening: the techniques used in motivational interviewing are only applicable when a practitioner has first devoted sufficient time to fully listening to and understanding a client's issues, and to developing trust and rapport.

Table 5.1 A Basic Framework for Active Listening

Depending on the session, devoting dedicated time to active listening may be appropriate for the bulk of the session, the first few minutes, or not at all—use your instincts, proceeding from the student's emotional cues as to their affective state.

Listen

Devote your full attention to the student.	*Engage yourself fully in the task of trying to understand and appreciate the learner's point of view: what they are thinking, what they are feeling, and how they arrived at their current affective state.*
Demonstrate your active attention. • Verbally (e.g., vocalizations, approving noises, encouragement) • Nonverbally (e.g., eye contact, body language, facing toward the student) • By avoiding distractions in the environment (e.g., other people, noises) or within yourself (boredom, judgment).	*Verbal and nonverbal demonstrations of your active attention all serve to demonstrate to the student that you are fully focused on them, creating a safe and supportive environment for them to share within. Verbal and nonverbal demonstrations of your inattention, as well as distraction or multitasking, signal the opposite: that you have something else you'd rather be doing, or that you are having an internal reaction that is distracting you from listening.*

Reflect

Summarize or paraphrase what the student is saying.	*Using summarizing or paraphrasing to reflect back to the learner what you're hearing about their affective state (e.g., "It sounds like you're worried you're not going to pass this course, and that you won't be accepted to your major" or "I hear you saying that you feel overwhelmed") provides them with the security of knowing that you hear, value, and understand them.*

Ask

Pose clarifying questions to encourage the student to elaborate.	*Clarifying questions (e.g., "Do you feel worried that you don't have enough time to write this, or is it more that you're confused about what's expected of you?) help you to more fully understand the students' point of view, and also show the student that you are interested and want them to continue. They can also double as diagnostic questions, providing you with important information to guide the session.*

Sources: Atwater (1981), Gordon (1975), Reed (1985), Rogers (1951), Rosenberg (2003), Stanley, Markman, & Blumberg (1997).

The underlying tenet of motivational interviewing is that the motivation to change behaviors that are keeping individuals from achieving their goals, or that are in conflict with their values, must come from the individual: it can't be imposed from the outside. The insight that one's behaviors are at odds with one's goals, and the motivation to make changes accordingly, has to come from the individual. Miller & Rollnick argue that persuasion is not an effective tool for changing behaviors, because the motivation to make changes must come from within in order to result in true change. The role of a practitioner using motivational interviewing is to guide clients' attention toward these conflicts, helping them to identify, examine, and resolve them. The core method of doing this is to make dispassionate, nonjudgmental statements and questions that draw individual's attention to conflicts between opposing values, or between their stated beliefs and their goals. Practitioners then pose further questions, to help guide individuals toward a plan of action. Motivational interviewers don't judge, and they don't give advice. They respect the right and autonomy of interviewees to make their own choices, and they recognize the difficulty of change because they've taken the time to see things from the interviewee's point of view.

For peer tutors operating within an academic setting, the model offers a set of tools for helping students to identify conflicts between their goals (e.g., to get an A on a paper) and their behaviors (not starting it until a few days before it is due). A tutor utilizing a motivational interviewing approach would pose questions to direct students' attention to conflicts between their goals and behaviors (e.g., "What changes in your process would help you to do better on your next paper?"), build their motivation to make changes ("How important is it for you to do well in this class? What will happen if you don't make changes to your approach for the next paper?"), see the overall situation ("You're hoping to get As on your papers, but you're writing them in the two days before they're due, which keeps you from writing at your full potential. If you continue, you'll probably keep getting low grades for your writing."), and decide on a future course of action ("How do you plan to use these insights?").

CONCLUSION

Peer tutors meet learners where they are, providing students with the support that they need at whatever point they are at in their individual journey. As a tutor, you'll never encounter a session that takes place wholly within the cognitive domain. Students' attitudes about what they are learning, their previous experiences with academic support, their feelings of anxiety, the way that their day has gone so far, and many other emotional factors all play a role in the session. So, too, do the intangibles that you bring to the session: your enthusiasm, your vulnerability, your calmness, and your willingness to listen. By focusing on and planning for these aspects of the session, you can create a sense of rapport that will define its dynamic, beneficially shaping the learning environment that is set up within it. You help the learner to enter an affective state in which they can take full advantage of their mental faculties. You reinforce the learning center as an accepting, supportive environment. And perhaps most importantly, you invite students to participate in a greater community, fostering a sense of connection and investment that will sustain them as they work toward their long-term goals.

QUESTIONS TO DRIVE THE SESSION

Within a learning interaction, we are always confronted with the question "How can I help this student?" Based on the concepts in this chapter, these are questions that you can ask yourself, in the moment, to drive the decisions that you make as a peer educator.

- How can I learn more about the emotions, motivations, desires, and stresses of this learner, and how these factors may be affecting their ability to learn?
- How can I model positive affect (curiosity, enthusiasm, interest) toward this concept, course, and discipline?
- How can I increase this student's positive affect and reduce their stress level, optimizing their prefrontal cortex for the effective operation of working memory?
- How can I help this learner to feel included within the academic community that I tutor, and that they see me as a representative of?
- How can I ensure that this learner feels fully listened to?
- How can I direct this learner's attention to conflicts between their goals and behaviors?

WAYS TO ENGAGE

Questions for Discussion

1. What are some of the ways that learners' negative affective states (e.g., sadness, anger, stress) might materialize in tutoring sessions? How might you engage with these? At what point would you seek help from others, and who would you seek help from?
2. Students' previous educational experiences can result in a counterproductive mindset toward learning. Have you had educational experiences that negatively affected your attitude toward school/college and enthusiasm to learn? What were they (if you feel comfortable sharing them)? How did you emerge from the experience as a successful student, and how might

you apply your experience to working with students who may have had similar experiences?

3. What are some of the ways that you, as a peer tutor and as a student leader, can model the motivation and positive attitude that you bring to your studies?

4. Think of someone (a friend, a coworker, a fellow student, an adviser, a family member) who you think of as a particularly good listener. What is it about sharing with them that makes doing so satisfying? How do they signal their attentiveness and interest?

5. Imagine a student who comes into the center an hour before their assignment is due, highly stressed and seeking your help. What difficulties does the situation create for you, and for the student? How could motivational interviewing provide you with tools to negotiate the situation with the student, both respecting their affective state and taking advantage of the scenario as an educational opportunity?

Activities

1. Working in groups of three, develop a scenario in which a learner's (or learners') stress and anxiety is making it difficult for them to learn, or to accomplish their intended goal, in the learning center.
   a. Decide who is the tutor (or tutors), and who is the learner (or learners).
      i. For the learner(s): What are you stressed about? How is this stress materializing in your behavior?
      ii. For the tutor(s): What tools from this chapter would be relevant to the situation? How will you strategize the session, helping the learner(s) to overcome their stress so that they can focus and learn effectively?
   b. Act out the scenario you developed for the larger group. The larger group should discuss the following questions:
      i. Did you find the scenario realistic?
      ii. What tools did the tutors use to help the learner to manage their stress and anxiety? What did you find particularly effective?
      iii. Were there other approaches that you think could also have been relevant to the situation?

2. In this activity, you will reflect on the experiences of listeners encountering attentive and inattentive learning strategies while also practicing active listening.
   a. In an individual freewrite using five minutes for each prompt, answer the following questions:
      i. What was your morning like? What happened between waking up and your first commitment this morning? How was it?

      ii. What was a challenging/hard/frustrating/annoying thing that happened to you in your academic or work life this week?
- b. In a group of two, take turns sharing your responses from (a).
  - i. Take three-minute turns sharing what happened to you this morning. The listener should use every means at their disposal (verbally and nonverbally) to signal their disinterest and distraction.
  - ii. In the same group of two, take four-minute turns sharing the challenging thing that happened to you this week. The listener should use every means at their disposal (verbally and nonverbally) to signal their attention, interest, and empathy.
- c. In the large group, discuss the following questions:
  - i. How did it feel, in (b), to share? What emotions came up for you as you were trying to share, and experiencing not being listened to?
  - ii. How did it feel, in (c), to be the speaker? What was the experience like for you of talking about something that was challenging for you, and being listened to? What did your listener do that felt especially attentive or meaningful to you?
  - iii. Based on your experience of this exercise, how do you think tutors should respond to learners who are experiencing challenges in their own education?

Questions for Reflection

1. What is the relevance of emotional states to learning? Why is it important to attend to learners as complete individuals, encompassing both affective and cognitive concerns? How do you intend to do so, in your work as a peer tutor?

Chapter 6

Learning Strategies

Students' systems of knowledge, defined by schemas stored in long-term memory, are incredibly important for structuring their understanding of core concepts in a discipline, and for solving problems in ways that line up with approaches used by thinkers in the field. Another important set of factors influence students' success across *all* of their courses, acting globally on the entire way that an individual approaches being a student. The tools that define an individual's general strategy for being a learner—the ways that students study, take tests, manage their time, approach course readings, take notes, write papers, and otherwise engage with the work of being a student—are outsized predictors of their success in college overall. It's unfortunate, then, that students who are having issues with learning strategies often don't realize that they are having issues with learning strategies. A student who just failed their biology midterm generally knows that they need a biology tutor. A student feeling anxiety about an upcoming research paper knows to visit a writing tutor. A student who is having issues with learning strategies may simply feel like the water is over their head, often accompanied by a questioning of whether they belong in college (or, more specifically, at their college in particular). By helping learners to recognize situations in which the strategies they are applying to their education may not be serving them, and intervening in helping them to develop more effective tools, tutors provide an incredibly helpful service. One common outcome of both survey and longitudinal data from students visiting learning centers for peer tutoring is that doing so helps learners not only in the course for which they visited the center but for other courses as well. Engagement with learning strategies is the reason for this. When students interact with peer tutors, they're not only exposed to a more advanced learner's understanding of the course material. They also receive the benefit of having modeled for them the strategies that successful college students use to approach the endeavor of being a college student. By learning to recognize situations in which a student's learning strategies may be the underlying issue, and by developing a set of strategies for successfully intervening with them, you can fully embody the potential for peer tutors to serve as a guide and mentor for students looking to you as a model.

6.1 LEARNING STRATEGIES AND THE TRANSITION TO COLLEGE

The transition from high school to college is a time of intense transition for learning strategies, and the first year of college is a common time for stress and anxiety as many students realize that the strategies they developed and applied—often to highly successful effect—in high school may not serve them in college. Students entering college directly out of high school are in the process of undergoing a massive change in their lives, fueled by a potent combination of having more to do (learn, write, study, memorize, perform, and otherwise accomplish) than they have ever had to do before, and also having more freedom to structure their own time than they have ever before experienced. Whereas students' days in high school are generally tightly structured and monitored, students in colleges and universities have tremendous latitude to make their own choices (whether to study or attend a new club, whether to prepare for lecture or get breakfast, whether to go to 8:00 a.m. Algebra or sleep in after a late night of making new friends). The consequences of college students' choices relating to students' choices tend to be highly delayed—whereas a student skipping class or not doing their homework in high school will often face immediate ramifications, a college student failing to fulfill the implicit expectations for a course may not face any consequences until an ill-omened midterm or final exam. At the same time, students entering college from high school are undergoing a profound shift in social networks, leaving behind friends and relationships, and figuring out where they fit within the new landscape of college life and young adulthood. They are entering a new stage of life, departing both the restrictions and security of home and family, and entering a wholly new arena of thrilling choices about how to manage their priorities, spend their time, and express their identity, as well as less electrifying (but no less urgent) choices about how and when to eat, pay bills, and do laundry. Often, first-year students are accomplishing all of this while juggling work, athletics, or continuing obligations from home. For first generation to college students (students who are the first in their immediate family to attend college) these challenges can be heightened, as they do not have the benefit of family lore on college life and knowledgeable advice from family members on how to overcome the challenges of higher education. The transition is no less potent for non-traditional students (students who do not align with the typical profile of the recent high school graduate). Nontraditional students, who can span a wide variety of ages, may be entering their first year of college, returning to college for an additional degree, or resuming an interrupted education. For individuals whose lives have been shaped by the demands of career, parenthood, or military service, it can be a highly jarring shift to change gears to student life, and to operate within a campus culture often set by the habits and preferences of 18- to 22-year-olds. While older students may have the benefit of having accrued more life skills and self-awareness than recent high school graduates, the shift toward the rhythms of college life takes no less intentionality.

For every college student, support for learning strategies is important. Students continue to grow and develop throughout their time in college in the ways that they implement organizational and strategic approaches to their own education, and peer tutors have an important role to play in helping learners at every stage in their academic careers to assess these strategies. Students in their first year to college, however, are at a particularly crucial stage for attention to learning strategies. Engaging first-year students over learning strategies can both help them through one of the most challenging times they are likely to encounter in their time as a student, and support them in developing approaches that they can then apply throughout their entire time in college.

6.2 TIME MANAGEMENT

The thing about time management is that you never fully figure it out, you just figure out the right system for your current circumstances. Every major life change requires a new system for managing one's time and priorities (you may be, in your own life, currently working to manage the competing demands on your time of being a student and of being a peer tutor). Every set of circumstances requires its own set of tools and strategies, unique to you and to your situation, that will allow you to succeed at the expectations being currently placed on you. For college students, the fundamental challenge is that students have a tremendous amount to do, but that their time is relatively unstructured. In order to attain good grades, progress through courses, and succeed within a curriculum, students are expected to spend a large amount of time studying, writing, reading, and doing homework. One commonly cited rule of thumb is that for every one hour spent in class, students should be spending two hours outside of class, devoted to the course. While the amount of time that it will take for a student to excel within a course will vary according to the student and the course, this generalization is accurate. The time that professors expect their students to spend outside of class, focused on the course, is known to educators as time on task: time spent engaging with, thinking through, reflecting, and reinforcing the concepts covered during class time. Creating time on task is one major reason why professors assign homework, papers, and projects. In order to succeed in the course, professors expect their students to be putting in a large amount of time on task outside of class hours.

HIGHER EDUCATION AND THE CARNEGIE UNIT

Almost all U.S. (and most Canadian) colleges and universities use a credit system to structure degree and graduation requirements. While this system has earlier origins (Charles Eliot at Harvard University is widely credited with creating the credit system still used today), the system was standardized and popularized through the foundation established by American iron magnate and philanthropist Andrew Carnegie (1835–1919). The Carnegie Foundation created a pension fund for professors only available to institutions that adopted standards imposed by the Carnegie Foundation, which persist as common features of higher education in the United States and elsewhere. The fundamental unit of this system is the Carnegie Unit, which corresponds to 120 hours of instructional time. Within this system, one credit hour corresponds to 3 hours of student work/week, for a 15-week semester. One of these hours is contact time with a professor (typically, a lecture or seminar), while the remaining two are lab or homework. The most common version of this system is for students to receive 3 credits for a typical undergraduate course that meets 3 hours/week, and for a 4-year undergraduate degree to correspond to about 120 credits (other systems, with wholly different rationales, are used in different parts of the world—a common point of confusion for international students and students engaged in study abroad). The fundamental organizing principle of this system, then, is contact time with professors. To earn one credit hour, students will generally spend one hour (or, more typically, 50 minutes) in the classroom. The other two hours of time come outside of class.

This system has two important repercussions for higher education. The first is that professors have limited time with students. A three-credit course, for example, involves (in theory) nine hours/week of learning time, but a professor teaching such a course can only count on three hours with their students. It can be challenging to integrate active, constructivist approaches to learning within such a limited amount of time, and many faculty reasonably feel that it is most important to use the limited instructional time available to them to cover as much as possible in lecture. One important function learning centers provide is creating a space for the more global approaches to learning that this may preclude.

The second important repercussion of this system is that for every one credit hour, professors expect students to spend two hours of time devoted to the course, outside of lecture. For a typical three-credit course, then, faculty will expect students to attend three hours of class each week, and to devote six hours of time outside of class to work for the class: studying, doing homework, writing papers, reviewing notes, and doing assigned readings. Most of the work of being a college student, then, is unstructured: it is intended to take place at a time and place of the student's choosing. The implicit, often-unstated assumption that students in a course spend two hours outside of class for every one hour in class is a common source of misunderstanding, tension, and grief for many new college students who begin their first year feeling like they have a large amount of free time, not realizing until later in their careers (often following a crisis) the need for this time to be utilized studying. Creating clarity around these expectations, making the implicit explicit and helping students to quickly establish an effective routine, is an important part of the work of a tutor.

What may initially present to college students as a large amount of free time is, in fact, time that professors expect students to occupy with time on task devoted to their courses. One challenge for college students is structuring their time in a way that allows them to fully take advantage of their time to accomplish everything that they need to do; breaking up and organizing their schedule in a way that empowers them to take advantage of their time to accomplish their goals. For a student taking a typical course load of 15 credit hours, on track to graduate in 4 years with 120 credit hours, the student will spend 15 hours in class each week. The students' professors, collectively, expect the student to be spending a minimum of 30 hours outside of class, devoted to the course. Beyond this 45 hours/week—already exceeding a full-time job!—students work, sleep, participate in other aspects of student life (athletics, clubs, student government, etc.), attend to family obligations, maintain a social life, and make time for activities (e.g., working out, solitary time, reading, watching movies, playing video games) necessary to their own health and well-being. All of this takes an enormous amount of time, and it takes a high degree of intentionality for a student to structure their time in a way that makes it possible for them to excel as a student, and in everything else going on in their lives.

All of these obligations create stress, and stress makes it highly difficult to learn effectively. A core strategy in time management is to create blocks of time devoted to a single purpose (e.g., "on Mondays, Wednesdays, and Fridays, from 8am to 10am, I am working on Biology 382"). During that time, students should attend to everything that they need to do for that course: meeting upcoming deadlines, daily reading, homework, and all other responsibilities. At the end of that time, they should put the course away and move on to other topics which are equally deserving of their dedicated attention, making sure that each course gets its full allotment of time. Critically, during the time allotted for a course or project, students should try not to worry about *anything else*. Trying to simultaneously keep in mind everything that one has to do for every course is a common mental strategy for students, hoping to make sure that nothing gets overlooked, to apply. Focusing on one course and/or assignment at a time is one critical way of managing the demands of working memory, devoting as much as possible of one's conscious attention to the task at hand. It's also an incredibly important way to manage and reduce stress. Bringing attention and mindfulness to one thing at a time, applying ones full capabilities to that task, is the way to do one's best work and to learn effectively. Writing things down in a plan, list, or calendar provides the security of knowing that an item can be dismissed from conscious attention without fear that it will be forgotten.

MULTITASKING: WHAT THE RESEARCH SAYS

Our society places a high premium on multitasking, and the intense demands placed upon the time of college students would seem to make multitasking a desirable strategy for college students. What does the research say about the efficacy of multitasking, while engaging in learning tasks?

True multitasking occurs when an individual's cognitive resources are simultaneously devoted to more than one task (e.g., talking on the phone while driving a car). Research consistently clearly indicates that speed and accuracy are significantly decreased when we divide our available resources among undertakings (Marois & Ivanoff, 2005; Pashler, 1994; Tombu & Jolicoeur, 2004). On the other hand, the human ability to multitask does seem to improve with practice, an effect that may be due in part to the routinization of schemas that comes with repetition of a task (Schumacher et al., 2001; Van Selst et al., 1999). If it is a desired outcome to be able to engage in two specific tasks simultaneously (e.g., for a medical professional to be able to make decisions while monitoring health data), then practice doing so is beneficial.

More commonly, when we refer to multitasking, what we are actually referring to is task-switching: alternating between different types of cognitive tasks (e.g., taking breaks to check your email while doing your homework). Rapidly switching back and forth between tasks is something that humans are good at, and that in many ways our cognitive architecture is designed to do. There is, however, a clear cost associated with task-switching: people are reliably slower at accomplishing the same amount of cognitive processing when they need to switch back and forth between tasks than when they are allowed to complete one task before moving on to another, because of the time associated with retrieving the relevant schemas from long-term memory (Rogers & Monsell, 1995; Yeung & Monsell, 2003). The more complex or unfamiliar the task that people are switching to, the more time is required for switching (Rubinstein, Meyer, & Evans, 2001)—an extremely important consideration when students are operating within their ZPDs, engaging with tasks at the limits of their abilities.

Humans are capable of both multitasking and task-switching, and can become better with practice. But it does come at a significant cost in processing time and cognitive resources. If the goal is to learn as much as possible, accomplish tasks (writing papers, mastering concepts, memorizing information, solving problems) well, and to do so in a way that makes efficient use of time, then it's to a learner's advantage to devote as much continuous time as possible to one task (or one type of task) before switching to another.

As a tutor, you can help students to manage their own time by keeping an eye out for signs that time management may be an issue (stress, a feeling of being overwhelmed, inability to focus on one task at a time during the session, issues with deadlines, expressed difficulty with managing priorities). You can also watch for red flags (e.g., a first-year student expressing pleasant surprise at how much free time they have in their schedule, a learner allocating only two hours/week of time to a course that you know to be extremely time-intensive, a student new to a challenging major expecting to be able to take 18 credits/semester while also working 15 hours/week). Motivational interviewing (see chapter 5) is a tool particularly well-suited to helping students to identify tensions between their goals and behaviors, which is reliably a crux at the center of time management issues. You can encourage students to devote time to the process of planning out how they manage their time, and you can provide strategies and tools that are helpful for doing so. You can then provide scaffolding, in the form of hints, questions, and suggestions, for students as they apply these strategies.

Successful students have in common that they've arrived at some sort of system, however informal, for managing their time and priorities. Such systems are highly varied, shaped by and suited to each person's values and approach. Students with well-formed systems will utilize tools (e.g., web calendars, devices, or planners), approaches (e.g., conceptualizing all of their obligations as items on a list, as calendar entries, or as priorities), and routines (e.g., beginning every day by creating a new to-do list, using time on social media as a reward for completing an item, starting the semester by transmitting all syllabus deadlines to a planner) in different ways. The goal for tutors in working with students on time management is to provide a basic set of tools that students can learn, practice, and then use a basis for customization, refinement, and improvisation as they develop their own unique, individual system. Table 6.1 provides a basic framework for students to use in creating or refining a weekly schedule, which table 6.2 provides a sample of. Table 6.3 provides a basic framework for students to use in creating a plan for each of their courses, which table 6.4 provides a sample of. Table 6.5 provides a basic framework for students to use in approaching each individual study session, which table 6.6 provides a sample of.

STRUCTURING STUDY SESSIONS FOR EFFECTIVE LEARNING: DISTRIBUTED PRACTICE, REPEATED RECALL, AND INTERLEAVING

As a peer tutor, you're cognizant that the underlying goal for learners is to develop robust knowledge structures for the concepts and problem-solving strategies that are important to a course or curriculum. Complex, well-entrenched schemas are what will allow students not only to accurately and rapidly recall information and perform tasks in assessments but also to retain information in long-term memory where it can serve as a foundation for further development toward mastery. Three important, interconnected concepts from research on memory and learning provide a set of principles that tutors can draw on in coaching students on effective learning strategies:

> **Distributed Practice** is the habit of spacing out study sessions, reviewing the same material or practicing the same kind of task repeatedly over a span of time. The effect of distributed practice is a powerful, reliable, and frequently replicated finding for multiple kinds of learning (Benjamin & Tullis, 2010; Cepeda et al., 2006; Janiszewski, Noel, & Sawyer, 2003). The clear finding from a large body of research on distributed practice is that it is both more effective and a better use of time to study a topic in small pieces of time distributed over a span of days than to devote the same amount of time in a single session.
>
> **Repeated Recall** is the related practice of continually bringing a concept or piece of information to one's conscious awareness (as happens in

Table 6.1   A Basic Framework for Time Management

Creating a Weekly Schedule

A weekly schedule allows students to always know what they should be doing (and, by extension, what they can not worry about in that moment). It essentially makes concrete one's values: What is important to me, and how much time am I according it? Creating a weekly schedule is a valuable exercise for students in thinking through how to manage and prioritize their time. It also makes time management into an active learning task that can bring more concrete structure to how students think of the time available to them. Creating a weekly schedule can be accomplished on paper, in a planner, on one's phone, or using an online calendar.

1. Enter your classes.	• *Your class schedule is at the core of your life as a student. Everything else in your schedule is built around the basic structure provided by your class schedule.*
2. Enter other inflexible commitments.	• *Do you have any other commitments that are both mandatory, and occur at a set time (e.g., athletics practice, student employment, meetings of clubs or other organizations, ROTC drilling)? If so, enter them now.*
3. Enter time for sleep.	• *The amount of sleep required for good health and for optimal learning varies by individual, but eight hours/ night is a good baseline. Allow an additional hour for "winding down" at night, and as much time as is required for your morning routine.*
4. Enter allocated study time for each course, clearly labeling blocks of time according to what course they are devoted to. This is your allocated time for completing all of the work associated with that course: studying, homework, readings, writing papers, and projects.	• *Allow two hours of allocated (and clearly labeled, by course) out-of-class time for each hour of time spent in class. For courses that you know are work-intensive, or that you anticipate being a particular challenge for you, you may want to allocate additional time.* • *In scheduling these blocks of time, consider when you do your best work. Do you do your best work and thinking in the morning, or evening? Accordingly, what time do you want to allocate for writing-intensive courses? For courses requiring concentration and problem-solving? Creativity? Memorization? Repetitive tasks? Avoiding scheduling study for times that simply won't work for you is an important part of creating a realistic schedule.* • *Consider whether you may want to schedule blocks of time immediately preceding class (so that you can prepare for it) or after (so that you can review and decompress it).* • *Time at the learning center is time on task for a course, so be sure to include it in your allocated study time.*
5. Enter time for eating.	• *Nutrition, like sleep, is prerequisite to effective learning. Overlapping meal time with study is both possible and reasonable, but mealtimes are also excellent opportunities for creating breaks between study sessions—studying is mental labor, and rest is required. If you use meals as times to socialize or get down time, be sure to give them allocated time.*

(Continued)

Table 6.1   A Basic Framework for Time Management *(Continued)*

6. Enter time for other obligations.	• *Any other commitments that require time but that are within your power to schedule should be added now, within available blocks of time.*
7. Enter time for personal commitments.	• *The things that make you you, that are important to your well-being, or that are otherwise valuable to you (visiting home on the weekends, spending time with friends, working out, reading, hobbies) are important, and should be reflected in your schedule. If you don't plan time for them, they'll either end up not ever happening, or they'll disrupt other aspects of your calendar when they do.*

common study strategies such as flashcards and practice quizzes). Repeated recall is a highly efficient means of storing information in long-term memory, and is one reason why distributed practice is so effective: through repetition, learners entrench schemas and routinize their activation, making them more persistent in memory and easier to recall for later use (Krug, Davis, & Glover, 1990; McDaniel & Masson, 1985; Smith et al., 2016). A core strategy in utilizing repeated recall is to allow time for a piece of information to pass from one's conscious attention before again recalling it to working memory.

Interleaving refers to switching, within a study session, between different kinds of related problems and information (e.g., by spending a few moments on each topic or by mixing the order of practice problems so that the learner is moving back and forth between multiple problem-solving strategies). Interleaving facilitates the formation of robust and complex schemas, helping learners both to discriminate between and to see connections among related concepts (Carpenter & Mueller, 2013; Richland et al., 2005; Rohrer, 2012; Rohrer, Dedrick, & Stershic, 2015). Interleaving also takes advantage of repeated recall, encouraging learners to continually reactivate schemas (Carpenter, 2014). Taking advantage of the effect of interleaving is accomplished by moving between multiple topics and problem types within a single study session, rather than devoting large blocks of time to a single concept.

Taken together, distributed practice, repeated recall, and interleaving are a powerful set of strategies for deep learning. Students can take advantage of the combined effects of these principles by spacing out repeated study of a topic over time, and by combining multiple topics within a single session (e.g., if a student has three topics to cover in three study sessions, they should cover all three topics in every session rather than dedicating a single session to each topic). Tutors can also take advantage of the effects

Table 6.2 Sample Weekly Schedule

	Monday	Tuesday	Wednesday	Thursday	Friday	Saturday	Sunday
7:00 a.m.–8:00 a.m.	Wake up and get ready, grab coffee and breakfast	Wake up and get ready, grab coffee and breakfast	Wake up and get ready, grab coffee and breakfast	Wake up and get ready, grab coffee and breakfast	Wake up and get ready, grab coffee and breakfast	Sleep	Sleep
8:00 a.m.–9:00 a.m.	Math 242 (class)	Gym	Math 242 (class)	Gym	Math 242 (class)	Sleep	Sleep
9:00 a.m.–10:00 a.m.	Bio 170 (class)	Anthropology 370 (study)	Bio 170 (class)	Anthropology 370 (study)	Bio 170 (class)	Wake up and get ready, grab coffee and breakfast	Wake up and get ready, grab coffee and breakfast
10:00 a.m.–11:00 a.m.	Bio 170 (study)	Anthropology 370 (study)	Bio 170 (study)	Anthropology 370 (study)	Bio 170 (study)	Gym	Laundry
11:00 a.m.–12:00 p.m.	Bio 170 (study)	Anthropology 370 (study)	Bio 170 (study)	Anthropology 370 (study)	Bio 170 (study)	Bio 170 (study)	Call home
12:00 p.m.–1:00 p.m.	Lunch & quick nap	Lunch & quick nap	Lunch & quick nap	Lunch & quick nap	Lunch & quick nap	Lunch	Work
1:00 p.m.–2:00 p.m.	Psychology 101 (study)	Psychology 101 (class)	Psychology 101 (study)	Psychology 101 (class)	Psychology 101 (study)	Free	Work
2:00 p.m.–3:00 p.m.	Psychology 101 (study)	Psychology 101 (class)	Psychology 101 (study)	Psychology 101 (class)	Psychology 101 (study)	Math 242 (study)	Work
3:00 p.m.–4:00 p.m.	Free	Work	Free	Work	Free	Math 242 (study)	Work
4:00 p.m.–5:00 p.m.	Sociology 200 (class)	Work	Sociology 200 (class)	Work	Sociology 200 (class)	Math 242 (study)	Free
5:00 p.m.–6:00 p.m.	Sociology 200 (study)	Sociology 200 (study)	Bio 170 (study)	Work	Sociology 200 (study)	Free	Free

(Continued)

Table 6.2 Sample Weekly Schedule (*Continued*)

	Monday	Tuesday	Wednesday	Thursday	Friday	Saturday	Sunday
6:00 p.m.–7:00 p.m.	Sociology 200 (study)	Sociology 200 (study)	Anthropology 370 (class)	Work	Sociology 200 (study)	Dinner	Dinner
7:00 p.m.–8:00 p.m.	Dinner	Dinner	Anthropology 370 (class)	Board Game Club	Dinner	Free	Free
8:00 p.m.–9:00 p.m.	Free	Free	Anthropology 370 (class)	Dinner	Free	Free	Free
9:00 p.m.–10:00 p.m.	Winding down	Winding down	Winding down	Winding down	Free	Free	Winding down
10:00 p.m.–11:00 p.m.	Getting ready for bed, reading, asleep by 11	Getting ready for bed, reading, asleep by 11	Getting ready for bed, reading, asleep by 11	Getting ready for bed, reading, asleep by 11	Free	Free	Getting ready for bed, reading, asleep by 11

Table 6.3   Creating a Plan for Each Course

In your very first allocated study session of the semester for each course, use your time to transfer all obligations for that course from the course syllabus to a new document. Accomplishing this task will help you to think through your approach for the course, and reduce extraneous cognitive load in all future study sessions by keeping all commitments for the course in a single document, organized in a way that is intuitive to you.

1. Make note of all deadlines.	• *Record every important deadline for the class, including homework, papers, projects, and any other assignments.* • *For every deadline, think about how far in advance you'll need to start the assignment in order to meet the deadline and accomplish the assignment well. Record this date as well.*
2. Make note of all important assessment dates.	• *Record the dates of every exam, quiz, or other assessment that you'll need to plan your studying around.* • *For every such date, think about when you'll want to begin studying in order to excel at it. Record this date as well.*
3. Make note of all daily or weekly obligations.	• *Record any regular expectations for the class regarding work that needs to be accomplished for every (or most) days/weeks that you have class. This could include readings, daily homework, online activities, reading responses, or anything else that will be a part of your daily or weekly routine for the course.*
4. Organize your plan in a way that is intuitive for you.	• *Transfer all of your entries to a planner or calendar, and/or keep them in a separate document that you can refer to when you study for that course. Do this in a way that works for you, but be sure to capture important dates and organize them chronologically.*

Table 6.4   Sample Course Plan

Political Science 250: Latin American Government and Politics

Deadlines
October 11: Project 1 due
November 19: Project 2 due
December 1: Draft of Final Paper due
December 8: Final Paper due
Other Important Dates
September 10: Quiz 1
September 24: Quiz 2
October 13: Midterm
October 29: Quiz 3
November 12: Quiz 4
December 8: Final Exam
Daily Obligations
• Complete the assigned reading before class
• Post a comment or question from the reading to the course's online discussion board
• After class, respond to one other student's comment or question on the discussion board

---

Table 6.5   Creating a Plan for Each Study Session

At the start of each of the blocks of time that you have allocated for a course, begin by creating a plan for the session. This plan provides structure for the session, and an opportunity to check in on one's overall progress in the course. To make your plan for the session, review your plan for the course and consider the following questions:

1. Are there any remaining, uncompleted items from your last session for the course?	• *If they're still relevant and important, carry them forward to your new plan. How much time will these items require?*
2. What important deadlines are coming up?	• *Is there anything coming up that you need to start working on? Are there upcoming projects you're worried about, that you'd feel better about if you started working on? What do you hope to accomplish in it today, and how much time would you like to allocate to doing so?*
3. What other important dates are approaching?	• *Is there anything else time-sensitive approaching? Are there quizzes or exams that you should start reviewing/practicing/ studying for? What do you hope to accomplish in it today, and how much time would you like to allocate to doing so?*
4. What daily or weekly obligations need attending to?	• *Is there anything you need to do before the next class (readings, homework, etc.)? How much time will it take?*
5. What is most urgent and important?	• *Rank the items in your list according to how urgently they need to be completed, and how important they are. (Does the item account for a significant portion of your grade? Will it help you learn the material?)*
6. Create a plan for the session, based on your answers to the questions above.	• *Indicate the order in which you will accomplish the items, and the time you plan to allocate for each.* • *Remember, you can't do it all in every session. Decide what is most urgent, and what can be accomplished within the time you have. Trust yourself to accomplish the rest in future sessions. A good plan is a plan that you can reasonably expect to complete.*

Table 6.6   Sample Study Session Plan

Music Theory 101: Introduction to Music Theory

Tuesday February 9, 10.00 a.m.–12.00 p.m.
1. Read and take notes, Chapter 5 (45 minutes)
2. Do homework for tomorrow (notation exercise—30 minutes)
3. Review the prompt for the paper due February 19, start a document for the paper and write down any initial thoughts (30 minutes)
4. Review mathematics of scales for Friday 2-12 quiz

of distributed practice, repeated recall, and interleaving by using them to structure the time that students spend in the learning center, and to drive their interventions with learners.

WHERE SHOULD I STUDY? LEARNING AND AUDITORY ENVIRONMENTS

Some students prefer to study in busy coffee shops, while others prefer quiet libraries. Many learners swear by listening to music while studying, while others prefer a silent environment. What can research literature tell us about the environments that are most ideal for studying, and the effect of background noise on learning, working, and memorization?

Physiological studies that have looked at the relationship between noise and stress have noted that unwanted noise increases stress levels (Cantell, 1978; Rahe & Arthur, 1978), which has an inhibiting effect on learning and concentration. Cognitive scientists have long been aware of the Irrelevant Speech Effect (Colle & Welsh, 1976; Jones & Macken, 1993; Salamé & Baddeley, 1986): when subjects are given the task of recalling a series of items in the proper order, they do so less effectively when they are in an environment with audible voices talking about unrelated things (suggesting that because speech processing places a significant load on working memory, it is better to perform learning tasks in an environment free of human voices). Based on findings such as these, the conventional wisdom has been that quiet study environments are always preferable. More recent research, however, has complicated the picture, examining different types of sound and pointing to specific factors that must be taken into account in assessing auditory environments for learning. Ellermeier & Hellbruck (1998) note that the distracting effect of speech is mitigated when an additional masking noise is introduced (an effect that helps explain while one conversation can be distracting, a busy environment in which individual voices are washed out by the general buzz of conversation can be less so). Hancock et al. (2007) argue that the volume of background noise matters, and that only at louder volumes does background noise introduce a level of stress that interferes with cognitive performance. Rausch, Bauch, and Bunzeck (2014) report that white noise can have a specifically beneficial effect on learning, improving attention, and memory formation. Lesiuk (2005), based on a study of software developers in a professional environment, notes that the presence of music facilitates better and faster creative work through a beneficial effect on mood.

In the absence of a clear consensus in the literature on what auditory conditions are most conducive to learning, it makes sense for learners to make decisions based on their own preferences: there's no reason not to take at their word a student who says that listening to music helps them to study, that they find silence challenging for getting work done, or that they find concentration easier in a busy environment. It may be helpful, however, for tutors to let students know that different types of environments may be suited to different kinds of learning tasks. It can also be affirming for students who may have been told that silence is always optimal for studying that the way they study is okay. The best advice for the student trying to figure out what study environments work for them (or who is simply having difficulty studying, for reasons they don't understand) is to experiment with different environments, pay attention to what works and what doesn't for different types of work, and do what works for them.

6.3 TAKING CLASS NOTES

The time on task that students spend outside of class is vitally important to their success in a course. No less, critical, however, is the time that students spend in class. One of the most common mistakes that college students make (particularly in large lectures, but in other types of classes as well) is to think of themselves as spectators. One aspect of this is related to time management: by using class time as an opportunity to engage critically with the material, students can reduce the time that they will need to spend working to master course concepts outside of class. Even more important, however, is that adopting a passive role in the classroom places a learner in the least advantageous role with respect to retaining and processing information. All learning is active learning. Nothing is retained in long-term memory, where it can be recalled for later use, until it is incorporated within an existing cognitive schema. The integration of new information with existing knowledge structures takes place as learners utilize, categorize, evaluate, and otherwise manipulate and apply new material. In some classrooms, the format of instruction is designed to provide students with these opportunities through practical labs, discussion, and problem-solving. In others, the format of the course tends to place learners in a more passive role. Learners can ensure that they reap the maximum possible benefit from all of their courses by making sure that they approach each class as an active learner, regardless of format. This will take on different meanings in different courses, but it always corresponds to a habit of mind of intellectual curiosity toward the material being covered. This means approaching lectures with clearly articulated questions and goals regarding concepts that the learner seeks to have clarified. It means taking every opportunity to ask clarifying questions of the instructor, and talking with other students (comparing notes, sharing impressions, debating ideas, and arriving at a shared understanding) about the material of the course. It also means actively engaging with the material of the course through effective note-taking.

Taking notes fulfills two important functions. The first is to create a record of the information covered in lecture in order to facilitate later studying. This goal is certainly an important one, as missing information reduces the utility of notes as a tool for review after class, and in preparation for quizzes and exams. This goal for note-taking will be familiar to most students, as it lines up with the way that most students think of class—their primary venue for getting the information that they will be accountable for in later assessments. The second, more valuable goal for note-taking is as a tool for learning in itself. Note-taking prompts students to organize the material (grouping similar concepts together, placing related concepts under headings, noting connections between old and new information, identifying points of uncertainty), helping them to far more effectively learn concepts and retain information. Notably, the second goal also serves the first: it's nearly impossible, without writing down every single word, to create a full record of a lecture. Organization is what makes it possible for note-takers to create useful documents for later studying.

TAKING NOTES: LAPTOPS, OR BY HAND?

There is a highly active debate in higher education on the role of laptops and other devices in the classroom. Proponents of Ubiquitous Computing (Brown, Burg, & Dominick, 1998; Brown & Petitto, 2003; Weaver & Nilson, 2005) argue that the presence of Wi-Fi and connected devices in classrooms increase opportunities for collaborative learning and student engagement, and provides students with valuable skills for learning in a connected world. Critics of the use of laptops by students have generally focused on the way that laptops can splinter students' attention and create distractions (Kay & Lauricella, 2011; Kraushaar & Novak, 2010; Skolnick & Puzo, 2008).

Social psychologists Daniel Oppenheimer and Pam Mueller, in a widely reported 2015 study, directly compared students' ability to recall information on lectures when they took notes written by hand, and typed notes on a laptop (the laptops were disconnected from the internet, controlling for distraction from online sources). The authors found two clear and apparently related findings: (1) the students who took notes on laptop wrote many more words than those who took notes by hand and (2) the students who wrote notes by hand had a much better ability to recall information from the lecture. The authors interpret their results to indicate that because note-takers are able to type more quickly than write, laptop users adopted a strategy of recording lectures near-verbatim. Students who took handwritten notes, on the other hand, were forced by the lower speed of handwriting to synthesize and summarize information—an active engagement with the material that resulted in better understanding and enhanced recall. Interestingly, this finding held even when students had the ability to review their notes before taking the assessment, a situation in which the students who took more copious notes on a laptop might be expected to excel. In addition, the authors found that explicitly instructing students taking notes on a laptop *not* to take verbatim transcriptions had no effect whatsoever: laptop users still wrote more words, and recalled the material less completely, than manual note-takers.

This is one study, and should be taken with a grain of salt, but it offers compelling findings. Students often take notes on laptops because it's easier, and because they are able to take more thorough notes. Oppenheimer and Mueller's research indicated that this ease, far from furthering learning, may come at the expense of it. Students who are not realizing a direct benefit from the connectivity that laptops afford (e.g., access to online resources, or the ability to collaborate with other learners in the course using shared electronic spaces) may wish to carefully consider the benefits that may accrue from manual note-taking.

The first rule in note-taking: Take notes. Any note-taking practice is orders of magnitude more effective than the extremely common (especially among new college students), and extremely ineffective, behavior of passively observing class. The most important intervention for tutors, in engaging learners over note-taking, is to encourage (and whenever possible, model) a consistent practice of constantly creating notes during class. The second: it's much more important to use notes as a tool for learning (by synthesizing ideas, and imposing a meaningful organization on them) than it is to create a full and accurate record of everything that happened in class. Less is more, and the goal is to process information rather than to transcribe the instructor.

As with time management, note-taking is highly personal and idiosyncratic. There are as many successful note-taking systems as there are successful students, each one reflecting the particular needs and habits of mind of its creator. But a system takes time and experience to create. In learning interactions with students who are working to develop a process for note-taking that both creates a useful record of class and maximizes class time as a venue for learning through active engagement, you will likely find it helpful offer a few basic principles to frame an effective approach. Table 6.7 provides a basic framework for learners to use in taking notes in class.

Table 6.7 A Basic Framework for Taking Notes in Class

Before Class

In order to approach their courses as active learners, students should enter every class with a clear sense of their own agency in the process of learning. One important way to accomplish this is to step into every class with a clearly articulated set of goals.

1. Identify your questions and goals for the day.	• *Based on the reading, on previous lectures, and on my own curiosity: What are the questions that I'm hoping to get answered in class?* • *Based on my understanding of the topics that will be covered today, what are my goals for the class? What outcomes do I hope to achieve in advancing my understanding of these topics?*
2. Write these at the top of the page or document that you'll be taking notes on.	• *These questions will guide the choices that you make in class that day: how you organize your notes, what questions you ask, and other ways you approach your role as a learner.*

During Class

Class time is an opportunity to engage critically with the material of the course. Effective note-taking fosters deeper learning, facilitating the process of synthesizing information, building schemas, and integrating new information with existing schemas.

1. Use topics and key terms as headings to organize information, labeling important concepts and leaving room under or next to it to take notes.	• *Listen and watch for cues from the instructor that call attention to key concepts (writing words on the board, emphasizing them in speech, using them as headings in visual presentations).* • *Keep an eye out for terms that were identified as important topics in readings.*
2. Place information and ideas relating to these concepts under your headings.	• *Identify information (facts, occurrences, entailments, quotes, elaborations) that will add to or support your understanding of the concepts you used as headings.*
3. As you take notes, annotate them according to how they relate to your questions and goals.	• *Using a system that is intuitive for you, identify information that addresses your questions (e.g., by underlining it), changes your understanding of a topic (e.g., with an exclamation mark in the margin), and/or raises new questions (e.g., with a margin question mark).*

After Class

After class, it's important to decompress large ideas and develop a plan, placing the day's class session in the context of one's larger journey toward mastery.

1. Look back at your questions and goals.	• *Did they get addressed? If yes, how? If no, why not?* • *What were your key takeaways from the day? What did you learn?*
2. What were the ramifications of the day's class for your next study session?	• *What concepts do you want to review or seek clarification on? Will it be most helpful to do this individually, with others in the class, at the learning center, or at the instructor's office hours?* • *Were there any important announcements or changes relating to upcoming deadlines, homework, papers, or assessments?*

6.4 READING

Reading, and especially the kind of highly dense reading encountered in textbooks for introductory courses, represents a very common stumbling block for college students. Reading for college courses is generally a very significant time commitment, often far exceeding what students may have encountered in their previous educational experiences. The issue is high-stakes: alongside lectures, course readings are one of the major sources of information for which students are held accountable in assessments. College reading is also a perennial source of confusion and frustration. It's a familiar experience for new and experienced college students alike to find themselves reading the same block of prose over and over without understanding it, or to complete a long reading without a clear sense of the overarching message or of how it applies to the concepts being covered in class. Approaching the copious time that they will spend reading in the most productive way possible is a very important skill for students to master quickly in order to succeed in college. Helping students to strategize their reading is a way that will result in comprehension and retention is a pivotal way that you can facilitate students' growth as independent learners, able to relate to their textbooks as resources rather than as obstacles.

Taking notes from readings is a crucial practice for students. Taking notes structures the process of completing course readings, giving students a clearly defined role. In taking notes, students engage in the active learning task of summarizing and synthesizing information. At the same time, they create a resource that they'll be able to return to in later review. Good reading notes present concepts in a consolidated, organized way that aligns with how the learner approaches the material. When students are later studying for assessments such as quizzes and exams, or incorporating material from course readings in papers and projects, they are likely to encounter far less extraneous cognitive load in engaging with their own notes than they would studying from the text itself.

READING AND ELABORATIVE INTERROGATION

Elaborative interrogation is a tool in which students articulate questions for themselves, and then seek to answer those questions as thoroughly as possible (McDaniel & Donnelly, 1996; Pressley et al., 1987; Pressley et al., 1988; Willoughby & Wood, 1994). It's a simple and highly effective tool for learning, because it gives students an active way of relating to content, and it supports the integration of new ideas with existing knowledge structures. By posing questions before engaging with new facts, learners give themselves a structure for contextualizing new information.

A number of studies (Menke & Pressley, 1994; Woloshyn at al., 1990; Wong, 1985) have indicated that elaborative interrogation is an extremely effective way for college students to approach the type of highly information-dense reading presented in college textbooks, which tend to convey knowledge as a series of facts. Using an elaborative interrogation approach, students engage with facts by converting them to questions ("Why would this fact be true? How would this work?") which they then proceed to answer based on their own experience and on subsequent reading. In the process, learners learn new information with schemas in long-term memory, and are able to later recall information more accurately than if they had spent the same amount of time reading passively (i.e., simply reading the prose as a series of facts and trying to remember them).

As with course lectures, in order to get the most from course readings, students should approach their readings with a sense of agency, and a clear sense of what they are trying to get from them. And as with note-taking in class, students will develop their own systems over time for processing readings in a way that will facilitate their own learning, and support their own habits for studying. In engaging learners over course reading, the goal for tutors is to impart useful strategies that students can use as a point of entry in beginning to developing their own system. Table 6.8 provides a basic framework for learners to use in taking notes on course readings.

6.5 WRITING PAPERS

Students develop as writers along many parameters during their years as college students, growing in their ability to craft effective arguments, fluently incorporate evidence, bring in other authors' ideas to support their own, and to change their writing for different audiences, disciplines, genres, and rhetorical situations. One aspect of writing that intersects with all of these, and also often represents a tremendous source of stress and anxiety for college students, is time management. Writing is both an effective means of demonstrating learning and a powerful tool for learning in and of itself. Novice writers tend to compress the writing process, devoting inadequate time and planning to its various parts and thereby hampering their ability to write in a way that effectively accomplishes either of these functions. One of the most important ways that learners develop as writers is in

Table 6.8   A Basic Framework for Taking Notes from Readings

Before you Begin

In order to build more complex knowledge structures and store information in long-term memory, learners should strive to approach course readings with a sense of inquiry.

1. Identify the questions that will drive your reading.	• *Look ahead through the reading, focusing on section headings.* • *Convert each topic (generally corresponding to a section heading) to a "why" or "how" question. For example: "The Economic Causes of the Civil War" → "How did economic factors contribute to causing the Civil War?" "Cell Division" → "How and why do cells divide?"*
2. Write these questions at the top of the page or document that you'll be taking notes on.	• *These questions will guide your reading and note-taking, determining where you spend time and what you write.*

As you Read

Consider how new ideas apply to the questions that are driving your reading of the text.

1. Look for information that bears on the questions you articulated.	• *As you read, scan for information that helps you to answer the questions that you articulated.* • *Focus on information that changes or enriches what you knew coming in to the reading.* • *Use your questions to focus your attention. Wherever information isn't relevant to your questions, move past it quickly.*
2. Record information and ideas that are meaningful to your question, using your questions to organize information.	• *As you take notes, condense the author's language and rephrase concepts in a way that makes sense to you.* • *Wherever the author's supporting arguments and facts lead to more questions, rephrase them as questions and record them in your notes.*
3. Note places where your questions were not answered to your satisfaction, or where the author's language was unclear to you.	• *What further clarification would be helpful to you? What ideas do you question? What arguments did you not find persuasive? Record this in your notes.* • *If a passage isn't clear to you, note your questions and move on. You can return to them later in class, study groups, with a tutor, or in later independent study.*

After Reading

Document how the reading changed your understanding of the concepts it covered.

1. What are your major takeaways from the reading?	• *How was your understanding of the concepts covered by the reading changed? What did you find most important or memorable?*
2. What clarifying questions do you have from the reading?	• *How does the reading inform your goals for the next class? What questions are you still seeking answers to, and how will you seek them?*
3. Based on the reading, what are you interested in learning more about?	• *What areas of intellectual curiosity did the reading raise for you? What do you hope to learn more about in subsequent readings or class meetings? What might you be interested in exploring in papers or projects?*

developing a beneficial process for writing that reduces stress, and allows adequate mental space for the fluidly interconnected activities of planning, drafting, and revision.

Technology is an important factor in composition. The ubiquity of laptops and other portable devices has completely changed the way that students write, and yet much of the way that we understand and talk about the process for writing remains rooted in an earlier era when "cutting" and "pasting" were literal terms, and when it was important to plan a piece of writing carefully before committing to an organization that would structure its final, typed form. These changes have been accompanied by contemporary theories of writing that have moved toward a more elastic view of the writing process, focusing more on the choices that writers make as they navigate continuously between processes of planning, drafting, and revision.

SCHEMAS, SHORT-TERM MEMORY, AND THE WRITING PROCESS

In 1981, composition theorist Linda Flower and cognitive psychologist John Hayes articulated a cognitive process model for writing (Flower & Hayes, 1981) that describes writing as a complex interplay of processes and subprocesses, each of which is governed by schemas that structure writers' procedural knowledge for engaging in fundamental tasks of writing (for writing a specific kind of text, for example, or for editing prose). Flowers and Hayes posited task-specific schemas for the planning, production, and review of writing. Critically, however, these concepts aren't used to label discrete steps in a linear progression, but rather cognitive processes that writers can invoke, and move fluidly between, at any stage of composing, or within a single passage. As writers move through the process of composing, they use these task schemas in the service of accomplishing their goals (which in turn change and multiply, as authors think through ideas in the act of writing). In 1996, both Hayes (Hayes, 1996) and Neuroscientist Ronald Kellogg (Kellogg, 1996) created updates of the Flowers–Hayes model that incorporated the role of working memory in the writing process, elaborating how the planning, production, and review of writing place significant, competing demands on the limited capacity of working memory.

This view of writing articulates composition as an incredibly complex cognitive task, involving a wide array of schemas recruited from long-term memory (knowledge of the social dimension for writing, of linguistic rules and conventions, of genres of writing, of content knowledge on the topics being written about) to working memory to be applied to the task at hand, in addition to the large inherent cognitive load imposed on working memory by the processes of planning, production, and review. The combination of all of these factors places extraordinary demands on working memory, limiting writers' fluency and ability to make effective choices. For peer tutors working to support learners as they engage in the intense mental labor of writing, one important goal is to reduce as much as possible the demand on working memory from composition. Tutors can accomplish this by encouraging writers to focus, in the moment, on a single stage in the writing process (planning, drafting, or review) rather than simultaneously engaging with all three. As learners become more experienced writers, their procedural schemas for engaging in these processes become more routinized and make less demand on working memory. Every opportunity to help writers to narrow their attention, breaking the large task of writing a paper into a series of smaller and more manageable goals, will allow writers to bring more of their attention and processing power to creating effective prose.

Writing is an incredibly effective means of thinking through ideas. The act of writing a paper is a process of fleshing out and organizing one's thinking on a topic, crafting arguments and filling in gaps in thinking. This is an amazing aspect of writing. It's also, at times, incredibly inconvenient. It can be unbelievably frustrating to complete half of an essay, and then realize that your thinking has changed in a way that alters the overall organization of the project. The goal is to do as much thinking and planning (and then more thinking, facilitated by writing) as possible before committing to a final organization. As a tutor, your aim when engaging learners as writers is to help them to develop rich procedural schemas for the various aspects of the writing process, and to create a timeline for writing papers spanning from a prompt to handing in the final product that reflects the writer's best effort, with no undue stress and no sleepless nights. In doing so, you accomplish a deeply meaningful act of mentorship. Writing is the common currency of the academy, and developing and sharing knowledge through writing is what scholars do. In helping students to develop a healthy process for writing and to find their voice as writers, you guide them in joining the academic and professional communities that exist within (and beyond) higher education. Table 6.9 provides a basic framework for learners in strategizing their approach to writing assignments, which you can use as a starting point in helping students to find a writing process that works for them.

Table 6.9   A Basic Framework for Writing Papers

Planning

Writing papers can be extremely stressful for students. A set of clear steps, beginning with the small one of getting started, can help scaffold students in the process of creating internal knowledge structures to articulate their own approach to writing.

1. Decide on a working title, topic, and thesis.	• *The most painful part of getting started on a paper is often deciding what you'll write about. Get it out of the way as soon as possible, so you can get to work. You can always change it later.*
	• *This is the best possible time to speak to a writing tutor. You can clear up any misunderstandings you have about the prompt before they become crystallized in your writing, and get feedback on your initial ideas while it's still easy to make changes.*
2. Start a document for your paper.	• *Writing generally becomes a lot easier once you've started setting pixels to pages. Create a file, and place your title, topic, and thesis at the top.*
3. Start taking notes for your project.	• *Use the document you created as a repository for all of your thoughts on the project. Make sure that every idea you have—things you want to talk about, topics you want to cover, sources you are interested in using, arguments you want to make—gets included. Don't worry about creating fluent prose or complete sentences, just get ideas down.*
	• *As ideas come to you, record them. As you go about your days, every time you have an idea related to the project, open the document and make a note of it.*
	• *As your thinking evolves, you may start to have ideas about specific sentences you want to write or paragraphs you want to include. Place these ideas in the document, close to other, related notes.*

Drafting

In each of your dedicated study sessions for the class, work on your document for a little bit. Writing is extremely cognitively demanding, so try to limit your writing sessions to about 45 minutes–1 hour.

1. Create an outline.	• *Move related notes, sources, and ideas adjacent to one another.*
	• *Consider what organization may be emerging, and what argument structure may suit your thesis.*
	• *Move sections into an intuitive order, and create headings to label your sections.*
2. Create a draft.	• *Begin writing wherever you have the clearest sense of what you want to say.*
	• *Within each section, use your notes as raw material.*
	• *As your writing spurs and changes your thinking, be sure to record your ideas in your notes for other sections.*
	• *Introductions and conclusions are hard to write until you have a clear vision of the overall project, so it often works best to save these for last.*

Reviewing

Devote the last week or few days to making changes to your draft, revising and editing your work to make it as effective as possible in accomplishing its purpose.

(Continued)

Table 6.9   A Basic Framework for Writing Papers (*Continued*)

1. Seek feedback.	• *Feedback can come from writing tutors, others in the class, your instructor, or others. Whoever you seek feedback from, be sure to give them clear guidance on what type of feedback you hope to receive.*
	• *If another reader isn't an option, give yourself enough time that you can approach your own writing with fresh eyes and try to see it as a reader. Record your feedback.*
2. Revise based on feedback.	• *Make changes, based on the feedback you received or on your own reading of the completed text.*
3. Repeat steps 1 and 2 as many times as possible.	• *Every cycle of feedback and revision will make your paper more effective.*
4. Edit.	• *Once your paper has been revised to its near-final form, you can edit to ensure final polish in word choice, citation, and sentence structure.*

CONCLUSION

Assistance in developing beneficial strategies for learning is one of the most important forms of support that you can offer for students, providing learners with tools that can be applied not just to one course but to all of them, and not just to the current term but to every term thereafter. They can also be one of the more elusive aspects of tutoring: learning strategies will rarely arise as an explicit focus of a session unless you perceive their importance and relevance to the session, and *make* them an explicit focus. Because many of the students you'll work with have not yet developed an understanding of learning strategies (much less a vocabulary for describing them), they will depend on you to guide them toward an understanding of how learning strategies can bear on their immediate scenario, and how attentiveness to learning strategies stands to impact their future success. Good students are good students because they've acquired a set of habits that equip them to meet the challenges of academic life. Through a conscious focus on learning strategies, you serve as an academic mentor, supporting students as learners in a way that will have an impact far beyond their time in the center.

QUESTIONS TO DRIVE THE SESSION

Within a learning interaction, we are always confronted with the question "How can I help this student?" Based on the concepts in this chapter, these are questions that you can ask yourself, in the moment, to drive the decisions that you make as a peer educator.

- How can I model, for this student, the habits that I've developed to help me succeed in my chosen course of study?
- How can I help this student to develop a system for managing their time that will help them to accomplish their goals?
- How can I support this student in making informed choices about what to do during their study sessions?
- How can I help this student to best take advantage of time spent in class as a learning opportunity?
- How can I provide support for this student in approaching their course readings with a sense of purpose and agency?
- How can I help this student to develop a process for writing that will empower them to create their best work, and to use writing as a tool for learning?

WAYS TO ENGAGE

Questions for Discussion

1. How have your approaches to time management, note-taking, reading, and writing changed over the course of your career as a college student? What do you know now that it would have been helpful for you to know in your first semester?
2. Were there any surprises for you in this chapter? Are there any changes that you are interested in making in your own strategies for learning, based on the principles outlined in it?
3. The transition from high school to college isn't the only important transition that students go through. What are some others transitions that take place within and beyond higher education? How might these changes implicate replanning learning strategies?
4. It can be challenging to redirect sessions to learning strategies, because students are focused on their immediate goals. At the same time, internalizing effective strategies for learning strategies can make an enormous difference for students. What might be some effective strategies that you could employ for shifting sessions toward learning strategies?
5. There is a rich cultural lore surrounding the rituals of college life, conveyed through movies, television, and elsewhere. How is the work of being a student (attending class, studying, reading, writing papers) portrayed in

the media? How might these representations affect how incoming students approach their classes?

Activities

1. Using the system outlined in this chapter plan your own weekly schedule for the current/upcoming term.
   a. Within a small group, share the challenges that you encountered in creating your schedule. Is the schedule that you created realistic for you? What challenges do you anticipate in supporting learners as they develop schedules for themselves?
2. Separate into five groups, with each group focusing on one type of learning strategy (time management, attending class, studying, reading, writing).
   a. Within each group, generate a list of signs students may be struggling with the issue in question (e.g., what might you observe during a tutoring session that might lead you to suspect that issues with effective time management may be at play?).
   b. Within the large group, have representatives from each group read an item from the list they developed and lead the class in discussing possible strategies for responding to the scenarios they describe. Repeat until all items have been covered.
3. Working in small groups, develop a list of diagnostic questions that may be helpful in gaining information about students' strategies for time management, attending class, studying, reading, and writing papers.

Questions for Reflection

1. In your work with students, how can you make sure you are noticing times that learning strategies are an important issue? How do you plan to engage students over these issues?

Chapter 7

Engaging a Diverse Student Body

Inequity is a reality of the world that we live in: within our society, some groups have significantly more access to wealth, power, and privilege than others. The interaction of higher education with inequity is complex and multilayered. On one level, higher education is an important equalizing force in society. Educational attainment is a significant predictor of social mobility and income for individuals from every segment of society. The knowledge, skills, social connections, and employment credentials received by individuals who attain a college degree allow access to a range of possibilities for employment and personal attainment that are inordinately more challenging for those without a college degree to access. On another level, higher education is simply another venue for inequity to play out within—every institution is a microcosm of the larger national and global environment that it occurs within. Income and race are both factors that have a large influence of the likelihood of an individual who begins college to complete their degree, because social inequity ensures that individuals from different segments of society receive different levels of preparation and support for the endeavor of receiving a college education, and because educational institutions tend to implicitly favor individuals from dominant social groups. One fundamental aspect of the work that peer tutors accomplish, deeply embedded in the origin and mission of learning centers, is to ensure that every student, regardless of background, has the support to succeed within the academy, and is able to realize their ability to accrue the benefits that higher education affords.

Yet another layer is represented by the inherent value of diversity within higher education. Within a socially homogenous group, everyone's values and beliefs are reinforced by the presence of others who share their beliefs, and by the absence of anyone presenting alternate points of view. The mixing of students from different social backgrounds results in students being exposed to viewpoints and cultural backgrounds different from their own, forcing learners to carefully consider, evaluate, defend, and (in many cases) change their values and beliefs. Approached from this point of view, the role of learning centers is to provide a space for learners' diverse points of view to come into conversation with one another, to ensure that every individual who wants it is afforded access to the scholarly dialogues that are nurtured within colleges and universities, and to further the goal that these dialogues include voices from all segments of society. Learning centers are hubs where individuals from every corner of the college and every part of society come into conversation with one another, engaging through collaborative learning in a mutually enriching dialogue on the questions that drive the human acquisition of knowledge. Learning centers empower every student to bring the literacies, values, and experiences of their own backgrounds to bear on their college experiences, and to assert their role and voice within the academy. In this chapter, we'll explore the ways that you, as a peer tutor, can support diversity on your campus, approach the students with whom you work with mindfulness toward their racial, cultural, linguistic, and neural uniqueness, and contribute to the work of the center in creating a welcoming and supportive environment for every learner.

7.1 EQUITY, ALLYSHIP, AND PEER TUTORING

Higher education can be a challenging place for people representing identities that have been historically marginalized within our society. Institutions of higher education were the explicit and sole purview of wealthy white men until very recently in history, and it has only been in the last half century that college has been reconceptualized as serving a broader social good than simply educating the elite. This history does not simply go away. For students of color, gender nonconforming students, LGBT students, female students, students with disabilities, and everyone else representing a group that has fought hard (and continues to fight) for equal standing in society, the trappings of colleges and universities—endless paintings of white and male former presidents, for example, or the overwhelming predominance of white and male voices on course syllabi—can serve as constant reminders of the assumption of whiteness, maleness, gender conformity, heterosexuality, and able-bodiedness that pervades higher education. Some students enjoy the privilege of being the default, assumed audience for instruction and programming; others experience the "othering" effect of an education that, while it may not in any formal way exclude them, was not designed with them in mind. More explicit forms of inequality are in no way a thing of the past, as discrimination, differential treatment, and hate crimes continue to be major issues on college campuses. Colleges and universities hold themselves admirably to progressive policies of equitability, often matched by genuine attentiveness to issues of diversity and inclusion. Even the best of intentions, however, can create challenging circumstances for students from marginalized minorities, as they may be called upon in classroom or other campus setting to serve as representative voices of the groups they represent, and often have the unfair burden placed upon them (not shared by other students) to serve as educators for their peers on issues of diversity and equitability.

Learning centers *must* not participate in cultures of noninclusion. In order to fulfill their mission of creating a welcoming and supportive environment for every learner, it is absolutely essential for learning centers to be safe spaces that embrace the unique identity of every single student that utilizes, or could potentially benefit from, the services that the center provides. There are important ways that you, in your work as tutor, can work in the service of this goal. Remember that your actions and attitudes affect different people in different ways. While a student who enjoys a privileged place in society may be inclined to interpret a lack of attention, eye contact, warmth, or friendliness as simply you having a bad day, a student who has experienced a history of discrimination may reasonably align your behavior with their previous experiences and perceive it as a hostility to their presence, based on their identity. Be a supportive, active listener to students who may be carrying with them the weight of harm caused by experiences related to their identity. Endeavor in all moments to be attentive to the possibility of implicit messaging, in your words and actions, that someone does not belong, or that they are in way less than others. Avoid normalizing whiteness, maleness, gender conformity, heterosexuality, and able-bodiedness, because doing so sends the clear message that other identities are abnormal. Equity is more than the absence of discrimination; it's the inclusion of diverse identities within the defaults of how we operate. The "center" described in our name must be a center broad enough to include all identities with which students enter our spaces.

IMPLICIT BIAS, STEREOTYPE THREAT, AND MICROAGGRESSIONS

All of us carry within ourselves implicit biases: stereotypes and attitudes about groups of people that unconsciously shape the way that we think, act, speak, and interact with others. Implicit biases can coexist with progressive ideals and a belief in the value of diversity, because they exist at a level below our conscious awareness, influenced by our upbringing, the media, and our day-to-day experiences. Having implicit biases doesn't mean that you're a bad person. It means that you're a member (and product) of a human social environment in which bias exists. Implicit biases emerge from the same process whereby we develop schemas for all other aspects of our knowledge. Applied to the realm of schemas that emerge from social interactions, they drive implicit social cognition, of which implicit bias is simply one aspect (Banaji, Hardin, & Rothman, 1993; Devine, 1989; Greenwald & Banaji, 1995; Macrae, Bodenhausen, & Milne, 1995). Like many other aspects of our cognition, implicit bias is a tendency within our minds that it's important for us to be aware of as we work with students.

The sorts of stereotypes that we are we exposed to in culture and in the media (which inform our implicit biases, and which we may in turn expose others to if we do not work consciously to counter our own biases) cause genuine harm to individuals from marginalized groups. A large body of research demonstrates that people who have been exposed to negative stereotypes about groups they belong to internalize them in ways that affect their performance (Croizet et al., 2004; Major et al., 1998; Schmader, Johns, & Forbes, 2008; Steele, 1997; Stone, Perry, & Darley, 1997). This effect is particularly well documented in academia, where stereotypes pertaining to intelligence and to the suitability of different groups of people to different areas of study are rampant and have a significant effect on student performance (Aronson & Inzlicht, 2004; Aronson, Fried, & Good, 2002; Good, Aronson, & Inzlicht, 2003; Spencer, Steele, & Quinn, 1999; Steele & Aronson, 1995). The very real effects of stereotypes on performance, including anxiety, self-doubt, and the fear of aligning with negative stereotypes, is collectively known as stereotype threat.

In your work in the center, microaggressions are one of the most important ways that implicit bias may express itself, and through which students may be exposed to stereotype threat. Microaggressions are small words and acts that convey, often unintentionally, derogatory or discriminatory attitudes toward the individuals to whom they are directed. Psychologist Derald Wing Sue (2010) stresses that the individuals who perpetrate microaggressions are often well-intentioned, and unaware of the effects of their words and behaviors. Nonetheless, the cumulative effect of microaggressions can be enormously harmful to individuals who, because of their membership in marginalized groups, often find themselves on the receiving end of them. Consider the following utterances, and the implicit assumptions and attitudes that each conveys to the individual being addressed:

- [*To an Asian American student*]: Your English is so good! Where are you from?

- [*To a female student*]: You're really sharp at Math. That's great, this can be a hard major for women.
- [*To an African American Student*]: It's so inspiring what you overcame to end up studying here.

Critically, the individual who expresses a microaggression may or may not be aware of the discriminatory undertones of their works, and may or may not have spoken with harmful intent. The damaging effect on the individual being addressed remains, regardless. A fundamental aspect of microaggressions is how difficult they are to respond to. Because they are by nature subtle, it's challenging to decide in the moment whether or not one has even experienced a microaggression. Because perpetrators are often unaware of the harmful nature of their words or actions, individual calling attention to them often encounter defensiveness. Victims may worry about playing into stereotypes of the "angry minority." Sue stresses the importance of responding to microaggressions rather than sitting on one's anger, and recommends the strategy of conveying how one experienced the microaggression ("When you said my English was good, it seemed to imply that all Asians are recent immigrants.") rather than making judgments of the perpetrator. ("You're ignorant.") Often, the individual who experiences a microaggression is the person least equipped to handle it. Experiencing discrimination is hurtful, and someone who just experienced harm may not be in the best state to articulate a response. Nor should they have to. The responsibility to ensure that we all live in a fair and equitable society falls on all of us, and allyship means taking this responsibility seriously. When you find yourself in the position of a third-party observer to a microaggression, consider how you can play a role in helping the perpetrator to understand the harmful ideas that they may be conveying without intending to, and in making sure that the victim feels supported and welcomed in the space, institution, and society within which the experience occurred. You may also find yourself as the unintentional perpetrator of a microaggression, having the discriminatory nature of something you said or did pointed out to you. This isn't an easy situation for anyone, and there is always a temptation to become defensive rather than to listen. Remember, what matters isn't your intent, it's the harm caused. We are all people who grew up in a society, and have been affected by discriminatory ideas that exist in every culture. What matters is our ability to think carefully about our behaviors and actions, to acknowledge and apologize for our role in perpetuating unjust attitudes, and to grow from our experiences.

As important as it is for learning centers to attend to issues of equity and inclusion within the walls of our programs, to be truly perceived as welcoming spaces for a diverse student body, and to genuinely earn the identity of safe spaces for students from historically marginalized groups, it's necessary for us to turn our attention outward. Not just as a tutor, but also as a representative of the learning center, how you can engage in active allyship? How can you work to make diverse identities visible on your campus? How you can demonstrate the solidarity of the center with marginalized groups? How can the center help bear the burden of educating the student body on issues of equity and inclusion, so that it does not rest solely on the shoulders of students who are themselves experiencing oppression? How can we support and collaborate with campus programs that are devoted to serving the needs of marginalized groups? Learning centers can and should demonstrate allyship toward traditionally disenfranchised groups, in order to share fully in the responsibility to create a more just and equitable environment for every student, regardless of their identity. In doing so, we also earn trust and create an authentically welcoming, supportive space for diverse learners.

ANTIRACISM

Historian Ibram Kendi studies the origins of racist ideologies (Kendi, 2019, 2020). In examining the root causes of racism in society, Kendi finds two facts to be of interest. First, in the historical record, racist ideologies do not precede and cause racist policies. Rather, racist ideologies follow racist practices, created by groups in power in order to protect their own interests (e.g., slavery in the America did not arise from or codify a preexisting idea that individuals of Africans or origin were inferior to those of European origin—rather, the doctrine that individuals of African descent were biologically inferior to "white" individuals arose as a system to justify the interests of those who benefited from slavery). Second, he notes that the dominant current discourse around race is post-racism, the idea that progressive society has moved past racial discrimination. However, when it's taken as axiomatic that we live in post-racial society in which discrimination no longer exists, then the only possible explanation for racial inequity is inherent differences between races. The idea of post-racism, while a seemingly right-minded point of view and a comforting reality to live within, is a powerful framework for creating racist ideas. Kendi's work advances the view that the causes of racism are not ignorance and hate, but rather the justification of discriminatory social policies. Kendi argues that to truly work toward equity is to be an antiracist. Antiracists reject the false idea of biological differences between races. They further recognize that not only are different races biologically equal, they are also culturally equal: every culture is equally valid, and other cultures can't be judged through the lens of one's own culture. They reject the idea of inherent behavioral inequality between racial groups, noting that social factors such as poverty, not race, are the true causes of differences in levels of crime and violence between racial groups. And they think intersectionally, applying the idea of antiracism not only to the way that inequity interacts with race, but also gender, sexual orientation, religion, and other aspects of identity.

Kendi takes the position that in order to actively work against racism, to be antiracist, we should focus our attention on the root causes of racism rather than the effects. To do this, we must look to the policies and practices that promote racism and other, intersecting forms of discrimination by fostering racist ways of thinking in those that stand to benefit from them. For learning centers, the implication of an antiracist approach is that it is not enough to simply ignore race in our interactions with students, ignoring the reality of racial inequity. Nor is it sufficient (much as it's good) for us to avoid discrimination in our own work with learners. To be antiracist in our work is to actively identify and work against discriminatory policies, practices, and curricula, working directly against the causes of racism on our campuses and in our communities.

7.2 PEER TUTORING ACROSS LINGUISTIC AND CULTURAL DIVERSITY

We live among astonishing linguistic diversity. In the world, there are well over 6,000 languages. In the United States alone, tens of millions of people speak a language other than English at home, and there are more than 30 languages other than English that have more than 160,000 speakers. These include immigrant languages (Arabic, Polish), indigenous languages (Navajo), signed languages (ASL), and colonial languages that have been spoken in areas of the United States for longer than those areas have been part of the United States (Spanish, French). Canada is home as well to an incredible amount of linguistic diversity, with hundreds of thousands of speakers of languages other than the official languages of French and English, and with a particularly strong representation of indigenous languages. This diversity is very much to the good. Every language, and every language variety, is the ideal mode of expression for the community that speaks it, articulating perfectly the ideas, values, and ways of thinking of a culture and of a community. As a peer tutor, you'll engage with students entering higher education from a wide variety of language backgrounds, and widely varying experiences with English. Many of the international students you'll work with will be non-native speakers of English. You'll also work with various domestic non-English speaking populations, including immigrants, the children and grandchildren of immigrants, and speakers of the many heritage and indigenous languages spoken in the United States and Canada.

There is no one for whom getting a college degree is easy. Enormous expectations are placed upon students, and curricula can be highly demanding. For students navigating their education in a language that is not their native language, the challenge of being a student is multiplied exponentially. From a cognitive approach, students who are non-native speakers of the language of study have a tremendously high level of extraneous cognitive load placed upon every single educational task in which they engage. In the affective domain, students navigating the education in a non-native language must deal with the constant frustration of not being able to express themselves with their full, native fluency. Moreover, they have to deal with their peers and educators responding to their language rather than to their ideas, and to the versions of themselves that they have the linguistic skills to communicate rather than to their full, rich identity. Not surprisingly, international students and other speakers of non-English languages often report feeling highly isolated in higher education, both from their fellow students and from educators.

Languages are the vehicles of cultures, and differences in language are invariably accompanied by differences in culture. Language and culture is the water in which we as humans swim, structuring our understanding of the world so thoroughly that we often fail to perceive ways in which our understanding of the world is specific to our own culture group, rather than universal across the human experience. Even such basic-seeming concepts as directions, time, and color are construed in wildly different ways in different languages, reflecting and structuring deeply divergent ways of understanding these concepts. Students approaching their education from the lens of a linguistic and cultural background different from the dominant culture of higher education may encounter, in many and often extremely subtle ways, situations in which cultural differences represent a significant obstacle. Essays, plagiarism, problem-solving, exams, and any of the other bread-and-butter concepts of college life are all culturally grounded concepts that play out in different ways in different parts of the world. For a student approaching their education from a different cultural background than that of the dominant, assumed culture, prompt, exams, and classrooms are all veritable minefields of cultural misunderstandings.

LANGUAGE RIGHTS

All human cultures are associated with a language variety (a language or a dialect of a language). A culture's language is the hallmark of that group's identity, and of the unique way of looking at and engaging with the world represented by that culture. Language rights is the concept that cultural groups have a right to their own languages and dialects. This is a deeply important idea in our world, as a long history of colonization, explicit efforts by governments to enforce cultural homogeneity, and changing global forces have dramatically reduced the number of human languages in the world, and left many cultures having lost their language or in an active struggle to maintain it. Work within communities to revitalize dying languages, and legislative work to protect the legal rights of speakers to their native languages, have serious implications for the future. Language rights is a concept developed and collaborated on by scholars from a variety of disciplines, including linguistics, anthropology, psychology, education, composition, and law (Hale et al., 1992; NCTE, 1974; UNESCO, 1996). The most important work on language rights occurs within communities, where speakers of heritage languages work to ensure the ongoing intergenerational transmission of the language.

Education is also an important venue for language rights. Fluency in the language of one's culture is an important connection to one's heritage, and educational institutions have a history of complicity in enforcing students' acculturation to the linguistic standards of the dominant culture. As a peer tutor, you'll work with many students who are working to become more fluent in the language varieties that are favored by the dominant society, in order to be able to find success in that society. One question to consider is how language rights plays into these tutoring interactions. How, in your work, as a tutor, can you both support learners in their goals and honor the rights of individuals to the native language and dialects? How can learning centers support linguistic diversity within the academy and within society?

As a tutor, you'll often work with students who are engaged in the process of becoming more fluent in the dominant language of your institution. They may be doing so with the goal of making their education easier, of attaining the cultural currency of multilingualism, or in order to accrue the social and career benefits that accompany fluency. Language acquisition among adult learners is a complex, highly specialized field of knowledge. As a tutor, the most important thing for you to know is this: overwhelmingly, language acquisition is a function of time and practice. The human mind is highly evolved for language, and with the relevant input, it can and will develop and routinize the cognitive schemas that facilitate fluency. Explicit coaching is, as a general rule, not especially helpful in this process. You should feel free, in your work with learners, to set aside issues of language and engage with the student themselves. It is your patience, your understanding, your empathy, and your willingness to see the thinker, writer, and learner *behind* the linguistic issues that will ultimately be of the most benefit to the student, not your attention to (or, much less, correction of) their language. Helping students to bridge cultural differences, on the other hand, can be a profoundly helpful service. In your sessions with multilingual learners, you can be attentive to students who may be struggling with understanding prompts or assignments, helping students coming from different frames of cultural reference to understand the work that they are being asked to do. You can help students who may be struggling to follow course material that assumes knowledge of the dominant culture, making explicit the substantial background knowledge that is related to a specific culture or history (but that is not explicitly covered by the course). You can be mindful of areas of potential discomfort, being aware that topics such as sexuality, criticism of authority, political beliefs, personal expression, and religious beliefs are subject to differing levels of comfort among students of different cultural backgrounds. You can also be on the lookout for unintentional violation of American and Canadian standards around academic honesty, helping students to understand culturally bounded conventions around citation, plagiarism, citation, and textual borrowing.

ADDRESSING LANGUAGE ISSUES

One of the challenges for tutors engaging with learners across language boundaries is that linguistic issues can be overwhelming and confusing. In situations when it is necessary to address language issues directly (e.g., when a student is facing a situation in which they will be assessed on the formal correctness of their language), you may find it helpful to allow the following principles to guide and focus your efforts.

1. **Avoid Intensive, Sentence-by-Sentence Commentary**
   Identifying and commenting on every error in a students' work focuses the session on the errors rather than on the thinking underlying the language, and is generally more demoralizing than helpful.
2. **Concentrate on Errors that Impede Comprehension**
   There are many ways that language learners can deviate from the phrasing that a native speaker would use that will change their intended meaning (e.g., using the wrong word or selecting the wrong tense). There are many other cases in which disfluencies will result in speech that may not sound like what a native speaker would produce, but does not affect comprehension (e.g., using "to" rather than "in" as a verb auxiliary). As a tutor, focus your efforts on the former.
3. **Concentrate on Patterns of Errors, Rather Than on Isolated Mistakes**

By calling attention to patterns of errors (e.g., subject-verb agreement) and spending time on the principles that underlie them, you help language learners to become more effective editors and proofreaders of their own work. Focusing on patterns rather than "one-off" errors will also help you to utilize your time in a way that will have the greatest possible benefit for the learner.

In engaging with learners from a different cultural background than your own, allow yourself to be curious. People generally enjoy talking about themselves, their homes, and their cultures, and much of the isolation that international students (and others from cultural groups other than the regional standard) often feel in higher education results from an unwillingness, on the part of their peers, to demonstrate inquisitiveness about culture, often from a misplaced fear that doing so will be perceived as rude. As a tutor, you should feel free to ask questions about learners' homes, cultures, and backgrounds. At the same time, allow students to drive the extent to which their cultural identity and personal story play a role in the session, taking your lead from the student based on their enthusiasm for the topic. In your conversation, avoid ethnocentrism, the application of values and standards from your own culture to the practices of others. Be aware that the rules governing eye contact, physical contact, gender dynamics, and physical proximity in conversation vary widely across cultures. Be open to interactions that may unfold in ways that you aren't used to, and on the guard against misinterpreting cultural difference for rudeness or lack of engagement.

7.3 PEER TUTORING ACROSS NEURODIVERSITY

Neurodiversity refers to the full range within which how we process information and express emotion varies. Every individual has a unique set of characteristics, corresponding to strengths of weaknesses in their ability to function and/or excel in different situations. Individuals who vary in ways that fall outside of the socially accepted norms (those with autism, dsylexia, ADHD, Tourette Syndrome, or other cognitive differences that may affect learning, emotion, memory, and self-control) face the challenge of having to operate in environments that may not be designed with their unique needs in mind, and to accomplish tasks to which it is difficult to bring their strengths to bear. In many cases, these challenges are accompanied by significant social pressure to express as neurotypical in their interactions with others, and discrimination that results from the inability to do so.

The transition to college is challenging for nearly everyone. For non-neurotypical students, the transition can be overwhelming. Higher education, while it can take many forms, tends to throw a similar set of tasks at learners (e.g., write papers, do homework, study, read, take tests). These tasks align closely with culturally defined expectations of what it is to be intelligent, and what a "normal" person should be able to do. For individuals whose intelligence does not express itself in ways that make all (or any) of these tasks easily attainable, colleges and universities can be extremely challenging place to succeed. On top of this, colleges and universities tend to operate on a model that expects students to meet a certain bar of accomplishment: at any given point in the curriculum, if students have mastered the relevant set of skills and information, they proceed. If they don't, they do not. This is a significant difference from K-12 education, where the focus for students with cognitive differences is generally on providing the support to advance in their studies. The difference can be extremely jarring, and the first year of college is often particularly difficult for non-neurotypical students who may be accustomed to receiving a high level of individual attention, but who in college receive only accommodations such as having more time to complete exams and assignments.

UNIVERSAL DESIGN

Universal design, a concept developed by architect and wheelchair user Ron Mace, is the idea that spaces should be designed with the needs of all of their users in mind (Story, Mace, & Mueller, 1998). Rather than planning for the "typical" (adult, non-disabled, average height) user and then either excluding or making special accommodations for everyone else, Mace argued that designers should create inclusive spaces that take into account, at every stage of planning, users from the full range of ages, abilities, and sizes—at the same time, they'll be making the space more comfortable for all users (e.g., wide spacing between tables that makes a learning center accessible to wheelchair users also has the effect of creating more sound buffering between adjacent tables). The concept of universal design was extended to the domain of education by educational theorist Anne Meyer and developmental neuropsychologist David Rose (Rose & Meyer, 2002). Rose and Meyer argued that instead of separate educational spaces for learners with unique needs, educators should design approaches to education in a way that takes into account the needs of learners across the full range of linguistic and cultural background, ability, disability, age, and genders. Many of the core tenets of universal design for learning will sound familiar to you, because they have been incorporated within the core pedagogies of learning centers: using multiple sensory strategies, materials, and formats to present information; providing learners with multiple ways to engage with, and demonstrate their knowledge of, the material; and responding to students as unique learners, allowing for students to learn in a way that builds on and proceeds from their strengths.

Universal design is the most powerful tool at your disposal in attending to neurodiversity. By asking diagnostic questions, mastering a large and diverse toolkit of tutoring strategies, making generous use of cognitive scaffolding, and providing learners with maximum flexibility in the format (individual, drop-in group) and physical space (quiet alcove, busy arcade) in which tutoring takes place, you make the center more accessible for students across the full spectrum of neurodiversity.

While educational systems are designed to treat students as groups, learning centers are designed to treat students as individual learners. As a peer tutor, you are uniquely positioned to provide every learner with the conditions that they need to learn. In engaging non-neurotypical learners, the general guiding principles of peer tutoring all apply, but a higher degree of flexibility should be considered in how they apply to the learner across the table from you. Be open to approaches that may diverge from your usual practices in working with students (being more directive, for example, or less discursive in your approach). Listen to the learner about what works for them, and do your utmost to honor their preferences. The physical space within which the session takes place is a particularly important area to take your lead from learners. Environments that minimize visual and auditory distractions can be extremely important in optimizing learning for individuals who process information in ways that fall outside of the generally accepted norm. Consider referrals to other formats of tutoring (e.g., individual appointments, online tutoring) that may align more closely with students' expressed preferences. As you would with any learner, engage across multiple sensory modalities, providing learners with multiple options for processing information in a way that fits with how they think. And finally, leverage the support network that is available to you, drawing on your fellow tutors and on the professional staff as a resource in helping you to make the decisions that will best support the learner in their journey toward mastery, and in directing the student to the available support that is most relevant to their needs. As you do so, be sure to consider every student's right to privacy. A learner's disclosure to you of a special need (and, in particular, a diagnosis) does not imply, unless explicitly stated, permission to share that information with others.

CONCLUSION

Supporting students as unique learners is at the very heart of what learning centers do. The high ratio of educators to learners, the absence of a perceived authority figure, and the intimacy of the peer-to-peer dynamic all make peer tutoring an ideal venue for attending fully to the singular backgrounds, particular considerations, and unique set of previous experiences with which learners enter the center. This opportunity is only realized, however, through active effort to engage with diversity. One way that you, as a tutor, can engage with this work is through your participation in creating a center that is fully welcoming, inclusive, and supportive of the full range of identities that are represented on your campus. Another is by considering, in your interactions with learners, how identity intersects with pedagogy, being fully responsive to the individual needs of every student. Spread across our own centers and campuses, each of us within the field of peer tutoring works toward a vision for higher education that is fully inclusive, ensuring that every learner has the support to succeed and that students of every background have a seat at the table for the conversations that take place within the academy.

QUESTIONS TO DRIVE THE SESSION

Within a learning interaction, we are always confronted with the question "How can I help this student?" Based on the concepts in this chapter, these are questions that you can ask yourself, in the moment, to drive the decisions that you make as a peer educator.

- How can I be an ally, in this tutoring interaction, to this student?
- How can I avoid causing unintentional harm to this student through my words and actions?
- How can I empathize and relate to the learner in front of me, rather than focusing on their use of language?
- How can I help this student to understand culturally grounded concepts that are prerequisite to their ability to understand and succeed at the task in which they are engaged?
- How can I ensure that this learning interaction takes place in a space, format, and manner that minimizes areas of difficulty for this learner, and takes advantage of their unique strengths?

WAYS TO ENGAGE

Questions for Discussion

1. Learning centers are physical spaces, and physical spaces have cultures. What could your learning center do at any and all levels (mission, decorations, policies, etc.) to create a culture of equity and inclusion, fully welcoming to a diverse student body?
2. How might your center engage (or fully engage) in allyship, engaging in advocacy for a just and equitable campus? What can you, personally, do to help this happen?
3. Have you had the experience of studying within an educational environment that did not use your native language? What was it like for you, intellectually? What was it like for you, emotionally?

Activities

1. In this activity, you'll be using image searches to look at cultural ideas around college students and tutoring. As you complete the activities, discuss the things you are noticing with others in your group.
   a. Working in small groups, do an internet image search for "college student" and look at the images that are returned.
      i. What do the images you see look like? Do you notice any patterns in visible aspects of identity, such as race, gender, and age?
      ii. What might these patterns reveal about social assumptions about who a "normal" college student is, and who the default audience for college instruction is?
   b. Do an internet image search for tutoring, and look at the images.
      i. Can you generally tell who the tutor is, and who the tutee is? How can you tell?
      ii. Do the tutors tend to be older or younger than the tutees?
      iii. When there is a student of color in the learning interaction, do they tend to be the tutor or tutee?
      iv. Try the same exercise, but for "college tutoring" and "peer tutoring." Do you notice any differences?
      v. What might these patterns reveal about social assumptions about tutoring? Are there any that you find troubling? If so, how can you subvert them in your work and in your center?
2. Great universal design results in changes that not only make an environment more usable and inclusive for individuals falling outside of the

socially accepted norm but for everyone else as well (the classic example is sidewalk ramps, which not only make sidewalks friendlier to wheelchair users but also to the elderly, parents pushing strollers, and bicyclists). Your center has been awarded an anonymous grant of $250,000 to implement universal design. Working in a group with three to five others, develop a plan for utilizing the grant funds to implement universal design in your center. Think of both the physical space and the programming within it, and include every type of diversity discussed in this chapter.

   a. What changes would you implement?
   b. For each change, how would it improve accessibility and usability for members of particular, historically underserved populations? How would it improve access and usability for everyone else?

3. Working in groups of three, develop scenarios in which you witness a microaggression taking place in the learning center, and intervene using the tools that Derald Wing Sue suggests. The microaggression could be between tutors, between a tutor and a student, or between students. Remember, microaggressions aren't explicitly hostile. Rather, they are generally unconscious statements that revel implicit bias, often by well-meaning individuals. Decide who the perpetrator of the microaggression is, who the victim is, and who will intervene (these roles may overlap).

   a. Act out your scenario for the larger group.
   b. After each scenario, discuss in the large group:
      i. What microaggression took place?
      ii. What discriminatory attitude was revealed by it?
      iii. How did the intervention address it?

4. Separate tutors into groups of four to six, and discuss the following scenarios:

   • You are reviewing a student's paper. The student has stated that they are concerned about their grammar as English is not their first language. You look at the paper, which articulates a carefully conceived, although at times a little bit hard to follow, argument. You think some transition sentences would help. There are indeed many grammar errors. You notice lots of issues with the use of the definite article "the," and some word choices that make sentences confusing. How do you help?

   • A student who is not a native speaker of English (you do not know what country they are from) has come to you in deep confusion over how to prepare for class the next day. The professor has let the students know that there will be a fun in-class activity in which students work in groups to prepare for a rap battle on schools of thought in moral philosophy. The student has had a week to work on this, but has not made any significant progress and is extremely stressed out.

- An international student is in tears because they have been accused of cheating on an essay exam. The professor has given them the chance to revise the short essay they wrote before being reported to the dean of students. You note that the student includes extended blocks of prose that are not set in quotes, but clearly are the words of the author that the question is about. How do you help?

Questions for Reflection

1. What is the role of a learning center in facilitating and empowering diversity in higher education? In your work as a peer tutor, how will you attend to issues of diversity?

Chapter 8

Critical Thinking and Disciplinary Ways of Knowledge

Critical thinking is both an incredibly important and an incredibly nebulous concept. Nearly all instructors agree that critical thinking is something that they want from their students. There is very little agreement, however, on what critical thinking *is*, or how to teach it. Part of the issue is that critical thinking is an idea with a long history, and that the term critical thinking does not label so much a set of cognitive operations as it does a list of high-level outcomes for education. While the structure of our minds is relatively fixed, the things that instructors want from students vary across groups and over time. As a result, there are countless definitions, theories, and pedagogies of critical thinking that have been advanced, all equally valid, and all driven by the hopes, desires, and cultural frames of their authors. The ways in which people have thought about critical thinking have changed over time, and they also vary tremendously by academic discipline. Physicists construe good thinking in ways different from philosophers, geologists from geographers, and accountants from art historians. There simply is no fixed definition of critical thinking, and it is not the goal of this text to advance one. Broadly, however, when people talk about critical thinking, they are talking about clear logic and rational thought. They are talking about evaluating sources, ideas, and arguments in a way that proceeds from solid principles rather than form one's preexisting beliefs. They are talking about making decisions and judgments in a way that takes fully into account the evidence at hand. And they are talking about effective habits of mind that help thinkers to overcome their own biases, and to think in a way that is driven by evidence rather than by preconceptions. In this chapter, we will consider the ways that you, as a peer tutor, can mentor students as critical thinkers, applying reason in ways that will help them to succeed as college students, disciplinary thinkers, and individuals in the world.

A SAMPLING OF RESEARCH IN THE COGNITIVE SCIENCES ON CRITICAL THINKING

The term *critical thinking* labels a large, complex aggregate of different skills and process. While these diverse facets of cognition have in common that they are desired outcomes of education, they do not represent, in terms of processing, a discrete set of cognitive operations. Nonetheless, a number of compelling findings have emerged in the cognitive literature on adult learners.

- **Huber & Kuncel (2016)**, in a meta-analysis of studies on the gains that college students make in critical thinking during college, find that college is effective in facilitating critical thinking. Students make continuous, significant gains in critical thinking throughout their college years.
- **Sanz de Acedo Lizarraga, Sanz de Acedo Baquedano, & Ardaiz Villanueva (2012)** associate critical thinking with executive functions, which are rooted in the prefrontal cortex and which are central to how individuals navigate new, complex scenarios. They note that the primary differences between critical thinking and executive functions aren't at the level of processing, but of goals, with the former operating to solve complex issues with novel solutions, while executive functions coordinate thought processes in ways that are responsive to an individual's environment and goals.
- **Butler, Pentoney, & Bong (2017)** found that critical thinking is a more effective predictor than intelligence of adults' ability to make beneficial real-world life decisions.
- **Shehab & Nussbaum (2015)** found that the critical thinking task of taking supporting arguments and counterarguments into account in crafting arguments makes significant cognitive load demands upon the working memory of college students, due to the need to hold disparate, multiple points of view in working memory. They argue that college students engaged in critical thinking tasks benefit from robust scaffolding.
- **West, Toplak, & Stanovich (2008)** argue, on the basis of a study that examined the correlation between college students' abilities to overcome the effect of cognitive biases against more traditional indices of critical thinking, that critical thinking is in large part rational thought: the ability to think in a way that counters the effects of cognitive biases.

8.1 CRITICAL THINKING AND BLOOM'S TAXONOMY: LEVELS OF LEARNING

One way to think about critical thinking is using Bloom's Taxonomy, a tool used by psychologists and educators to organize learning according to the type and complexity of the learning task being accomplished.

BLOOM'S TAXONOMY

Bloom's Taxonomy is a tool that has had a remarkably long and far-reaching impact in education. While now a staple of K-12 Education programs, it had its origins in higher education, and while associated with the name of a single individual, it was in fact the result of a remarkably collaborative process (Anderson & Kratwohl, 2001; Pickard, 2007). Following World War II, veterans utilized the G.I. Benefit in large numbers. This original group of "nontraditional students" forced a reconceptualization of an institution that had long been considered the sole provenance of 18- to 22-year-olds. Challenged to account for the considerable life knowledge of students who had been to war and received extensive military training, colleges set out to determine a system of awarding course credit for examinations. The psychologists (many of them graduate students) who designed and implemented these examinations met under the auspices of the American Psychological Association (APA), designing over the course of several APA conferences a system (inspired by the Kingdoms of Life Taxonomy used by biologists) for designing examinations, and classifying the types of knowledge they assessed. Benjamin Bloom chaired the APA committee that created the taxonomy, and edited the volume in which it was first published (Bloom, 1956), but in other regards was simply one voice among many in a group containing both men and women (an important fact to note, given the decade in which it was published and the widespread impact of the document).

The taxonomy recognized three domains for learning: the cognitive (knowledge-based), the affective (emotion-based), and the psychomotor (action-based). Within each, the taxonomy established a hierarchy of levels of learning that range from the simplest, most concrete forms of learning to the most complex, abstract forms of learning. The taxonomy is, by design, an evolving tool. The original group fully articulated the cognitive domain, leaving the affective and psychomotor domains to be more fully developed in later updates (Harrow, 1972; Krathwohl, Bloom, & Masia, 1973; Simpson, 1972). In 2001, the taxonomy received its most significant recent update, to the form in which it is presented in this chapter.

The taxonomy established by Bloom and his colleagues continues, scores of years later, to provide a useful framework for the types of learning that take place in higher education. For tutors, Bloom's Taxonomy provides a compass, directing our work toward the ultimate goal of deep learning even as we spend time with students engaging at shallower levels of learning.

Bloom's Taxonomy organizes cognitive learning into six levels: remembering, understanding, applying, analyzing, evaluating, and creating. The basic logic of the taxonomy is that these levels occur in a continuum. At one end are forms of thinking that are simpler and more common. They require only a shallow understanding of concepts, involving only the memorization of information. As the continuum moves toward more complex and less common forms of learning, the tasks that learners accomplish require them to engage at a progressively deeper level with concepts, ultimately applying and extending on them to create new works and new knowledge. As learners progress in their understanding of a concept, they are able to engage with it in deeper ways (figure 8.1).

These six categories organize a number of more specific cognitive processes. These are the activities that students are asked to perform in assigned work and assessments. Table 8.1 shows the six categories of the cognitive process dimension, with related cognitive processes, from Bloom's Taxonomy.

When people talk about critical thinking, often what they are talking about are the deeper forms of learning referred to by Bloom's Taxonomy. These categories—interpreting, exemplifying, classifying, summarizing, inferring, comparing, explaining, differentiating, organizing, attributing, checking, critiquing, generating, planning, producing—are collectively referred to as higher-order thinking. They require learners to involve cognitive processes that go beyond simply remembering information. Generally, professors want students to use higher-order thinking skills. Students, especially less experienced students, tend to assume that their professors want them to perform lower-order thinking skills (this can become more complicated by the fact that professors may want critical thinking skills from their students, but be

Figure 8.1   Levels of learning in the cognitive domain. *Dan Sanford.*

Table 8.1   The Six Categories of the Cognitive Process Dimension and Related Cognitive Processes. Adapted from Anderson & Kratwohl (2001, p. 31)

REMEMBER
Retrieve relevant knowledge from long-term memory
- Recognizing   *e.g., recognize the dates of important events in U.S. history*
- Recalling   *e.g., recall the dates of important events in U.S. history*

UNDERSTAND
Construct meaning from instructional messages, including oral, written, and graphic
   communication
- Interpreting   *e.g., paraphrase important speeches and documents*
- Exemplifying   *e.g., give examples of various artistic painting styles*
- Classifying   *e.g., classify observed or described cases of mental disorders*
- Summarizing   *e.g., write a short summary of the events portrayed on*
      videotapes
- Inferring   *e.g., in learning a foreign language, infer grammatical principles*
      from examples
- Comparing   *e.g., compare historical events to contemporary situations*
- Explaining   *e.g., explain the causes of important eighteenth-century events*
      in France

APPLY
Carry out or use a procedure in a given situation
- Executing   *e.g., divide one whole number by another whole number, both*
      with multiple digits
- Implementing   *e.g., determine in which situations Newton's second law is*
      appropriate

ANALYZE
Break material into constituent parts and determine how parts relate to one another
   and to an overall structure or purpose
- Differentiating   *e.g., distinguish between relevant and irrelevant numbers in a*
      mathematical word problem
- Organizing   *e.g., structure evidence in a historical description into evidence*
      for and against a particular historical explanation
- Attributing   *e.g., determine the point of view of the author of an essay in*
      terms of his or her political perspective

EVALUATE
Make judgments based on criteria and standards
- Checking   *e.g., determine whether a scientist's conclusions follow from*
      observed data
- Critiquing   *e.g., judge which of two methods is the best way to solve a*
      given problem

CREATE
Put elements together to form a coherent or functional whole; reorganize elements
   into a new pattern or structure
- Generating   *e.g., generate hypotheses to account for an observed*
      phenomenon
- Planning   *e.g., plan a research paper on a given historical topic*
- Producing   *e.g., build habitats for certain species for certain purposes*

assessing them based on their ability to remember information). Helping students to think critically helps them to meet their professors' expectations. To do this, tutors can look for opportunities to encourage students to understand, apply, analyze, evaluate, and create.

Bloom's Taxonomy is an incredibly useful tool for you to make use of in guiding your sessions with students. The categories of learning are progressive, with each level building on the level of preceding it (e.g., students must understand information before they can apply it, apply it before they analyze with it, analyze with it before they can evaluate it, etc.). Because of this, the levels articulated in the taxonomy provide a useful tool for framing diagnostic questions and for planning a strategy to guide learners toward an increasingly deep, thorough understanding of a topic. The specific processes provided under each category provide explicit active learning tasks that can be used to direct student learning (and to provide scaffolding for learners as they work to accomplish them). Importantly, not only does higher-order thinking empower critical thinking; it also facilitates lower-order thinking: recognizing and recalling information is much easier when drawing on a more robust understanding of a concept created through deeper learning tasks. Bloom's Taxonomy is also a useful guide to active learning tasks: the cognitive processes under each dimension correspond neatly to types of active learning tasks that tutors can scaffold student in accomplishing.

8.2 CRITICAL THINKING AND BLOOM'S TAXONOMY: WAYS OF KNOWING

Bloom's Taxonomy also articulated, for the cognitive domain, a typology of the four types of knowledge involved in learning: factual knowledge, conceptual knowledge, procedural knowledge, and metacognitive knowledge. Whereas the levels of learning described in the previous section are sequential, with learners progressing from one level to the next and growing in their depth of mastery as they do so, the four types of knowledge are cumulative: learners steadily acquire knowledge in all four areas as they progress toward mastery, and deep learning requires engagement with all types of knowledge. The four domains of knowledge intersect with the levels of learning: for any particular curriculum or concept, each level of learning implicates all four domains of knowledge. Table 8.2 shows the major types and subtypes of the knowledge dimension of Bloom's Taxonomy.

Critical thinking is highly disciplinary. Another thing that people mean when they talk about critical thinking is the habits of thought that are cultivated within academic disciplines—thinking (in analyzing data, in evaluating

Table 8.2   The Major Types and Subtypes of the Knowledge Dimension. Aadapted from Anderson & Kratwohl (2001, p. 29)

FACTUAL KNOWLEDGE

The basic elements students must know to be acquainted with a discipline or solve problems in it

• Knowledge of terminology	*e.g., technical vocabulary, musical symbols*
• Knowledge of specific details and elements	*e.g., major natural resources, reliable sources of information*

CONCEPTUAL KNOWLEDGE

The interrelationships among the basic elements within a larger structure that enable them to function together

• Knowledge of classifications and categories	*e.g., periods of geological time, forms of business ownership*
• Knowledge of principles and generalizations	*e.g., Pythagorean theorem, law of supply and demand*
• Knowledge of theories, models, and structures	*e.g., theory of evolution, structure of Congress*

PROCEDURAL KNOWLEDGE

How to do something, methods of inquiry, and criteria for using skills, algorithms, techniques, and methods

• Knowledge of subject-specific skills and algorithms	*e.g., skills used in painting with watercolors, whole-number division algorithm*
• Knowledge of subject-specific techniques and methods	*e.g., interviewing techniques, scientific method*
• Knowledge of criteria for determining when to use appropriate procedures	*e.g., criteria used to determine when to apply a procedure involving Newton's second law, criteria used to judge the feasibility of using a particular method to estimate business costs*

METACOGNITIVE KNOWLEDGE

Knowledge of cognition in general as well as awareness and knowledge of one's own cognition

• Strategic knowledge	*e.g., knowledge of outlining as a means of capturing the structure of a unit of subject matter in a textbook, knowledge of the use of heuristics*
• Knowledge about cognitive tasks, including appropriate contextual and conditional knowledge	*e.g., knowledge of the types of tests particular teachers administer, knowledge of the cognitive demands of different tasks*
• Self-knowledge	*e.g., knowledge that critiquing essays is a personal strength whereas writing essays is a personal weakness; awareness of one's own knowledge level*

sources, in solving problems, in creating arguments) like a biologist, a sociologist, a mathematician, a creative writer, or any of the professions/mindsets associated with areas of scholarship. Every academic discipline has its own unique way of approaching the construction of knowledge, and of communicating it to others. As a peer tutor, one of your most important roles is as a guide and mentor to the communities that exist within the academy, and to the ways of thinking and writing that define them.

Peer tutors are advanced learners. You are, relative to the students you work with in the learning center, a student who is at a more advanced stage in the journey toward mastery. The four types of knowledge, and subtypes under each, are a guide for you in thinking through the types of knowledge that you have, and that less advanced learners would benefit from. Every academic discipline approaches and construes knowledge in a different way, but the levels and subtypes articulated in the taxonomy apply equally to each. In considering the typology of knowledge presented here, how do these ideas play out, in the area that you tutor? What facts, vocabulary, sources, and types of information are students expected to retain in long-term memory? What classifications, categories, principles, theories, models, and structures should students develop robust, complex schemas for? For what skills, algorithms, techniques, methods, criteria, and procedures should learners devote their energy to creating well-entrenched procedural schemas? What knowledge of how to learn, of the types of assessments (writing, exams, homework) used in the field, and of their own strengths and weaknesses would it benefit students to develop? As a more advanced learner, what do you know that less advanced learners could benefit from? How can you share your knowledge? The typology of knowledge presented in Bloom's Taxonomy is a source of insight for you in directing your energy as a mentor to an academic discipline. Every academic discipline has its own way of constructing knowledge, and its own tools for critical thinking. An important part of your role is to be a mentor to students who are entering these fields and to help them understand how knowledge is constructed, tested, evaluated, and applied in your field. Disciplinary modes of critical thinking are habits of mind that people successful in the field have mastered. The most important way that you can be a mentor to students entering your discipline is to encourage them to think like a member of the academic community you represent (and, in the process, help them to join it) by encouraging and prompting them to use these tools.

Metacognitive knowledge—the most recent addition to the taxonomy—is also one of the most important areas for tutors to focus their efforts. While factual, conceptual, and procedural knowledge are generally made explicit in courses and curricula, metacognitive strategies are, very often, not. Students may be left largely to their own devices in determining how to approach common tasks (e.g., taking notes, doing readings, writing papers) in the discipline, how to succeed at the type of assessments used in the field (multiple choice exams, essay exams, story problems), and how to approach their own processes for learning (how to study, how to learn, and how to figure out what works for them as a unique individual in doing so). It may even be a part of the culture in some departments to foster a culture of "sink or swim": students either figure out the implicit metacognitive knowledge that will enable them to develop toward mastery in a discipline, or they will fail out. As a tutor, you are in a position to ensure that the student who wants to succeed also has the tools to do so (a review of the concepts in chapters 2 and 6 may be helpful to you as you consider how to offer support). In your work with students, consider the ways that you can incorporate higher-order thinking skills, in discipline-appropriate ways.

8.3 CRITICAL THINKING AND COGNITIVE BIASES

As humans, we like to think of ourselves as fully rational animals. Our minds, however, are not instruments designed expressly (or even primarily) for rational thought. Our cognitive faculties are the results of innate tendencies emerging from our evolutionary history and routinized pathways resulting from all of our previous experiences. The gap between completely rational decision-making (assessing all of the available information and using logic to determine the best course of action) and the ways that we do in fact tend to make decisions is labeled by the term cognitive biases. In our daily lives, we are called upon constantly to engage in complex cognitive tasks, determining the relevance of new information to our existing beliefs, making judgments about new people and new scenarios, and making decisions about how to proceed in difficult decisions and how to plan our time. In all of these cases, we rely upon cognitive shortcuts that allow us to go about our lives without devoting inordinate time and mental effort to the countless judgments, decisions, and evaluations that we make on a daily basis. Cognitive biases are the systematic tendencies, universal to all humans, to think in ways that depart from fully rational thought. Table 8.3 provides a list of common cognitive biases, with examples of ways that they can arise within a college setting.

Critical thinking, on the other hand, explicitly involves making decisions, evaluating ideas, and crafting arguments in a way that proceeds logically from all of the available information. Correcting for cognitive biases—our ingrained tendencies to think in non-rational ways—is an important aspect of achieving the kind of critical thinking that is prerequisite to college success. Helping learners to depend on disciplinary modes of inquiry in evaluating, utilizing, and reporting ideas and information, and to make rational decisions about how to strategize their own success, is one important aspect of peer tutoring. Understanding the way that cognitive biases influence our thinking is an invaluable part of this work.

One place that cognitive biases emerge and cause difficulties for college students is in the reasoning that they bring to their writing and problem-solving. When instructors and educational institutions talk about critical thinking as a

Table 8.3 Common Cognitive Biases

There are many more cognitive biases than the ones listed here; this is a sampling of biases that are particularly relevant to college students and that are particularly well-attested in the experimental literature. The term heuristic *refers specifically to strategies that serve as a cognitive shortcut in decision-making and judgments (while they are treated as essentially the same thing here, in a technical sense, biases are instances in which heuristics result in erroneous conclusions).*

Actor–Observer Asymmetry (Jones & Nisbett, 1971)

We tend to explain our own actions and behaviors using external factors, while attributing others' actions and behaviors to internal factors.

"I didn't get my paper in on time because my parents came to visit, and then the week after that I had a cold. He didn't get his paper in on time because he's lazy and doesn't plan well."

Anchoring Bias (Sherif, Taub, & Hovland, 1958)

In making decisions, we tend to attach irrational levels of significance to initial information, using it as a frame (or "anchor") for all subsequent decision-making, even when this information is arbitrary.

"Olu said that he studied for this test for three hours. I want to do a really good job, so I'll study for four."

Availability Heuristic (Tversky & Kahneman, 1974)

People tend to assess the probability of an event based on how easily they can recall an example or instance of that type of event, not on the objective frequency of the event.

"Hardly anyone passes this class—I have three friends who failed it."

Belief Bias (Markovits & Nantel, 1989).

We tend to accept the conclusions of arguments as true when they align with our beliefs about the world, even when the process of arriving at the conclusion was objectively flawed.

"As an environmentalist, I know that this hurricane was caused by global warming because global warming causes more extreme weather."

Confirmation Bias (Koriat, Lichtenstein, & Fischhoff, 1980; Perkins, Farady, & Bushey, 1991; Wason, 1968).

As we seek out, interpret, and remember information, we tend to unconsciously focus on information that supports our preexisting views, and to disregard information that does not.

"In conclusion, these five instances in which a private citizen with a gun prevented a crime demonstrate that gun control would lead to more gun violence."

Dunning–Kruger Effect (Kruger & Dunning, 1999)

We tend to overestimate our own expertise when we are ignorant about a topic, because we don't yet understand the topic well enough to understand how much there is to know about it.

"I already know a ton about Physics from watching documentaries, so I think this class is going to be pretty easy for me."

Hindsight Bias (Fischhoff & Beyth, 1975)

When we know the outcome of a series of events we tend to see that outcome as inevitable and overestimate the extent to which it was certain to happen, when at the time it was just one of many possible outcomes.

"It should have been obvious to anyone paying attention to economic indicators in 2007 that the economy was due for a crash in 2008."

(Continued)

Table 8.3   Common Cognitive Biases (*Continued*)

Illusory Correlation (Chapman & Chapman, 1967, 1969, Hamilton & Gifford, 1976).

We tend to observe a correlation in data, even when none exists, when linked pairs are especially noticeable or when they align with our expectations.

"I always do best on tests when I'm wearing my lucky hat."

Outcome Bias (Baron & Hershey, 1988)

A decision that led to a desirable outcome is evaluated after-the-fact to be a good decision, even when the outcome was determined by complex variables or partially random.

"I got an A on the test, so my decision not to study for it was the right one."

Overconfidence Effect (Alpert & Raiffa, 1982)

Our confidence in what we know, our predictions about the future, and our judgments tends to far exceed their objective accuracy.

"More than half of college students don't graduate within 4 years, but I will, because I'm a better student than most."

Planning Fallacy (Kahneman & Tversky, 1979)

We tend to be over-optimistic in assessing how long it will take us to complete future plans, utilizing best-case scenarios rather than accurate generalizations over previous experience.

"I should be able to get this paper done by Thursday, assuming I can get in 3 solid days of good writing and nothing else comes up."

Sunk Cost Bias (Arkes & Blumer, 1985; Garland, 1990; Whyte, 1986)

We tend to make decisions about whether to invest additional resources (e.g., time, money, effort) into an endeavor based on how much we have previously invested, rather than on a current, accurate assessment of how worthwhile the endeavor is.

"I'm not enjoying this major, but I'm already 2 classes into this progression of courses. I should just stick with it."

---

desired educational outcome, this is a large component of what they mean—reasoning in a clear-eyed manner, crafting arguments and making evaluative judgments in a way free from bias. Cognitive biases are important parts of how we navigate our day-to-day lives, providing a streamlined processing route for making snap decisions and judgments. Critical thinking demands precisely the opposite—that we bring our full conscious attention to a task, carefully reasoning it through rather than depending on cognitive shortcuts. Cognitive biases detract from critical thinking, subtly affecting the ways that we evaluate information, draw conclusions, and make decisions. There are several ways that you, in your role as a peer tutor, can help learners to think more critically by overcoming the effects of bias. One is simply by recognizing it, and pointing it out to them. As an observer who is privy to learners' process of reasoning but does not have the same particular set of biases, you are in a position to point out to learners instances in which their biases may be affecting the way that they are approaching ideas, analyses, decisions, and information. As you do so, you may consider sharing information on cognitive biases, helping learners to recognize situations in which common cognitive biases may detract from critical thinking. Finally, you can model for learners the mental habit of thinking carefully about how someone with an opposing viewpoint would approach the same assignment, paper, source, or set of data. Activities that help learners to step outside of their own point of view (e.g., "If you were someone who was opposed to the legal right to abortion, what types of sources would you be looking for in writing this paper? How could you incorporate those points of view in to your argument?").

Cognitive biases also interact with learning strategies. Biases can affect the way that we allocate time, decide on plans for approaching important tasks, and even make important (perhaps life-altering) decisions about our course of study. In your work as a peer tutor, one of the most important ways that you can help learners to apply critical thinking to decisions on how to approach their studies is to explicitly address learning strategies, using the strategies discussed in chapter 6: by coaching awareness of learning strategies, you provide students with a set of tools other than their own biases for making decisions on how to manage their time, study, take notes, read, and write. A strategy that you may find helpful in working with learners who make poor decisions on learning strategies is to think about the worst-case scenario in approaching their studies (e.g., "What if tomorrow something else comes up, and you can't work on your paper?" "What if this course turns out to be more challenging than you expect it to be?").

Cognitive biases can also, perhaps most insidiously, affect the way that we see ourselves, others, and our place in the world. Cognitive biases can affect our awareness of our own expertise, our personal narratives of how we attained success, our view of others (and other groups, perhaps in ways that intersect with gender, race, class, and culture), and our willingness to critically assess our own beliefs and values. Both in your work with learners and in considering your own status as a successful student fortunate enough to serve in a student leadership position, it can be painful, challenging, and ultimately profoundly powerful and self-revealing to consider the ways that cognitive biases may have affected ones narrative of oneself and the ways we think about our own expertise and relationships.

CONCLUSION

When students develop the capacity for critical thinking, they practice deeper engagement with course material, engaging with ideas in a way that develops true mastery rather than simply the retention of information. They acquire disciplinary habits of mind and modes of inquiry, learning to approach the construction of knowledge and solving of problems in the ways that define academic fields. They also become more objective, overcoming the limitations and tendencies innate to all of us as humans and as members of a society. In supporting the acquisition of skills for critical thinking, peer tutors help students to learn more effectively, engage fully with academic disciplines, and develop habits of mind that will help them to be more clear-eyed, global, and expansive thinkers in all aspects of their lives.

Critical thinking is also, however, an essential lens for the work that you do as a tutor. To engage with peer tutoring as a critical thinker is to carefully consider the ramifications of everything you've learned about tutoring to the work that you do as a tutor, allowing your practice to be informed by the scholarship of learning center theory (as well as the scholarship of teaching and learning more broadly) while also adopting a critical intellectual stance, considering everything you learn as tutor from the perspective of whether (and how) it applies to your work with students. It means working within the disciplinary habits of mind that define learning center theory as a field of academic inquiry and also thinking across disciplinary boundaries, allowing your work as a tutor to take place in conversation with (and informed by) your emerging identity as a thinker in your primary field of study. To think critically, as a peer tutor, is to reflect carefully on your values and beliefs that you hold as an educator, and then to let these principles, rather than personal habits, biases, or preconceptions, drive every choice that you make in your work with students.

QUESTIONS TO DRIVE THE SESSION

Within a learning interaction, we are always confronted with the question "How can I help this student?" Based on the concepts in this chapter, these are questions that you can ask yourself, in the moment, to drive the decisions that you make as a peer educator.

- How can I encourage this student to engage with the material using deeper forms of learning and utilizing higher-order thinking?
- How can I model and coach the critical thinking strategies that are unique to my academic discipline?
- How can I help this student to understand the implicit forms of knowledge that help learners to succeed in this field?
- How can I help this student to overcome the effects of cognitive biases in evaluating sources, ideas, and information, in crafting arguments, in solving problems, and in arriving at conclusions?
- How can I help this student to overcome the effects of cognitive biases in making decisions about learning strategies and planning?

WAYS TO ENGAGE

Questions for Discussion

1. What was a time when you were asked to think critically in/for a class? In the context of that course, what did it mean to think critically? What did the instructor do to prompt you to think critically? What did you gain from the experience, in your understanding of the material or the way that you approach being a student? How might this experience translate to your work in the learning center?
2. Which of the common cognitive biases listed in this chapter do you remember experiencing personally? Which do you think are especially relevant to people in your major? Which biases would affect learning strategies? Which would affect how people analyze data, evaluate sources, and construct arguments? Which would affect how people see themselves? What strategies would you use to counter each one, in tutoring?

Activities

1. Working in groups of three to six organized by academic major (e.g., biology, economics) or by larger groupings of majors (e.g., natural sciences, social sciences, humanities), consider the ways that critical thinking plays out in the disciplines that you tutor.
   a. Discuss the following questions. Record your answers on whiteboard, chalkboard, or other way you'll be able to easily share your answers with the larger group.
      i. In your discipline, how do people construct knowledge? How do they find things out? (e.g., do researchers make use of ethnography? Observation? Introspection? Formal logic? Experimentation? Surveys?)
      ii. In your field, what does it mean to think critically? How are ideas evaluated? How are they put to the test? How do people in your field evaluate facts, and how do they decide if something is a good theory/idea or a bad theory/idea?
      iii. As peer tutors, how can we support learners in mastering the disciplinary modes of critical thinking that you've identified?
   b. Share your responses with the larger group.
2. Working in partners, consider the ways that Bloom's Taxonomy can be used as a helpful tool for driving active learning and higher-order thinking in tutoring interactions.
   a. Develop a tutoring scenario in which a student arrives in the center focused on lower-order learning tasks, but it seems apparent to the tutor that higher-order thinking is required.

   b. Using the cognitive process dimensions and related cognitive processes, how would you drive the session toward deeper forms of learning?
     i. What active learning tasks, aligning with cognitive processes, would you direct the student(s) toward?
     ii. How would you scaffold the learner(s) in achieving them?
   c. Switch partners with another group. In the new pairings, take turns explaining your scenarios and the strategies that you used to address them and providing ideas and feedback.

Questions for Reflection

1. What does critical thinking mean to you, and what does it mean to people in your academic discipline? In your work as a peer tutor, how will you work to support students in mastering the disciplinary modes of critical thinking that will help them to succeed and excel in their studies?

Chapter 9

Tutoring in Online Environments

Online tutoring takes place where tutoring sessions are mediated by the internet, via computers or connected devices. It occurs in a wide variety of forms that only become more varied with time as bandwidth increases, new learning technologies develop, new platforms for online interactions emerge, and as learning centers respond to new venues for online education. Online tutoring can be text-, video-, or audio-based (or involve any combination of these). It can take place via dedicated software platforms or mobile apps, or through general-purpose tools such as email or social media. It can occur within the learning platforms of online courses, or be accessed through a separate platform maintained by learning centers. One of the few accurate generalizations that can be made of online tutoring sessions is that learners and tutors are separated by physical distance, and must therefore depend on the tools made available by the online environment to accomplish their goals for the session.

The potential advantages offered by online tutoring are considerable. Online tutoring is an excellent option for students who aren't able to access tutoring in person, because they are at a physical remove from the learning center (because they commute to campus for class and do their studying at home, because they are distance education students, because they are traveling for athletics, because they are studying abroad, or for any of a host of other reasons). Depending on the form that online tutoring takes, it can be a good option for students seeking support outside of the center's usual hours, during a late night study session or a weekend devoted to a large project. It may be an ideal choice for the student for whom disability or illness makes communication via writing preferable to spoken communication or a physical visit to the center impractical. It's also an excellent option for the student who may simply prefer, based on their own mood or proclivities, to remain in their dorm room rather than visit the highly social, interactive environment of a learning center. The convenience of online tutoring can make it prefer-able for a student to send a query via chat from the student union building, or a video call from a coffee shop, rather than to pack up their books and hike across campus to the learning center. For many learning centers, the imple-mentation of online tutoring was originally driven by the needs of groups of student learners who were not able to physically access the learning center. Increasingly, however, online tutoring has simply become an alternate mode of tutoring, preferred by many. Online environments make learning centers larger than their physical spaces, able to accommodate even the student who can't, or simply would rather not, visit them in person.

One of the most significant assets that online tutoring environments offer to tutors and learners is the ease of accessing online resources. Every academic discipline has its own online resources (tutorials, guides, references, wikis, instructional videos, podcasts, apps, etc.) that are helpful for learners, and/ or are tools often utilized by individuals in the field. Introducing learners to such resources is an important part of any tutoring session. Learners who are familiar with the resources at their disposal are better able to operate as independent learners, and familiarity with the tools that people use to learn, engage in research, and connect with others is an important part of gaining entry to an academic community. Within an online environment, it's natu-ral and easy to provide a link or engage in screensharing that makes such resources immediately accessible to students. Perhaps most importantly, it's a fundamental part of the world that the internet has created that people are able to quickly and easily connect to vast repositories of knowledge, and to participate in enormous, interconnected networks of individuals. These changes have fundamentally altered the ways that humans in technological societies relate to knowledge. Online venues offer tutors and learners alike the environment most ideally suited to embracing these changes.

CONNECTIVISM

Connectivism is a theory of learning in digital environments articulated by educational and organizational theorist Mark Siemens (2005) and philoso-pher Stephen Downes (2010), a pair widely credited with teaching the first Massive Open Online Course (or MOOC), a 2008 course on connectivism and connective knowledge offered through the University of Manitoba. Connectivism argues that technology has fundamentally reshaped what learning is and that theories of learning that preexisted the internet com-ing into everyday use simply aren't adequate to accounting for the way that learning works in a hyperconnected society. Platforms such as email, social media, and wikis have enabled vast networks of individuals to share information with one another with a speed and ease unprecedented in human history. As the rate of technological change increases, new, less formal methods of instruction are necessary to deploy skills so that people can navigate them in the narrow window of time before they become obsolete. The networked nature of human knowledge and the way significant aspects of human cognition interplay with technology (technologies that we surround ourselves with and use to navigate the world, including mobile devices that we can use to access the vast repositories of knowledge that exist on the internet) force us, connectivists argue, to redefine learning not as increasing what individuals know, but as increasing what human societies are able to accomplish in partnership with technologies that we have created.

In connectivist approaches, the role of educators is to help learners to navigate the vast amounts of information that are available through peer-to-peer networks via the internet. Connectivism suggests that the role for tutors in online environments is to guide learners to appropriate resources and information, to support them as they evaluate and incorporate these resources into their own knowledge structures, and then to facilitate and encourage learners' processes of becoming active participants in online communities of knowledge-sharing.

There is no clear distinction between in-person and online tutoring. Rather, the two represent ends of a continuum, with any number of intermediate points between the two (e.g., in-person sessions that take advantage of online resources, or a session in which the tutor and learners are engaging in an in-person conversation while navigating an online platform together). All peer tutoring sessions are of a kind. They vary in the degree to which they incorporate technology, but the same fundamental concerns apply. Whether you engage students in a physical or online environment, your goals remain the same: to facilitate the formation of complex, robust schemas for course concepts, to provide scaffolding for learners to operate at the limits of their abilities, and to help students to be aware of their own processes for learning. Online tutoring is best understood not as a discrete form of tutoring, separate from individual appointments, drop-in labs, and group learning venues, but rather as an alternate form that any of these can take. Within the tutoring interaction, all of the goals, tools, strategies, and concerns articulated in chapter 4 apply. They will play out, however, in ways particular to the online environment. Online spaces have their own unique cultures (e.g., the intensely critical and frequently unkind nature of online commenting, the terse, transactional nature of customer service chats, or the self-conscious creation of highly curated versions of our own identity that takes place via social media).

Learners entering online learning spaces bring with them expectations based on these cultures and on their previous online experiences, which may affect the learning interaction in unexpected ways. Every platform for online learning introduces its own, highly particular set of constraints. Each content area (e.g., math, music, writing) brings, as well, its own concerns with respect to how it how it plays out in an online learning environment. The online tutoring session itself is a complex, emergent space where these factors can interact in surprising ways.

Broadly, approaches to online learning fall into two categories. In *synchronous* learning interactions, the tutor and learner(s) communicate in real time. Whether this be via text, audio, or video, synchronous tutoring allows tutors and learners to participate in a back-and-forth dialogue (examples could include group chats, collaboration within a shared document, an interactive whiteboard, or an audio conversation). While participants in synchronous learning interactions are separated by physical space—an important consideration that must by all available means be attended to—they occupy the same time. The dialogic nature of tutoring can unfold in a way that is very analogous to in-person tutoring. *Asynchronous* learning interactions, on the other hand, are those online sessions in which there is a significant time delay between the learners' and the tutors' communications (e.g., email-based systems, message boards, and online tutorials). In asynchronous tutoring interactions, participants compose a message, send or post it, and then wait for a reply. On the surface, it may seem that synchronous tutoring environments, because they allow for a rapid, fluid exchange similar to in-person dialogue, are preferable to asynchronous environments. It is indeed the case that the formats (and methods and strategies for each) discussed in chapter 4 map most cleanly on to synchronous online tutoring. Asynchronous environments, however, precisely because they are so unlike physical conversation, create opportunities for learning that are unique to the format. Asynchronous tutoring allows tutors to be highly strategic and planful in their interactions, because it provides the space to fully consider responses before posting. It can facilitate a level of careful review of student work that isn't possible in in-person or synchronous online environments. It can also create a more comfortable learning environment for the student who prefers to carefully control the wording of their communications. In addition, asynchronous formats offer the advantage that the learner and the tutor do not need to be online at the same time: learners are able to send queries at any time that they happen to be working, irrespective of the schedules of learning centers.

Online learning environments are rapidly changing, and the development of new approaches for supporting learning in online environments is an exciting area of applied pedagogy. No text could hope to fully orient tutors to the full range of online environments that they may find themselves engaging students within, because the technology changes so quickly. There are, however, a number of categories that existing platforms fall into, which together account for a majority of extant systems. Invariably, these categories will fail to fully account for tutoring platforms in place at many colleges and universities. As in chapter 4, however (with individual appointments, drop-in labs, and group learning venues), formats of tutoring that do not align with these categories can generally be viewed as a hybrid of, or intermediate between, two or more of the categories outlined here. For example, many of the content management systems utilized by institutions of higher education to provide platforms for online courses, and which are commonly used for tutoring as well, frequently incorporate both a message board function and a way to engage in direct messaging. Many platforms designed specifically for tutoring provide both a whiteboard tool and a channel for text chat. The sections that follow (which progress broadly from least to most synchronous) will consider the relative strengths and drawbacks of each of these formats, with considerations for operating within them.

COMPUTER-MEDIATED COMMUNICATION

The study of computer-mediated communication (CMC) is a major area of inquiry for communications theorists. Researchers of CMC (common forms of which include texting, email, and social media) study the ways that cultural communication has been changed by the increase in communication by means of computers, and the attributes particular to forms of communication that take place in digital environments. One of the core questions posed by CMC researchers is how communicative competence—a speaker's ability to convey information to others, to present the image of themselves that they hope to project, to persuade others, to form relationships, to avoid misunderstandings, or to otherwise attain the goals of an interaction—can be defined in online environments. Brian Spitzberg (2006) identified four parameters that can be used to measure competence in a CMC context:

Attentiveness: Demonstrating concern, interest, and attention to the individuals one is communicating with
Composure: Demonstrating assertiveness, confidence, and control in the interaction
Coordination: Demonstrating skillful conversation behaviors such as timing, topic management, and the introduction and closing of topics
Expressiveness: Demonstrating energy and animation in expression

Online tutoring is a unique venue of computer-mediated communication, with its own specific goals (e.g., the attainment of learning outcomes and the modeling of effective learning strategies) specific to the genre. It shares with all forms of CMC, however, that success in achieving the goals of the interaction will depend on a communicator's competence. As a tutor operating in online environments, the concepts of attentiveness, composure, coordination, and expressiveness are rubrics that can be applied to your interactions with learners, predicting the degree of success that you will have in attaining the goals that you and the student(s) you are working with have articulated for the session. In your growth and development as on online tutor, they are useful concepts to frame your reflections on your work.

9.1 DIRECT MESSAGING

In tutoring via direct messaging, learners send queries to tutors, and tutors send replies. Common variants include email-based systems, forms embedded in learning center websites, and direct messaging functions included in classroom content management systems. One of the most popular and widely utilized forms of tutoring via direct messaging is systems in which learners submit papers to writing tutors, who review them and reply with critical feedback, suggestions for revision, and responses to areas of writers' particular concern.

Email is one common instance of a direct messaging tutoring platform. Tutoring via email offers the significant advantage that the platform is so completely familiar to the vast majority of learners. Online environments created specifically for learning (or even specifically for tutoring) may offer far more powerful tools for interaction, but generally any increase in complexity is accompanied by a corresponding increase in the learning curve required to master the platform. Learners who feel intimidated by technology, or who simply would prefer to invest their limited time in solving the problem at hand rather than mastering a new platform, may prefer the simple, intuitive nature of email-based systems (or other, similar systems for direct messaging). Little or no coaching on the tool itself is needed, and very little of a learners' cognitive resources need to be devoted to navigating the platform itself.

Direct messaging is highly asynchronous, and asynchronous learning interactions tend to unfold in a unique way. Because participants have to wait for responses, and cannot depend on immediate, real-time feedback (questions, encouragement, responses) to ensure the clarity of their communications, messages tend to be longer and more thorough. In asynchronous tutoring interactions, learners often take great time and care in articulating their questions and concerns in a carefully crafted message: they want to ensure, when the tutor replies, that they have all of the information needed for them to do so in a helpful way. The process that students undergo of creating full, comprehensive descriptions of the issues that they are facing (often guided by a template or questionnaire created by the center) can be an important part of the learning process, encouraging learners to reflect on gaps in their own knowledge structures and processes for solving problems. Tutors in asynchronous learning interactions likewise tend to create more protracted, exhaustive responses to student queries. Because they can't depend on the cues that are at their disposal in dialogue-based sessions to indicate when learners are not following along, tutors in asynchronous tutoring environments often feel a pressure to explain themselves as thoroughly as possible, anticipating and addressing in advance any questions or concerns that may arise. Many tutors operating in an asynchronous learning environment find it challenging, as they seek to fit as much content as possible into their communications, to avoid becoming more directive in their tutoring. It's all the more important, when operating within an asynchronous tutoring environment, to recall that learning is an active process. Scaffolding that supports learners in solving problems for themselves is always, in every tutoring environment, ultimately more productive than explicit directives on how to proceed (figure 9.1).

9.2 MESSAGE BOARDS

In message board–based environments, interactions take place via threaded conversations that make it possible to respond to comments that have been left by other users. As with email, tutors can generally expect message boards to be a familiar format for most learners. Message boards are the basic mechanics of commenting systems on many internet sites and social media platforms. Message boards are also a central component in many platforms explicitly designed for managing the online components of college courses.

Like direct messaging, message boards are an asynchronous platform. Asynchronous learning environments, by their very nature, slow learning interactions down. In combination with a highly social aspect that allows for interaction between a large number of users, the format allows participants to undergo an intentional process of participation and reflection. As a dialogue emerges that captures, in sum, the unique contributions of discrete learners, individuals are able to benefit from the knowledge of others in a group and to participate in a highly effective mode of collaborative learning.

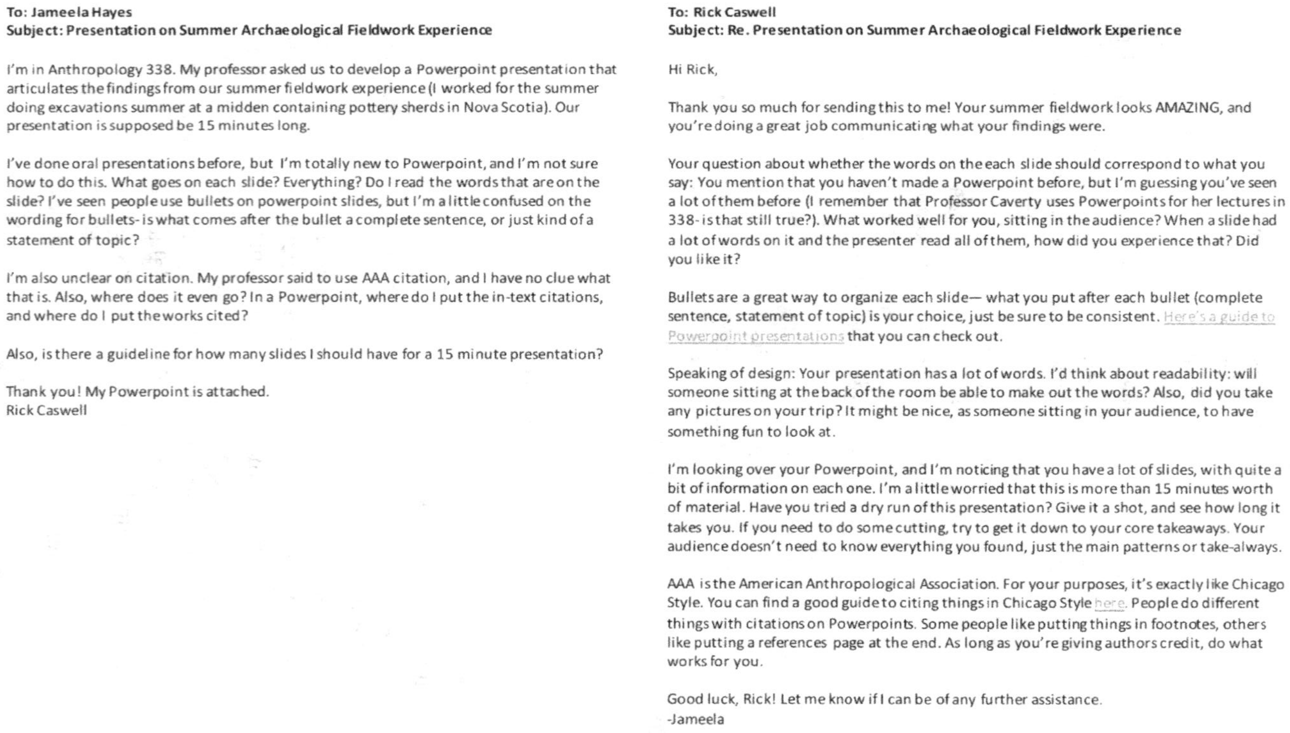

To: Jameela Hayes
Subject: Presentation on Summer Archaeological Fieldwork Experience

I'm in Anthropology 338. My professor asked us to develop a Powerpoint presentation that articulates the findings from our summer fieldwork experience (I worked for the summer doing excavations summer at a midden containing pottery sherds in Nova Scotia). Our presentation is supposed be 15 minutes long.

I've done oral presentations before, but I'm totally new to Powerpoint, and I'm not sure how to do this. What goes on each slide? Everything? Do I read the words that are on the slide? I've seen people use bullets on powerpoint slides, but I'm a little confused on the wording for bullets- is what comes after the bullet a complete sentence, or just kind of a statement of topic?

I'm also unclear on citation. My professor said to use AAA citation, and I have no clue what that is. Also, where does it even go? In a Powerpoint, where do I put the in-text citations, and where do I put the works cited?

Also, is there a guideline for how many slides I should have for a 15 minute presentation?

Thank you! My Powerpoint is attached.
Rick Caswell

To: Rick Caswell
Subject: Re: Presentation on Summer Archaeological Fieldwork Experience

Hi Rick,

Thank you so much for sending this to me! Your summer fieldwork looks AMAZING, and you're doing a great job communicating what your findings were.

Your question about whether the words on the each slide should correspond to what you say: You mention that you haven't made a Powerpoint before, but I'm guessing you've seen a lot of them before (I remember that Professor Caverty uses Powerpoints for her lectures in 338- is that still true?). What worked well for you, sitting in the audience? When a slide had a lot of words on it and the presenter read all of them, how did you experience that? Did you like it?

Bullets are a great way to organize each slide— what you put after each bullet (complete sentence, statement of topic) is your choice, just be sure to be consistent. Here is a guide to Powerpoint presentation that you can check out.

Speaking of design: Your presentation has a lot of words. I'd think about readability: will someone sitting at the back of the room be able to make out the words? Also, did you take any pictures on your trip? It might be nice, as someone sitting in your audience, to have something fun to look at.

I'm looking over your Powerpoint, and I'm noticing that you have a lot of slides, with quite a bit of information on each one. I'm a little worried that this is more than 15 minutes worth of material. Have you tried a dry run of this presentation? Give it a shot, and see how long it takes you. If you need to do some cutting, try to get it down to your core takeaways. Your audience doesn't need to know everything you found, just the main patterns or take-always.

AAA is the American Anthropological Association. For your purposes, it's exactly like Chicago Style. You can find a good guide to citing things in Chicago Style here. People do different things with citations on Powerpoints. Some people like putting things in footnotes, others like putting a references page at the end. As long as you're giving authors credit, do what works for you.

Good luck, Rick! Let me know if I can be of any further assistance.
-Jameela

Figure 9.1   Direct messaging tutoring interaction. *Dan Sanford.*

ONLINE COLLABORATIVE LEARNING THEORY

Online collaborative learning theory, developed by educational theorist Linda Harasim (2012), focuses on the profound potential for online learning spaces to serve as vehicles for collaborative learning. Harasim argues that the unique features of text-based, asynchronous learning environments that allow for threaded conversations are ideal, when shepherded by an educator who can provide appropriate guidance, for facilitating the shared construction of knowledge. Threads allow ideas to be explored in fine-grained detail, while the overall conversation documents the shared progress of the group toward a common understanding.

Online collaborative learning articulates three steps in the co-construction of knowledge that can take place within such an environment. In the *idea generating* phase, students articulate their individual ideas and positions. In this phase, the diversity of thinking that exists within the group is captured in a way that is accessible to everyone in the group. In the *idea organizing* phase, learners react and respond to one another's ideas. A rough organization is imposed on what was previously an unstructured collection of individual positions as learners compare, contrast, evaluate, and categorize the comments of their peers. In the *intellectual convergence* stage, learners work together to accomplish a shared outcome (e.g., a paper, project, or assignment) and through doing so arrive at a shared understanding of the material. Through this process, a group arrives at an understanding more rich and textured than that originally held by any single individual. This shared understanding is in turn distributed among the individuals who participated in the process, each of whom ends up knowing more than they did at the outset. This theory suggests that a beneficial role for tutors in online environments is to guide groups of learners through these stages.

When working within a message board environment, your role as a tutor is to facilitate group learning: framing activities that engage the group in productive learning tasks, ensuring equal participation, and providing scaffolding (questions, hints, redirections, prompts) that lead learners toward new insights and toward a greater capacity for independent learning. Peer tutors facilitate the process of moving from generating ideas, to organizing them, to arriving at synthesis through a shared goal. As they do so, tutors can act as representatives of the communities of knowledge that are represented by academic disciplines, encouraging students to engage with the material in ways that are appropriate to the discipline (figure 9.2).

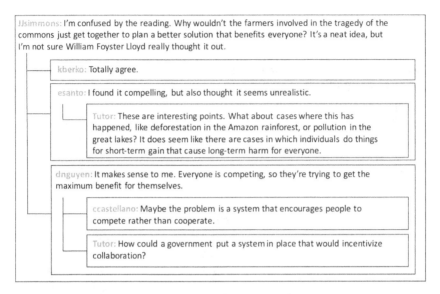

JJsimmons: I'm confused by the reading. Why wouldn't the farmers involved in the tragedy of the commons just get together to plan a better solution that benefits everyone? It's a neat idea, but I'm not sure William Foyster Lloyd really thought it out.

> kberko: Totally agree.

> esanto: I found it compelling, but also thought it seems unrealistic.

>> Tutor: These are interesting points. What about cases where this has happened, like deforestation in the Amazon rainforest, or pollution in the great lakes? It does seem like there are cases in which individuals do things for short-term gain that cause long-term harm for everyone.

> dnguyen: It makes sense to me. Everyone is competing, so they're trying to get the maximum benefit for themselves.

>> ccastellano: Maybe the problem is a system that encourages people to compete rather than cooperate.

>> Tutor: How could a government put a system in place that would incentivize collaboration?

Figure 9.2   Message board tutoring interaction. *Dan Sanford.*

9.3 TEXT CHAT

In text chat, users interact with one another by means of brief, written messages, delivered in real time. Like direct messaging and threaded chats, tutors can expect text chat to be highly familiar for most learners: it is, indeed, one of the basic engines of modern communication, occurring in personal communications among smart phones, customer service chats, instant messaging systems, and many other widespread venues for both internet and cellular communication.

Text chat is in some ways very much like direct messaging, in that users are exchanging text-based messages in an interaction taking place, generally, between two individuals. The similarities, however, stop there. The two platforms highlight the difference between synchronous and asynchronous communication. The time delay inherent to direct messaging means that both learners and tutors tend to create long, carefully worded communications. In text chat, the opposite is true. The fact that both users are online at the same time, awaiting one another's replies, creates a pressure to communicate rapidly. The format values brevity, and conciseness is the norm. An entire set of linguistic conventions, including alternate spellings (k), abbreviations (ttyl), and grammatical conventions (you good?) has arisen around text chat, where a high premium is placed on ease and rapidity of communication. The short, terse nature of text chat communications create a unique situation for online tutors to operate within.

As we explored in chapter 7, tutoring has an extremely significant emotional and interpersonal aspect. Learners' attitudes and emotions play an important role in tutoring sessions, as does the dynamic of the interaction between the learner and the tutor. As anyone who has participated in an email chain that escalated to conflict or a video interview that went poorly can speak to, the subtle cues that help humans to navigate the delicate arenas of feelings, attitudes, and relationships can translate poorly to online environments. Just as in face-to-face learning interactions it is an important part of the session to make learners feel welcome and oriented to the center, it's central to the work of tutors working in online environments to set a welcoming, friendly culture for the virtual space and to set learners' expectations for operating within it. Because interpersonal cues can be more challenging to relay in text-based online environments, it's helpful for you (always, but *especially* when operating in on online environment) to avail yourself of every opportunity to express warmth, receptivity, and acceptance.

AFFECT AND ONLINE ENVIRONMENTS: PUNCTUATIONS, EMOJIS, AND EMOTICONS

Undercurrents of emotion are important to all human communication. In face-to-face conversation, humans use complex, culturally specific systems of gesture, facial expression, posture, and intonation to signal their own attitudes and emotions. They also use these cues to interpret the attitudes and emotions of individuals addressing them. In text, these cues are absent, often leading to ambiguity in what a speaker "means" by a comment and how it should be interpreted.

Online spaces have developed their own conventions for addressing this issue. In computer-mediated communication, punctuation, emoticons, and emojis play an essential role in helping participants in a dialogue to interpret the intent behind comments. These signals provide much the same function as nonverbal cues in face-to-face communication, helping interlocutors to detect sincerity (Gunraj et al., 2016), interpret emotions (Derks et al., 2008), and understand intent (Thompson et al., 2016). Consider, for example, the difference between the sentences on the left and the sentences on the right:

It's fine	It's fine!
You messed up big time.	You messed up big time :p
I ended up going by myself.	I ended up going by myself :)

These conventions can be powerful tools for avoiding misunderstandings, and making sure that comments are received in the spirit that they were intended, in online tutoring interactions. They can also be a good way to signal to learners that the online tutoring environment is an informal space, within which (like the physical learning center) students do not need to hold themselves to the standards of behavior that govern more formal educational environments.

Text chat tutoring, unlike other text-mediated environments that entail a longer delay, allow tutors to take advantage of the rapid back and forth of real-time dialogue to ask diagnostic questions, probe for gaps in learners' understanding, and assess comprehension (figure 9.3).

ksmith: For Psych 101, we had to design an experiment and write up the methods section for it. My professor is asking me to rewrite it, because "I'm not adequately testing whether the independent variable affects the dependent variable." I'm not sure what to do.
Tutor: Okay, that makes sense. So what was the assignment, exactly?
ksmith: We had to set up a psychological experiment to test a hypothesis.
Tutor: What's your hypothesis?
ksmith: My hypothesis was that people who vape will be less likely to accept that vaping could have any negative health effects, because they want to believe that it is a healthy alternative to smoking.
Tutor: That's a solid hypothesis! So in your experiment, what's the independent variable and what's the dependent variable?
ksmith: I guess I'm not sure.
Tutor: Would it help if we took a minute to review those concepts? What is an independent variable, and what's a dependent variable?
ksmith: I'm... not totally sure. I know we covered those terms.
Tutor: No worries! Take a look back at your notes from lecture and see if you can find definitions. I'll wait.
ksmith: Ok- independent variable is the thing you are trying to test, dependent variable is the thing that it will affect.
Tutor: That puts it really well. So for your experiment, which is which?
ksmith: I guess I'm saying the independent variable is whether someone vapes, and the dependent variable is whether they accept vaping could have potential health risks.
Tutor: Nice! Ok: what's your experiment?
ksmith: I outlined an experiment to ask 10 people who vape the question "Do you think that there are any potential health risks associated with vaping?" I'm analyzing their responses to see if there is a correlation between whether someone vapes and whether they think it could be unhealthy.
Tutor: Got it. Okay, I think I'm up to speed. So in your experiment, what's your experimental group and what's your control group?
ksmith: ?
Tutor: I think maybe this is a good place for us to spend some time. Does it work for you if we spend this session talking about experimental and control groups? I think it will really help you to understand your professor's comment.
ksmith: That sounds great.

Figure 9.3 Text chat tutoring interaction. *Dan Sanford.*

9.4 VIDEO CHAT

In peer tutoring via video chat, tutors and learners are able to use a web platform to both see and hear one another, and are able to engage in a conversation in real time. The introduction of speech makes communication more rapid and efficient than text-based mediums, while the ability for tutors and learners to see one another's faces and hear one another's voices makes interpersonal communication considerably easier than in other modes of computer-mediated communication. In many ways, video chat recreates the experience of in-person conversation. As a tutor operating in a video chat environment, you can explore a student's understanding of course content, assess factors that may be affecting their success in the course, and implement a plan based on your understanding of the unique needs of that individual as a unique learner. Unlike in a text chat, you'll have access to many of the same verbal (e.g., intonation, tone) and nonverbal (e.g., facial expression, posture) cues that speakers use to signal their attitudes toward the material or toward the tutoring session, and to signal conversational turn-taking behavior (e.g., leaning forward to indicate that one wants to speak).

The format of video chat introduces issues of technology that raise the barrier of entry for peer tutoring. While nearly any functioning computer will allow a student to participate in text-based communications, video chat requires a functioning microphone and camera, as well as sufficient bandwidth for a quality connection—issues that, particularly considering how socioeconomic status affects access to technology, may represent significant barriers for many students. Video chat also requires relative privacy for users. While direct messaging and message boards can be comfortably accessed from any physical location, many people prefer to engage in video chat only from quiet, secluded locations. Finding such a place can be challenging, in the life of a college student on a busy campus.

Video chat facilitates tutors and learners speaking face-to-face, which is helpful in creating a feeling of connection in a tutoring session. It may or may not, however, line up with the needs of the session in terms of the content being tutored. A face-to-face conversation may ideally suit the needs of a learner using a tutoring session to practice speaking in a foreign language, engage in a dialogue over a complex topic, or participate in a question-and-answer session. It may be less helpful in the highly common situation that the focus of the session is a task that a learner is trying to accomplish. In these cases, it may be far more helpful for tutors and learners to be able to simultaneously look at and interact with the same thing, rather than to be able to see one another (this issue plays out in physical sessions as well, in which tutors and learners may choose to sit side-by-side so that they can look together at a book, screen, or the students' work, rather than to sit face-to-face across a table from one another). Video chat may be less well-suited to facilitate this kind of shared engagement with material (e.g., a student paper, a challenging problem, a data set, a diagram) (figure 9.4).

9.5 WHITEBOARDS

Whiteboard systems allow for tutors and learners to look at and interact simultaneously with a shared virtual space. Within the category are tools that allow users to draw and write in a blank visual field (e.g., a music theory tutor using a whiteboard to draw on a piece of musical notation written out by the student) or to concurrently view and comment on a document (e.g., a tutor marking and commenting on a learner's homework or piece of writing). Whiteboard systems are commonly centerpieces of online platforms designed specifically for tutoring, where they are often combined with either a video- or text-based chat system (or both). Tools that incorporate whiteboard systems are, in many cases, incredibly powerful platforms, creating unique opportunities for interaction and for multimodal learning. The ability for tutors and learners to simultaneously contemplate and edit the same live document facilitates learner-oriented situations in which tutors can provide scaffolding as students engage in tasks. Because tutors are able to actually observe learners working as they solve problems and apply concepts, they are able to intervene meaningfully with learners' processes for doing so. In many ways, whiteboard systems are an optimal solution to the challenge of creating online tutoring environments that allow the work of being a student to be at the center of the learning interaction.

One important consideration in engaging students within whiteboard environments is that they are considerably less likely than any of the other types of online tutoring to be familiar to learners, and can therefore present as intimidating and off-putting. Platforms that offer a variety of tools and features may be extremely appealing to tutors and to experienced online learners. As a general rule, however, the more complicated and powerful a software platform is, the less intuitive it is for new users. Learners are likely to have had less experience with whiteboard systems than with direct messaging, message boards, text chat, or video chat. As a result, such platforms can introduce significant extraneous cognitive load to the learning task, taking learner's cognitive resources away from the task at hand (the concept they are trying to master, the problem they are trying to solve, the idea that they are trying to articulate, the information that they are trying to retain) and focusing it on navigating the learning environment (how to switch between windows, how to delete a mark made in error, how to type a mathematical symbol). A learners' comfort with navigating a particular online learning environment will depend completely on the schemas they have developed, based on their previous experience,

Tutor: Hi, Xiao! What are we working on today?

Learner: Hi Azra. Okay, so we have to do a poster presentation that incorporates peer-reviewed sources. This is a little embarrassing but I have no idea what that actually is.

Tutor: It's all good! We're in school to learn, right? Okay, so peer reviewed just means that other scholars in the field have looked at the piece of writing, made comments, and evaluated it as a publishable piece of scholarship. Does that sound familiar?

Learner: So...like a journal article?

Tutor: Yes! Books and book chapters can be peer reviewed too, but definitely, yes, journal articles.

Learner: Oh, okay. That's easy I guess. But how am I supposed to know if something is peer reviewed? And where am I supposed to go for Journal articles? I've had them assigned as readings, but I don't think I've ever, like, actually seen a journal.

Tutor: Okay – we have a great resource to help with this. What you need is a research librarian. The school subscribes to a bunch of journals so we have free access, and they can show you how to browse them and find articles on your topic. It's super easy once you know how to do it, and they'll guide you through the whole process.

Learner: Ugh. I just want to get this project done.

Tutor: I hear you! The research phase can be pretty fun, though – there are such cool ideas out there, and it's great to see what actual scholars are doing. Do you know where you're headed for the research librarian?

Learner: Is it the big round desk in the middle of the library?

Tutor: Yep! Let me know how it goes, okay?

Figure 9.4   Video chat tutoring interaction. *Dan Sanford.*

with navigating similar environments. When operating in online spaces that may be unfamiliar to learners, it's helpful for you to make as explicit as possible for learners the way that the environment functions. Whenever it's in your power to steer learning interactions toward environments similar to ones that learners are likely to have had previous experience with (e.g., video chat, email, IMing), it will free up more cognitive resources for the goals with which learners entered the session. Alternately, when effective tutoring is dependent on the tools made available in platforms (such as whiteboards) that may be unfamiliar to learners, it's important for tutors to devote time to allowing learners to become familiar within an environment, practicing basic interactions within it, before tackling progress on the learning task.

In a whiteboard environment, you're sharing a space in which a learner is accomplishing the work of being a student. The technology gives you the ability to participate fully—to draw, write, and edit, alongside the student. Just as with face-to-face tutoring sessions, it's essential to remember that if the student is going to retain anything from the session in long-term memory, develop more robust schemas, and grow toward mastery, it's essential for them to be the one doing the work. The tools that are provided within the platform for engaging with student work should be treated as ways of communication and of drawing learners' awareness to specific issues, and (when called for) to provide examples and visual explanations. In face-to-face sessions, it's not helpful to take a students' work and begin editing or completing it yourself. Whiteboard technology shouldn't be taken as a license to do so. As in all peer tutoring, a learner's active engagement in the process of learning is essential to their growth and development (figure 9.5).

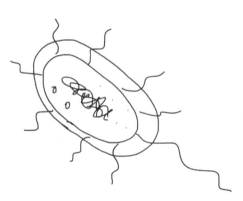

Tutor: Welcome! What can I help you with, Aaron?
asimms: So I have a quiz in Bio tomorrow, and I have to label the parts of a bacterium. I'm not feeling prepared.
Tutor: Ok, we can definitely work on that. To start with, could you draw me a bacterium, based off of what you remember? The drawing tools are at the bottom left of your screen.
asimms: Okay, I see them. Give me a minute...
Tutor: Great! So walk me through this- what are the squiggly lines? What do they do?
asimms: the little ones on the side are pilli, and they help the bacterium attach to things or reproduce. That big one is a flagellum for swimming.
Tutor: Excellent- so that's a lot you have down. Let's focus on the middle parts, then.
asimms: This is what I'm confused about. I know that there are chromosomes and ribosomes, but I'm not sure what the difference is or what's what in the diagram.
Tutor: Okay- how does it sound if we spend some time with that?
asimms: Really good! Where do we start?

Figure 9.5   **Whiteboard tutoring interaction.** *Dan Sanford.*

CONCLUSION

A very wide variety of factors are at play in online learning interactions. Each of the formats of tutoring above introduce their own particular considerations that may influence the choices that you and the learners you work with may make in deciding on a venue for tutoring, and on the way that learning interactions unfold within them. Individual software platforms, exemplifying these formats or hybrids thereof, all introduce their own unique, idiosyncratic concerns relating to usability, ease of use, and specific tools available. In addition, every area of tutoring plays out in unique ways in online environments, introducing new elements that tutors must consider. For example, the specialized systems of notation used in mathematics, formal logic, and music theory can make it highly challenging to engage with them in text-based environments, while writing and language tutors may find them to be ideal for engaging with queries from learners. The highly dialogic pedagogy favored in the humanities can thrive in video chat, while the problem-based learning often found within the sciences can be more well-suited to whiteboard environments. Any one individual tutoring interaction is best understood as jointly influenced by factors arising from all of these areas (figure 9.6).

Most importantly, however, the key considerations in online learning environments are fundamentally the same as in any learning environment, and the most important goals for tutors operating in online environments are the same as in any learning center interaction: to make students feel welcome and

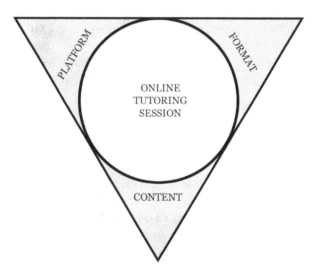

Figure 9.6 Factors in online tutoring interactions. *Dan Sanford.*

invited to the space; to facilitate students' development of complex, robust schemas for core concepts; to seek opportunities for active and collaborative engagement with the material; to engage with each student as a unique learner, honoring their unique background and meeting them where they are in their journey as a learner; to guide and mentor students in their entry to the communities of knowledge represented by academic disciplines; and to foster independent learning. Online environments extend the reach of learning centers, and enrich the work that we do with tools and approaches that are fostered by digital domains. But the guiding approach for tutors operating in online environments should always be driven by the same goals as tutors working in brick-and-mortar venues, and the technology underpinning online interactions should always empower, rather than in any way detract from, the core values and approaches of peer tutoring.

QUESTIONS TO DRIVE THE SESSION

Within a learning interaction, we are always confronted with the question "How can I help this student?" Based on the concepts in this chapter, these are questions that you can ask yourself, in the moment, to drive the decisions that you make as a peer educator.

- How can I take advantage of the online environment, by helping the learner to find, evaluate, and utilize online resources that are used in the discipline?
- How can I help this learner to participate in, and benefit from, knowledge-sharing in online communities of knowledge?
- How can I, in this online interaction, encourage the learner to be active and engaged in their own process for learning?
- How can I take advantage of the conventions that have developed for communication in online spaces to convey warmth, attentiveness, and empathy?

WAYS TO ENGAGE

Questions for Discussion

1. Think of a time that an online communication went poorly. What went wrong? How did the format play in to the problem? If you were able to do it again, is there anything you could do to make it go better?
2. What are the formats for online learning that exist on your campus? How do they align with the formats above? What has been your experience using them? How do you think they could be improved?

3. What are the formats for online tutoring that are available through your center, and how do they line up with the formats for online tutoring listed in this chapter? What are the situations in which you would refer a student to each of these formats?

4. What are some of the online resources, communities, and tools that are utilized by people in the discipline? How might you make use of these in online tutoring sessions?

5. For the area that you tutor, do you think online tutoring is more effective, as effective, or less effective than in-person sessions? Why?

Activities

1. Working with a partner, use your phones to participate in a five-minute-long text chat to describe to one another the best thing that happened to you in the previous week. Be sure to ask questions of your partner, to get as much information as possible.

   a. Were there any moments in which it was frustrating to be texting, rather than speaking? What were they, and what was the source of your frustration?

   b. Looking over the messages you received from your partner, how did they signal affect (how they felt about the topic they were discussing and about the conversation) in their communications?

2. Working with a partner, think about the various social media platforms that you engage with and consider how online platforms affect tutoring practice:

   a. If you were to implement peer tutoring through each of the major social media platforms that you're familiar with, what would it look like?

   b. What would be the relative strengths and drawbacks of each platform be, for the purposes of peer tutoring?

   c. How could the various tools and functionalities available in each platform be used for learning interactions?

3. Working in a small group, consider the following scenario: A team of software engineers is developing an online tutoring platform for tutors to engage with learners, in your content area. You've been asked, as an experienced and knowledgeable tutor, to consult on the project as lead designer. Your role is to determine the features and interface of the platform. In return for your participation, your center will have free access to the platform, and you will be able to use it in your work as a tutor.

   a. What are the unique needs of the content area that you tutor, that the platform needs to be able to account for?

    b. Describe the interface of your platform. How will learners seek support? How will tutors deliver it?

    c. Which of the formats of tutoring articulated in chapter 4 (individual appointments, drop-in labs, group learning venues) will be supported?

    d. Is your platform synchronous or asynchronous? What drove your choice?

    e. Does your platform use direct messaging, text-based chat, message boards, video chat, a whiteboard, some combination of these, or a different type of format altogether? How did you decide among these options?

Questions for Reflection

1. How does (or will) your unique philosophy as a peer educator play out when you engage learners in an online environment? How do/will you alter your style and approach to accommodate the opportunities and constraints of tutoring mediated by the internet?

Chapter 10

Other Ways to Engage as a Tutor

You are a leader on your campus. In your work as a peer tutor, you demonstrate what it is to be a good student, and you guide others toward the strategies, tools, resources, and self-awareness that will allow your fellow students to find success in attaining their own academic goals. You model how to excel within the environment of higher education (and, in many ways, beyond it). Just as importantly, you demonstrate how to do so in a way that builds and supports community. The work that you and your coworkers in the center do sends the clear message that no one is alone in the work of being a student, and that everyone benefits from participation in a community of learning that supports the success of every learner. You are also, as you advance in your work as a peer tutor, a leader (whether formally though a supervisory position, or informally by virtue of your status as a veteran peer educator) within your center. Leaders in any context are most effective when they exert influence through persuasion, inspiration, and the example they set for others, rather than through explicit authority. This is particularly true within the community-oriented environment of a learning center, where leadership means showing, by example, what peer tutoring looks like when it's done with excellence, a positive attitude, and mindfulness toward the theory that underlies it. Leadership also means taking responsibility, being proactive in addressing any issues that arise within the center either by taking the initiative to resolve a problem yourself or by letting a supervisor know about it.

In the same way that learning is a process of continuous development toward mastery, development as a tutor is a process of continuous development toward deeper insight into how to facilitate students' progress toward their academic goals. The materials in this chapter will provide you with guidance as you push toward deeper engagement with your center, and with the work of peer tutoring. Know, as you do so, that while there is much more to learn about the field than what is covered in this text—learning center and writing center theory is a large, rich field offering endless opportunities for scholarly exploration—your growth will ultimately depend on your own contribution rather than on any received wisdom. The work that you do with students matters, in a very real and immediate sense—it makes an enormous difference to the students you work with. Your voice within the center matters as well, and you have opportunities to contribute to its vision and leave a lasting mark on it. You also have the opportunity to contribute to the broader scholarship of learning centers, and of teaching and learning more broadly.

10.1 BEING A LIAISON FOR THE CENTER

Learning centers support academic curricula, and the connections between centers and the departments they support are critical to both. In serving as liaisons with departments (a role that may be, depending on the structure of your center, formally assigned to specific, experienced tutors, or an informal part of every tutor's position), peer tutors take advantage of their dual status as representatives of the center and as students seeking degrees within departments to facilitate healthy communication between the center and the academic programs, ensuring the two-way sharing of information to support healthy collaboration. Tutors can also serve as liaisons to nonacademic programs (teams, clubs, organizations, other student support programs) to support awareness of the center among targeted student populations. Programs and departments can be essential allies to the work of the center, but only if they're fully aware of center programming, feel invested in it, and have the opportunity to voice concerns and feedback about it. Liaisons provide the structure to make this possible.

Liaisons devote time on a weekly basis to checking in (through emails or in-person meetings) with members of the faculty who teach courses supported by the center, maintaining connections to staff in related programs, and attending events in the department as a visible representative of the center. These activities provide a channel of communication providing you with information that you can then pass along to others, ensuring that everyone in the center has all of the information they need to support students from the department. This may include information about assignments, instructor concerns, the dates of upcoming major exams, and anything else that will provide helpful context for you and other tutors in anticipating student needs, planning programming, and providing relevant guidance to learners. Meetings also provide an opportunity to make sure that faculty and staff have a thorough understanding of the center, providing them with all of the information they need to make informed recommendations to students on using the center. Finally, maintaining a relationship with partner units can facilitate collaborative programming (e.g., exam reviews, in-class workshops, guest tutor trainings by faculty, tutoring sessions offered in departmental lounges) designed to support the unique needs of specific groups of students.

One essential aspect of being a liaison to a department or program is ensuring that every student in the department is aware of the relevant services that are offered within the center, who the tutors are, and how to access support. Visits to the classes that you support as a tutor are one of the most important tools at your disposal for educating students about the services that you and your fellow tutors provide, and for building a broad awareness on campus of the work of the center. Students have the opportunity to see, in-class visits, what tutors are like—warm, friendly, approachable, unintimidating, and supportive. Class visits also lay the groundwork for a productive relationship with the instructor of the course. Generally, it works best to do class visits in the first week or two of the semester, when the center is at its least busy and students are still setting their strategies for the term. Class visits can also, however, work well in the lead-up to major projects and assessments, when students may be actively wondering about support options. Table 10.1 provides a basic framework for visiting courses to advertise the services of the center.

10.2 PEER OBSERVATIONS

We are fortunate, operating within the environment of a learning center, to be surrounded by colleagues who we can connect to over our roles as educators. The day-to-day of tutoring, however, can leave little time for comparing notes on our shared work. Peer observations, in which tutors observe, reflect on, and offer feedback regarding their fellow tutors interactions with learners, are an opportunity for co-mentorship. Everyone, regardless of where they are in their own personal journey as an educator, has avenues for growth, and everyone has things that they can learn from the example of others. Peer observations allow tutors to receive thoughtful feedback from an informed third party to think about how others have responded to the common challenges of tutoring, and to share approaches to that work. Observations can take place between tutors with the same level of experience or between tutors with different levels of experience, depending on the goals of the observer and the observee.

To complete a peer observation, you'll need to identify a time that you can clear at least an hour out of your schedule for you to observe and report on a session. It's essential to make sure that every student who the tutor works with during your time as an observer is aware of who you are, and that your goal is to observe and evaluate the tutor as they work (as opposed to observing and evaluating the student as they learn). Learners should always have the opportunity to decline having an observer present during their session.

Table 10.1   A Basic Framework for Class Visits

Before the Visit	
Decide what class(es) you hope to visit.	*The goal is to visit every class you support, but this may be impractical. When it is necessary to focus your efforts on a subset of courses, large introductory classes are the most important to visit. If you work as part of disciplinary team of tutors, strategize together to make sure all important courses get visits.*
Contact the instructor seeking permission to visit the class, and setting a time for the visit.	*Class time is highly important to faculty! Communication in advance of a visit is an important courtesy, and you should never visit a class the instructor of which you have not communicated with in advance. Timing the visit to minimize disruption is important as well (generally, the first or last five minutes of class will work best).*
Visiting the Class	
Introduce yourself.	*Let the class know who you are, and what your position is. Make sure they know that you're a student yourself. If you've taken the class you're visiting, that's also very good information to share.*
Tell the class about your center.	*What are the most important things for any student to know about your center? What is its core mission? Who are the tutors? What services does it offer?*
Tell the class about the services that you provide.	*What are the services that you, specifically, provide for the course you are visiting? Why would a student come to see you? Be as specific as possible, thinking about students who may be totally unfamiliar with peer tutoring: what are two or three specific scenarios in which a student from the course might come to see you?*
Tell the class about all of the services that the center provides that are relevant to the course.	*Are there other services provided by your center that are relevant to the class (e.g., workshops, writing support, other formats of tutoring)? Make sure the students in the course are aware of all options within the center, not just the ones you specifically offer.*
Make sure students have all of the information they need to access the learning center.	*One of the most important goals for your visit is to make sure that everyone in the class has everything they need to follow up: the center's location, hours, and contact information, information on how to make an appointment, the center's website, and anything else they may need to utilize services.*
Close with Q&A.	*Allow time for any students who may have questions to ask them. You may find it helpful to get things going with one or two pre-prepared questions ("one question I often get asked is . . .").*
Thank the class and instructor for their time.	*Show your appreciation for the time that the instructor and class gave you, and express that you're looking forward to working with the class.*
After the Visit	
Send a thank-you email.	*A follow-up email to the instructor is both an appreciated courtesy and an opportunity to set up a channel of communication for questions and potential issues that may arise at any point during the term.*

A simple rubric can help the observer to frame their feedback, and to keep in mind questions to consider as they seek to gain insight into how other tutors approach the fundamental challenges of engaging students as learners. The guide presented here, grounded in the core principles presented in this text, is one possible framework for a peer observation. You can and should consider altering and/or adding to it, according to your goals and to the particular needs of your center.

PEER OBSERVATION FEEDBACK FORM

Who is the tutor doing the observing? _____

Who is the tutor being observed? _____

What format of tutoring is the session? _____

What was the date and time of the session? _____

As you observe the session, place a check mark next to categories that you observe and take brief notes on what you see.

• Making learners feel welcome and at ease
Notes:

• Asking diagnostic questions to fully understand learners' understanding of a concept/task/assignment
Notes:

• Working with learners to create a plan for the session
Notes:

• Helping learners to build a complete, complex understanding of a concept or process
Notes:

• Helping learners to practice and routinize applying a concept in action
Notes:

• Managing learners' stress
Notes:

• Attending to learners' emotional states
Notes:

• Managing the constraints of learners' working memory
Notes:

- Taking advantage of multiple sensory channels
Notes:

- Scaffolding learners in engaging in tasks that push the limits of their abilities and knowledge
Notes:

- Making students active in their own processes for learning
Notes:

- Facilitating collaborative learning between students
Notes:

- Engaging over learning strategies
Notes:

- Responding to students as individual learners, considering their background, attributes, and unique strengths
Notes:

Following the session, reflect on what you observed by answering the following questions.

1. Choose five of the categories above to expand on. What did you see that was especially interesting or noteworthy?
2. Based on your observation, what do you feel the tutor you observed is especially effective at in their work with learners?
3. Based on your observation, what do you feel the tutor you observed should focus on in further developing their practice?
4. What did you observe that you would want to incorporate within your own tutoring practice?

10.3 CREATING A PROJECT FOR THE CENTER

Special projects that you pursue on behalf of the center are opportunities for you to share the expertise, experience, and insight that you've gained as a peer tutor with other tutors, to pursue deeper study in learning center theory, and to enrich the center with new programming and resources. Projects allow you to step back from direct engagement with students, and take the resulting space to reflect on the work that you do as a peer tutor and build on it in ways that will ultimately enhance not only your own tutoring practice but that of your fellow tutors as well.

Projects that you undertake for the center could take the form of trainings or resources for your fellow tutors, giving them guidance based on your experience, background, or research that you've undertaken. They could be decorations or displays for the center that help set a welcoming tone for the center or that provide learners with useful guidance. They could be marketing initiatives, student workshops, or new programming initiatives. Aside from the absolute requirements that they be driven by your passions and interests, motivated by the mission of the center, and that you can make a clear case for their feasibility, cost-effectiveness, and utility, there are no limits to the possibilities for the work that you can accomplish on behalf of your program. You are an accomplished peer tutor, with significant experience engaging your fellow students as learners. You are also an experienced learner, who understands the challenges faced by students in your discipline. No one is more qualified than you are to speak to what would help tutors in your center to do their job well, and what would help students in your field excel as learners. In deciding on how to invest your time, let your insight based on these experiences drive your choices.

As you consider project ideas that you wish to pursue, one thing that you may wish to consider is the type of professional experience that it would benefit you to accrue. What are your professional interests, and how might you apply them within the center? What types of experience and skills would you like to be able to put on your resume? When you are sitting in future job interviews, what types of accomplishments would you like to be able to speak to? The projects that you complete in your work as a tutor can not only enrich the center with your skills and aptitudes but also provide you with professional accomplishments that you can use to leverage your experience as a tutor in attaining your career goals.

SAMPLE IDEAS FOR PROJECTS

- Create a poster to be displayed in the center, showing a visualization of a core concept in your field or reporting your research on a topic in learning center theory.
- Create an online video tutorial for a concept that comes up often in your work with students.
- Create a guide to studying/writing/taking exams/solving problems in your discipline, to be made available as a handout in the center.
- Develop and lead a workshop on a topic of recurring interest to learners in your field, incorporating collaborative learning techniques.

- Lead a training for your fellow tutors on working with a student popu-
lation that you have particular insight into based on your background
(e.g., veterans, non-traditional students, international students, deaf
students).
- Lead a training for the tutors in your center on a pedagogical approach
from your field that would be helpful in peer tutoring more broadly.
- Select one of the formats of tutoring outlined in chapters 4 and 9 (or
another format of your own design) that isn't used on your campus, and
pilot it in your center.
- Develop and report on an assessment/survey project to find out what
impressions students (or particular groups of students) have of the
center.
- Create a series of social media posts that provide students in a major
with tips for how to succeed in that discipline.
- Design a flyer for the center, incorporating core aspects of learning center theory and your center's mission.

10.4 DEVELOPING A STATEMENT OF
PEER EDUCATOR PHILOSOPHY

A statement of peer educator philosophy is an articulation of your beliefs
and values as a peer tutor. For you, a peer educator philosophy represents the
chance to articulate everything that you've learned in your work as a peer tutor,
expressing the values that guide your work, the aspects of tutoring that are
most important and meaningful to you, the principles of learning center theory
that are most relevant to your practice, and the hard-won lessons that you have
learned in implementing them in interactions with learners in the center. A
statement of peer educator philosophy is an expression of your growth as a peer
tutor, showing the ways that you've developed as an educator. As such, it's a
living document. A statement of peer educator philosophy should be revised
periodically to reflect your ongoing growth as a tutor as you gain experience,
progress in your own field of study, and incorporate new aspects of the scholarship of teaching and learning in your practice. The process of creating a statement of educational philosophy—fully describing the motivations that underlie
your work with learners—is a practice in both learning and reflection, helping
you to connect theory to practice, to identify the things you've learned through
your work in the center, and to consider who you aspire to be as an educator.

A statement of peer educator philosophy is a powerful tool in your role as
a liaison. Your statement provides a highly effective means (included as an
attachment or signature to an email, posted on a personal website, or included
by your request on the website for a course you support) to introduce yourself

to students in a class or department who you hope to see in the center, faculty with whom you seek a working relationship, and potential campus partners with whom you seek to collaborate. Your statement, in this context, is a chance to introduce yourself, show who you are as a tutor, and to actively engage with any flawed, negative preconceptions students and educators may have of tutoring and academic support.

Finally, a statement of peer educator philosophy is a valuable professional document. As a part of your professional portfolio, it's a way to demonstrate to employers not only the specific outcomes of your work as a peer educator but the depth and seriousness with which you approach your work more broadly. A statement of educational philosophy demonstrates to employers in educational fields your familiarity and experience with implementing core concepts in educational theory. To employers in any arena, it shows an attribute that all employers want to see in the people they hire—a sincere desire to do their work as well as possible, implementing their training in informed practice, to the best of their ability. Your statement of peer educator philosophy can, with a small amount of effort, be recrafted as a statement of educational philosophy, a professional document frequently requested from job applicants in education (both in K-12 and for faculty positions in colleges and universities). Should you be an undergraduate student whose plans include graduate school, and if you hope to secure a teaching assistantship, your statement of educational philosophy—which demonstrates the depth of your training in educational theory and your thoughtfulness in the task of engaging undergraduate students as learners (rare and highly desirable attributes for beginning graduate students)—will provide you with a significant competitive advantage.

A statement of philosophy is generally a brief (approximately one to two double-spaced pages, or 250–500 words) written document. Statements of peer educator philosophy can also take the form of other multimedia documents (videos, slideshows, etc.), but brevity is a key component to any format. This represents much of the challenge of creating one: the limited space of the genre forces the author to carefully consider what the most important aspects of the work are to them. (It also creates a highly accessible document for potential employers and other audiences.) Answering the "Questions for Reflection" at the end of each chapter of this book will provide you with an excellent starting point for creating a statement of peer educator philosophy; your answers to these questions can then be revised and edited to create a coherent whole. Other questions that you may consider, as you articulate your philosophy, are the following: Why were you drawn to the work of being a peer tutor? Why is it important, and what is its value? Why do you do it, and what have you learned from doing it? Drawing on both your personal background and on the educational theory that undergirds learning centers, what are the beliefs and values that motivate your work with students?

ENGAGING IN THE SCHOLARSHIP
OF PEER-LED LEARNING

Do you have a research project, pilot initiative, or statement of peer educator philosophy that you're interested in sharing with a larger audience?
As a peer tutor, you're part of a national and an international professional
and scholarly community that is highly welcoming and supportive of
scholarship from undergraduate and graduate students. Publications and
presentations created by peer tutors can take many different formats,
forms, and lengths, depending on the venue, and can be either individually or collaboratively authored. The list below provides a starting point
in seeking venues for publishing/presenting student work; there are also
many regional conferences and associations (including regional meetings
of many of the organizations listed below) that you can learn more about
for your area by asking your learning center director or through an internet search. Many campuses provide grant funding for students to travel
to conferences.

Academic Conferences of Higher Education Peer Tutoring

- The CRLA (The College Reading & Learning Association) Conference
- The IWCA (International Writing Center Association) Conference
- The National Conference on Peer Tutoring in Writing (NCPTW)
- The NCLCA (The National College Learning Center Association)
  Conference
- The SI (Supplemental Instruction) Conference

Peer-Reviewed Journals of Higher Education Peer Tutoring

- The Journal of College Reading and Learning
- The Learning Assistance Review
- Praxis: A Writing Center Journal
- The Supplemental Instruction Journal
- The Writing Center Journal
- WLN: A Journal of Writing Center Scholarship

Other Venues for Publication

- The NCLCA Newsletter
- The Dangling Modifier (a student-produced newsletter associated with
  the NCPTW)
- Peer Centered (a blog for peer tutors of writing)

CONCLUSION

In every field of inquiry, there is a progression that learners undertake from the acquisition of knowledge (apprehending the foundational principles, tools, and information that form the basis for all subsequent learning) to the application of knowledge (practicing, ideally under the guidance of teachers and mentors, using what they've learned to engage as active participants in the work that people in the field do), to the construction of new knowledge (using the framework provided by the field to enrich it with new ideas, new findings, and new approaches). Peer tutoring is no different. There is a lot to know about the enterprise of helping your fellow students to learn. It's important and valuable to give yourself time to build, within your mind, the structures of knowledge that will guide your work with learners—the goal of this text has been to provide you with the background knowledge that you need to make informed decisions as you do so. Pushing yourself forward, engaging with learning centers and with peer tutoring in new ways by participating in other aspects of the center and the field (outreach, administration, programmatic innovation, scholarly engagement), and demonstrating intellectual and professional leadership within your program in the same way that you demonstrate intellectual and professional leadership on campus are the ways forward in your growth as an educator. Know, as you grow toward mastery and begin to develop your own signature approach to peer-led learning, that there is room for the unique competencies and assets that you bring to the work. There are no rules in peer tutoring, only guiding principles. Allow your insights and intuitions, guided by the fine-grained understanding of learning and pedagogy that you've developed, to drive the choices that you make in sessions. And know that the insights that you have to contribute—based on your singular strengths and on your own personal and scholarly history—are welcome, within your center and within the field.

QUESTIONS TO DRIVE THE SESSION

Within a learning interaction, we are always confronted with the question "How can I help this student?" Based on the concepts in this chapter, these are questions that you can ask yourself, in the moment, to drive the decisions that you make as a peer educator.

- How can I demonstrate leadership within my learning center, using my experience and training to support others peer tutors in their own growth?

- How can I facilitate connections between the learning center and other communities (e.g., academic departments, clubs, teams, other student-serving programs) on campus?
- How can I apply my unique skills, strengths, and background to supporting the mission of my center?

WAYS TO ENGAGE

Questions for Discussion

1. On your campus, how do people think about your center? What reputation does it have? What would people who use and like it say? What would people who do not like it and who do not use it say? How might you engage with these perceptions, in outreach work (both in liaison activities and in marketing materials) for the center?
2. What topics in learning center theory have been most interesting and resonant for you? What would you be interested in exploring further?
3. What ideas, concepts, and pedagogical tools from your own discipline might be relevant to tutors in other disciplines, providing them with tools or insights in their work with students?
4. Imagine yourself in the situation of a student entering the center for the first time. How could you make it more welcoming and inclusive for them?
5. What resources would be helpful for students in your discipline as they study and work in the center, or in their own spaces using resources provided by the center (e.g., through the center's website)?
6. What resources would be helpful for tutors in addressing recurring issues that arise in the center?

Activities

1. Pair off in groups of two to practice delivering a class visit.
   a. Individually, create notes for a visit to a class that you tutor based on the outline in this chapter. Review your talk to yourself.
   b. In pairs, take turns practicing delivering your class visit. The person in the "audience" role should provide feedback, using the framework as a guide.
2. Working in small groups, develop and seek feedback on project ideas.
   a. Individually, review the "Sample Ideas for Projects" sidebar in this chapter. Based on these examples, generate a list of at least 10 ideas for projects that you would be interested in accomplishing. Don't

worry about being thorough, but do provide enough detail that another person could understand your idea.

b. In a group of three or four, each individual participant should very quickly (about 10 seconds/idea) share their list of 10 ideas. The others in the group should provide feedback on which ideas they feel are most interesting, helpful, realistic, and implementable.

c. As a group, working on filling out each group member's two or three most promising ideas. How would it work? What would the final product look like? What would it mean for the project to succeed?

d. Individually, decide which project idea you are most interested in pursuing.

3. Working in a small group, consider the following scenarios. For each situation, how could you take initiative and/or leadership in addressing it?

a. While working in the center, you overhear a group of students that is having a loud social conversation, and you notice that the students around them look distracted and annoyed.

b. Over the course of several shifts, you've noticed that a particular student consistently makes subtle remarks to one of your fellow tutors about their physical attractiveness.

c. While eating lunch, you overhear a group of students complaining about a series of negative experiences in the learning center, involving a tutor who is consistently late for appointments.

d. You are attending the first day of class for one of your courses, and your professor makes an announcement about the learning center. It is full of inaccuracies, significantly misrepresenting the nature of the services provided by the center.

e. A student who is an acquaintance reaches out to you because they know you are a tutor. They will be studying abroad, and want to know if there is any way they could access tutoring from another country.

f. While studying in the center, you notice several students in the drop-in lab who are waiting for help, trying to make eye contact with one of the tutors. The tutors are having a conversation and do not notice the students.

Questions for Reflection

1. How should the scholarship of learning center theory change and develop? What do you feel are important directions for future growth, for the field as a whole and for your learning center in particular?

References

Alpert, M., & Raiffa, H. (1982). A progress report on the training of probability assessors. In D. Kahneman, P. Slovic, & A. Tversky (Eds.), *Judgment under uncertainty: Heuristics and biases* (294–305). Cambridge, England: Cambridge University Press.

Anderson, L., & Krathwohl, D. A. (2001). *Taxonomy for learning, teaching and assessing: A revision of Bloom's taxonomy of educational objectives.* New York, NY: Longman.

Angelo, T. A., Major, C. H., & Cross, K. P. (2001). *Collaborative learning techniques: A practical guide to promoting learning in groups.* San Francisco, CA: Jossey-Bass Pfeiffer.

Arco-Tirado, J., Fernández-Martín, F., & Fernández-Balboa, J. (2011). The impact of a peer-tutoring program on quality standards in higher education. *Higher Education, 62*(6), 773–788.

Arco-Tirado, J., Fernández-Martín, F., & Hervás Torres, M. (2019). Evidence-based peer tutoring program to improve students' performance at the university. *Studies in Higher Education,* 1–14. doi:https://doi.org/10.1080/03075079.2019.1597038

Arkes, H. R., & Blumer, C. (1985). The psychology of sunk cost. *Organizational Behavior and Human Decision Processes, 35*(1), 124–140. doi:http://dx.doi.org/10.1016/0749-5978(85)90049-4

Arnsten, A. F. (2009). Stress signaling pathways that impair prefrontal cortex structure and function. *Nature Reviews. Neuroscience, 10*(6), 410–422. doi:10.1038/nrn2648

Aronson, J., Fried, C., & Good, C. (2002). Reducing the effects of stereotype threat on African American college students by shaping theories of intelligence. *Journal of Experimental Social Psychology, 38,* 113–125.

Aronson, J., & Inzlicht, M. (2004). The ups and downs of attributional ambiguity: Stereotype vulnerability and the academic self-knowledge of African American students. *Psychological Science, 15,* 829–836.

Ashby, F. G., Isen, A. M., & Turken, A. U. (1999). A neuropsychological theory of positive affect and its influence on cognition. *Psychological Review, 106*(3), 529–550.

Atwater, E. (1981). *I Hear You.* New York, NY: Prentice-Hall.

Banaji, M. R., Hardin, C., & Rothman, A. J. (1993). Implicit stereotyping in-person judgment. *Journal of Personality and Social Psychology, 65*(2), 272–281. doi:10.1037/0022-3514.65.2.272.

Barkley, E. F., Major, C. H., & Cross, K. P. (2014). *Collaborative learning techniques: A handbook for college faculty.* Hoboken, N.J: John Wiley & Sons.

Baron, J., & Hershey, J. C. (1988). Outcome bias in decision evaluation. *Journal of Personality and Social Psychology, 54*(4), 569–579. doi:10.1037/0022-3514.54.4.569

Barsalou, L. W., Niedenthal, P. M., Barbey, A. K., & Ruppert, J. A. (2003). Social embodiment. In B. H. Ross (Ed.), *The psychology of learning and motivation: Advances in research and theory, Vol. 43* (43–92). New York, NY: Elsevier Science. doi:https://doi.org/10.1016/S0079-7421(03)01011-9

Bean, J., & Eaton, S. (2000). The psychology underlying successful retention practices. *Journal of College Student Retention, 3*(1), 73–89.

Beasley, C. (1997). Students as teachers: The benefits of peer tutoring. *Teaching and Learning Forum, 97,* 21–30.

Benjamin, A. S., & Tullis, J. (2010). What makes distributed practice effective? *Cognitive Psychology, 61,* 228–247.

Bergen, J., & Milem, J. (1999). The role of student involvement and perceptions of integration in a causal model of student persistence. *Research in Higher Education, 40*(6), 641–664.

Bloom, B. S. (1956). *Taxonomy of educational objectives.* New York, NY: David McKay Co., Inc.

Brown, D. G., Burg, J. J., & Dominick, J. L. (1998). A strategic plan for ubiquitous laptop computing. *Communications of the ACM, 41,* 26–35.

Brown, D. G., & Petitto, K. R. (2003). The status of ubiquitous computing. *Educause Review, 38,* 25–33.

Butler, H. A., Pentoney, C., & Bong, M. (2017). Predicting real-world outcomes: Critical thinking ability is a better predictor of life decisions than intelligence. Critical thinking, executive functions and their potential relationship. *Thinking Skills and Creativity, 25,* 38–46.

Cantrell, R. (1974). Prolonged exposure to intermittent noise: Audiometric, biochemical, motor, psychological and sleep effects. *Laryngoscope 84*(10), 1–55.

Carpenter, S. K. (2014). Spacing and interleaving of study and practice. In V. A. Benassi, C. E. Overson, & C. M. Hakala (Eds.), *Applying science of learning in education: Infusing psychological science into the curriculum* (131–141). Washington, DC: Society for the Teaching of Psychology.

Carpenter, S. K., & Mueller, F. E. (2013). The effects of interleaving versus blocking on foreign language pronunciation learning. *Memory & Cognition, 41,* 671–682. doi:10.3758/s13421-012-0291-4

Cepeda, N. J, Pashler, H., Vul, E., Wixted, J. T., & Rohrer, D. (2006). Distributed practice in verbal recall tasks: A Review and quantitative synthesis. *Psychological Bulletin, 132*(3), 354–380.

Chapman, L. J., & Chapman, J. P. (1967). Genesis of popular but erroneous diagnostic observations. *Journal of Abnormal Psychology, 72*, 193–204.

Chapman, L. J., & Chapman, J. P. (1969). Illusory correlation as an obstacle to the use of valid psychodiagnostic signs. *Journal of Abnormal Psychology, 74*(3), 271–280. doi:http://dx.doi.org/10.1037/h0027592

Chemero, A. (2009). *Radical embodied cognitive science.* Cambridge, MA: MIT Press.

Clark, A. (1997). *Being there: Putting brain, body, and world together again.* Cambridge, MA: MIT Press.

Colle, H. A., & Welsh, A. (1976). Acoustic masking in primary memory. *Journal of Verbal Learning & Verbal Behavior, 15*, 17–31.

Colvin, J. (2007). Peer tutoring and social dynamics in higher education. *Mentoring and Tutoring, 15*(2), 165–181.

Cooper, E. (2010). Tutoring center effectiveness: The effect of drop-in tutoring. *Journal of College Reading and Learning, 40*(2), 21–34.

Croizet, J. C., Després, G., Gauzins, M. E., Huguet, P., Leyens, J. P., & Méot, A. (2004). Stereotype threat undermines intellectual performance by triggering a disruptive mental load. *Personality and Social Psychology Bulletin, 30*(6), 721–31. doi:10.1177/0146167204263961

Derks, D., Bos, A. E., & Von Grumbkow, J. (2008). Emoticons in computer-mediated communication: Social motives and social context. *Cyberpsychological Behavior, 11*, 99–101.

Devine, P. G. (1989). Stereotypes and prejudice: Their automatic and controlled components. *Journal of Personality and Social Psychology, 56*, 5–18. doi:10.1037/0022-3514.56.1.5

Downes, S. (2010). New technology supporting informal learning. *Journal of Emerging Technologies in Web Intelligence, 2*(1), 27–33.

Duncan, S., & Barrett, L. F. (2007). Affect is a form of cognition: A neurobiological analysis. *Cognition and Emotion, 21*, 1184–1211.

Education Amendments Act of 1972, 20 U.S.C. §§1681 - 1688 (2019).Ellermeier, W., & Hellbruck, J. (1998). Is level irrelevant in "irrelevant speech"? Effects of loudness, signal-to-noise ratio, and binaural unmasking. *Journal of Experimental Psychology: Human Perception and Performance, 24*(5), 1406–14.

Estrada, C. A., Isen, A. M., & Young, M. J. (1997). Positive affect facilitates integration of information and decreases anchoring in reasoning among physicians. *Organizational Behavior and Human Decision Processes, 72*(1), 117–135.

Family Educational Rights and Privacy Act of (1974, 20 U.S.C.) §1232g.

Fischhoff, B., & Beyth, R. (1975). "I knew it would happen": Remembered probabilities of once-future things. *Organizational Behavior and Human Performance, 13*, 1–16.

Flower, L., & Hayes, J. R. (1981). A cognitive process theory of writing. *College Composition and Communication, 32*(4), 365–87.

Folkes, V. S. (1988). The availability heuristic and perceived risk. *Journal of Consumer Research, 15*(1), 13–23.

Freedom of Information and Protection of Privacy Act, R.S.O. (1990, c. F.31) s. 1.

Freire, P. (1972). *Pedagogy of the oppressed*. New York, NY: Herder and Herder.

Garland, H. (1990). Throwing good money after bad: The effect of sunk costs on the decision to escalate commitment to an ongoing project. *Journal of Applied Psychology, 75*(6), 728–731. doi:http://dx.doi.org/10.1037/0021-9010.75.6.728

Gibbs, R. (2006). *Embodiment and cognitive science*. Cambridge, England: Cambridge University Press.

Good, C., Aronson, J., & Inzlicht, M. (2003). Improving adolescents' standardized test performance: An intervention to reduce the effects of stereotype threat. *Journal of Applied Developmental Psychology, 24*, 645–662.

Gordon, T. (1975). *P.E.T.: Parent effectiveness training*. New York, NY: New American Library.

Gray, J. R., Braver, T. S., & Raichle, M. E. (2002). Integration of emotion and cognition in the lateral prefrontal cortex. *Proceedings of the National Academy of Sciences USA, 99*, 4115–4120.

Greenwald, A. G., & Banaji, M. R. (1995). Implicit social cognition: Attitudes, self-esteem, and stereotypes. *Psychological Review, 102*(1), 4–27. doi:10.1037/0033-295x.102.1.4

Grillo, M. C., & Leist, C. W. (2014). Academic support as a predictor of retention to graduation: New insights on the role of tutoring, learning assistance, and supplemental instruction. *Journal of College Student Retention, 15*(3), 387–408.

Gunraj, D., Drumm-Hewitt, A., Dashow, E., Upadhyay, S., & Klin, C. (2016). Texting insincerely: The role of the period in text messaging. *Computers in Human Behavior, 55*(B), 1067–1075.

Hale, K., Krauss, M., Watahomigie, L. J., Yamamoto, A. Y., Craig, C., Masayesva, L. J., & England, N. C. (1992). Endangered languages: On endangered languages and the safeguarding of diversity. *Language 68*(1), 1–42.

Hamilton, D. L., & Gifford, R. K. (1976). Illusory correlation in interpersonal perception: A cognitive basis of stereotypic judgments. *Journal of Experimental Social Psychology, 12*, 392–107.

Hancock, P. A., Ross, J. M., & Szalma, J. L. (2007). A meta-analysis of performance response under thermal stressors. *Human Factors, 49*, 851–877.

Harasim, L. (2012). *Learning theory and online technologies*. New York, NY: Routledge.

Harrow, A. (1972). *A taxonomy of psychomotor domain: A guide for developing behavioral objectives*. New York, NY: David McKay.

Hayes, J. (2000). A new framework for understanding cognition and affect in writing. In J. R. Squire (Ed.), *Perspectives on writing: Research, theory, and practice* (6–44). International Reading Association.

Huber, C. R., & Kuncel, N. R. (2016). Does college teach critical thinking? A meta-analysis. *Review of Educational Research, 86*(2), 431–468.

Janiszewski, C., Noel, H., & Sawyer, A. G. (2003). A meta-analysis of the spacing effect in verbal learning: Implications for research on advertising repetition and consumer memory. *Journal of Consumer Research, 30*, 138–140.

Jones, E., & Nisbett, R. (1971). *The actor and the observer: Divergent perceptions of the causes of behavior*. New York, NY: General Learning Press.

Jones, M., & Kolko, V. (2005). The psychosocial growth of peer mentors in a college program for students on academic probation. Unpublished manuscript, Indiana University, Bloomington, IN.

Kahneman, D., & Tversky, A. (1979). Intuitive prediction: Biases and corrective procedures. *TIMS Studies in Management Science, 12,* 313–327.

Kay, R., & Lauricella, S. (2011). Exploring the benefits and challenges of using laptop computers in higher education classrooms: A formative analysis. *Canadian Journal of Learning and Technology, 37*(1). doi:http://dx.doi.org/10.21432/T2S598

Keenan, C. (2014). *Mapping student-lead peer learning in the UK.* The Higher Education Academy. Retrieved from https://www.heacademy.ac.uk/system/files/resources/peer_led_learning_keenan_nov_14-final.pdf

Kellogg, R. T. (1996). A model of working memory in writing. In C. M. Levy, & S. Ransdell (Eds.), *The science of writing: Theories, methods, individual differences and applications* (57–72). Mahwah, NJ: Lawrence Erlbaum Associates.

Kendi, I. X. (2016). *Stamped from the beginning: The definitive history of racist ideas in America.* New York, NY: Nation Books.

Kendi, I. X. (2020). *How to be an antiracist.* New York, NY: One World.

Koriat, A., Lichtenstein, S., & Fischhoff, B. (1980). Reasons for confidence. *Journal of Experimental Psychology: Human Learning and Memory, 6,* 107–118.

Kostecki, J., & Bers, T. (2008). The effect of tutoring on student success. *The Journal of Applied Research in the Community College, 16*(1), 6–12.

Krathwohl, D. R., Bloom, B. S., & Masia, B. B. (1973). *Taxonomy of educational objectives, the classification of educational goals. Handbook II: Affective domain.* New York, NY: David McKay Co., Inc.

Kraushaar, J. M., & Novak D. C. (2010). Examining the effects of student multitasking with laptops during the lecture. *Journal of Information Systems Education, 21,* 241–251.

Krug, D., Davis, B., & Glover, J. A. (1990). Massed versus distributed repeated reading: A case of forgetting helping recall? *Journal of Educational Psychology, 82,* 366–371.

Kruger, J., & Dunning, D. (1999). Unskilled and unaware of it: How difficulties in recognizing one's own incompetence lead to inflated self-assessments. *Journal of Personality and Social Psychology, 77*(6), 1121–1134.

Kuh, G. D., Kinzie, J., Schuh, J. H., & Whitt, E. J. (2005). *Student success in college: Creating conditions that matter.* San Francisco, CA: Jossey-Bass.

Lakoff, G., & Johnson, M. (1980). *Metaphors we live by.* Chicago, IL: University of Chicago Press.

Landrum, R. E., & Chastain, G. (1998). Demonstrating tutoring effectiveness within a one-semester course. *Journal of College Student Development, 39*(5), 502–508.

Lesiuk, T. (2005). The effect of music listening on work performance. *Psychology of Music, 33*(2), 173–191.Luzzatto, E., & DiMarco, G. (2010). *Collaborative learning: Methodology, types of interactions and techniques.* New York: Nova Science Publishers.

Macrae, C., Bodenhausen, G. V., & Milne, A. B. (1995). The dissection of selection in-person perception: Inhibitory processes in social stereotyping. *Journal of Personality and Social Psychology, 69*(3), 397–407.

Major, B., Spencer, S., Schmader, T., Wolfe, C., & Crocker, J. (1998). Coping with negative stereotypes about intellectual performance: The role of psychological disengagement. *Personality and Social Psychology Bulletin, 24*(1), 34–50. doi:10.1177/0146167298241003

Markovits, H., & Nantel G. (1989). The belief-bias effect in the production and evaluation of logical conclusions. *Memory and Cognition, 17*(1), 11–17. doi:10.3758/BF03199552. PMID 2913452

Marois, R., & Ivanoff, J. (2005). Capacity limits of information processing in the brain. *Trends in Cognitive Sciences, 9*, 296–305.

McDaniel, M. A., & Donnelly, C. M. (1996). Learning with analogy and elaborative interrogation. *Journal of Educational Psychology, 88*, 508–519.

McDaniel, M. A., & Masson, M. E. J. (1985). Altering memory representations through retrieval. *Journal of Experimental Psychology: Learning, Memory, and Cognition, 11*, 371–385.

Menke, D., & Pressley, M. (1994). Elaborative interrogation: Using "why" questions to enhance the learning from text. *Journal of Reading, 37*(8), 642–645.

Miller, D. T., & Norman, S. A. (1975). Actor-observer differences in perceptions of effective control. *Journal of Personality and Social Psychology, 31*(3), 503–515. doi:10.1037/h0076485

Miller, W. R., & Rollnick, S. (1991). *Motivational interviewing: Preparing people to change addictive behavior.* New York, NY: Guilford Press.

National Council of Teachers of English. (1974). *Resolution on the student's right to their own language.* NCTE Annual Business Meeting. New Orleans, LA. Retrieved from http://www.ncte.org/positions/statements/righttoownlanguage

Nisbett, R., Caputo, C., Legant, P., & Marecek, J. (1973). Behavior as seen by the actor and as seen by the observer. *Journal of Personality and Social Psychology, 27*(2), 154–164. doi:10.1037/h0034779

Pashler, H. (1994). Dual-task interference in simple tasks: data and theory. *Psychological Bulletin, 116*, 220–244.

Perkins, D. N., Farady, M., & Bushey, B. (1991). Everyday reasoning and the roots of intelligence. In J. F. Voss, D. N. Perkins, & J. W. Segal (Eds.), *Informal reasoning and education* (83–106). Hillsdale, NJ: Lawrence Erlbaum Associates.

Pickard, M. J. (2007). The new Bloom's taxonomy: An overview for family and consumer sciences. *Journal of Family and Consumer Sciences Education, 25*(1), 45–55.

Pressley, M., McDaniel, M. A., Turnure, I. E., Wood, E., & Ahmad, M. (1987). Generation and precision of elaboration: Effects on intentional and incidental learning. *Journal of Experimental Psychology: Learning, Memory and Cognition, 13*, 291–300.

Pressley, M., Symons, S., McDaniel, M. A., Snyder, B. L., & Turnure, I. E. (1988). Elaborative interrogation facilitates acquisition of confusing facts. *Journal of Educational Psychology, 80*, 268–278.

Rahe, R. H., & Arthur, R. J. (1978). Life change and illness studies: Past history and future directions. *Journal of Human Stress, 4,* 3–15.

Rausch, V., Bauch, E., & Bunzeck, N. (2014). White noise improves learning by modulating activity in dopaminergic midbrain regions and right superior temporal sulcus. *Journal of Cognitive Neuroscience, 26*(7), 1469–1480.

Reed, W. H. (1985). *Positive listening: Learning to hear what people are really saying.* New York, NY: F. Watts.

Reinheimer, D., Grace-Odeleye, B., Francois, G., & Kusorgbor, C. (2010). Tutoring: A support strategy for at-risk students. *The Learning Assistance Review, 15*(1), 23–33.

Richland, L. E., Bjork, R. A., Finley, J. R., & Linn, M. C. (2005). Linking cognitive science to education: Generation and interleaving effects. In B. G. Bara, L. Barsalou, & M. Bucciarelli (Eds.), *Proceedings of the Twenty-Seventh Annual Conference of the Cognitive Science Society* (1850–1855). Mahwah, NJ: Lawrence Erlbaum Associates.

Rogers, C. R. (1951). *Client-centered therapy.* Boston, MA: Houghton-Mifflin.

Rogers, R., & Monsell, S. (1995). The costs of a predictable switch between simple cognitive tasks. *Journal of Experimental Psychology: General, 124,* 207–231.

Rohrer, D. (2012). Interleaving helps students distinguish among similar concepts. *Educational Psychology Review, 24,* 355–367.

Rohrer, D., & Taylor, K. (2007). The shuffling of mathematics problems improves learning. *Instructional Science, 35,* 481–498.

Rohrer, D., Dedrick, R. F., & Stershic, S. (2015). Interleaved practice improves mathematics learning. *Journal of Educational Psychology, 107*(3), 900–908.

Rose, D., & Meyer, A. (2002). *Teaching every student in the digital age: Universal design for learning.* Alexandria, VA: Association for Supervision and Curriculum Development.

Rosenberg, M. B. (2003). Non-violent communication: A language of life. Encinitas, CA: Puddle Dancer.

Rubinstein, J., Meyer, D., & Evans, J. (2001). Executive control of cognitive processes in task switching. *Journal of Experimental Psychology: Human Perception and Performance, 27,* 763–797.

Salamé, P., & Baddeley, A. D. (1986). Phonological factors in STM: Similarity and the unattended speech effect. *Bulletin of the Psychonomic Society, 24,* 263–265.

Sanz de Acedo Lizarraga, M. L., Sanz de Acedo Baquedano, M. T., & Ardaiz Villanueva, O. (2012). Critical thinking, executive functions and their potential relationship. *Thinking Skills and Creativity, 7,* 271–279.

Schmader, T., Johns, M., & Forbes, C. (2008). An integrated process model of stereotype threat effects on performance. *Psychological Review, 115*(2), 336–356. doi:10.1037/0033-295X.115.2.336

Schumacher, E., Seymour, T., Glass, J., Fencsik, D., Lauber, E., Kieras, D., & Meyer, D. (2001). Virtually perfect sharing in dual-task performance: Uncorking the central cognitive bottleneck. *Psychological Science, 12,* 101–108.

Shapiro, L. (2011). *Embodied cognition.* New York, NY: Routledge.

Shehab, H. M., & Nussbaum, E. M. (2015). Cognitive load of critical thinking strategies. *Learning and Instruction, 35,* 51–61. doi:https://doi.org/10.1016/j.learninstruc.2014.09.004

Sherif, M., Taub, D., & Hovland, C. I. (1958). Assimilation and contrast effects of anchoring stimuli on judgments. *Journal of Experimental Psychology, 55*(2), 150–155.

Siemens, G. (2005). Connectivism: A learning theory for the digital age. *International Journal of Instructional Technology and Distance Learning, 2*(1), 3–10.

Simpson, E. J. (1972). *The classification of educational objectives in the psychomotor domain.* Washington, DC: Gryphon House.

Skolnick, R., & Puzo, M. (2008). Utilization of laptop computers in the school of business classroom. *Academy of Educational Leadership Journal, 12,* 1–10.

Smith, E. R., & Semin, G. R. (2007). Situated social cognition. *Current Directions in Psychological Science, 16*(3), 132–135.

Smith, M. A., Blunt, J. R., Whiffen, J. W., & Karpicke, J. D. (2016). Does providing prompts during retrieval practice improve learning? *Applied Cognitive Psychology, 30,* 544–553.

Spencer, S. J., Steele, C. M., & Quinn, D. M. (1999). Stereotype threat and women's math performance. *Journal of Experimental Social Psychology, 35,* 4–28.

Spitzberg, B. (2006). Preliminary development of a model and measure of computer-mediated communication (CMC) competence. *Journal of Computer-Mediated Communication, 11*(2), 629–666.

Stanley, S. M., Markman, H. J., & Blumberg, S. L. (1997). The speaker/listener technique. *The Family Journal: Counseling and Therapy for Couples and Families, 5,* 82–83.

Steele, C. M. (1997). A threat in the air: How stereotypes shape intellectual identity and performance. *American Psychologist, 52*(6), 613–629. doi:10.1037/0003-066X.52.6.613

Steele, C. M., & Aronson, J. (1995). Stereotype threat and the intellectual test performance of African-Americans. *Journal of Personality and Social Psychology, 69,* 797–811.

Stone, J., Perry, W., & Darley, J. (1997). White men can't jump: Evidence for the perceptual confirmation of racial stereotypes following a basketball game. *Basic and Applied Social Psychology, 19*(3), 291–306. doi:10.1207/s15324834basp1903_2

Story, M. F., Mace, R. L., & Mueller, J. (1998). *The universal design file: Designing for people of all ages and abilities.* North Carolina: NC State University, Center for Universal Design.

Strayhorn, T. (2012). *College students' sense of belonging.* New York, NY: Routledge.

Sue, D. W. (2010). *Microaggressions in everyday life: Race, gender, and sexual orientation.* Hoboken, NJ: Wiley.

Sweller, J. (1988). Cognitive load during problem solving: Effects on learning. *Cognitive Science, 12,* 257–285.

Thompson, D., Mackenzie, I. G., Leuthold, H., & Filik, R. (2016). Emotional responses to irony and emoticons in written language: Evidence from EDA and facial EMG. *Psychophysiology, 53,* 1054–1062.

Thurston, A., & Keenan, C. (2014). *A pilot study of reciprocal peer tutoring in Irish medium schools.* Belfast, Ireland: Queen's University Belfast.

Tinto, V. (2015). Through the eyes of students. *Journal of College Student Retention: Research, Theory & Practice, 19*(3), 254–269.

Tombu, M., & Jolicoeur, P. (2004). Virtually no evidence for virtually perfect time-sharing. *Journal of Experimental Psychology: Human Perception and Performance, 30,* 795–810.

Tong, E. (2004). Tutoring aids tutors, learners. *Collaborative Learning, 661,* 253–257.

Tversky, A., & Kahneman, D. (1974). Judgment under uncertainty: Heuristics and biases. *Science (New Series), 185,* 1124–1131.

United Nations Educational, Scientific and Cultural Organization. (1996, June). Universal Declaration of Linguistic Rights. The World Conference on Linguistic Rights. Barcelona, Spain.

Van Selst, M., Ruthruff, E., & Johnston, J. C. (1999). Can practice eliminate the psychological refractory period effect? *Journal of Experimental Psychology: Human Perception and Performance, 25,* 1268–1283.

Varela, F. J., Thompson, E., & Rosch, E. (1991). *The embodied mind: Cognitive science and human experience.* Cambridge, MA: MIT Press.

Vygotsky, L. S. (1978). *Mind in society: The development of higher psychological processes.* Cambridge, MA: Harvard University Press.

Wason, P. C. (1968). Reasoning about a rule. *Quarterly Journal of Experimental Psychology, 20*(3), 273–281. doi:10.1080/14640746808400161

Weaver, B. E., & Nilson, L. B. (2005). Laptops in class: What are they good for? What can you do with them? *New Directions in Teaching and Learning, 101,* 3–13.

West, R., Toplak, M., & Stanovich, K. (2008). Heuristics and biases as measures of critical thinking: Associations with cognitive ability and thinking dispositions. *Journal of Educational Psychology, 100,* 930–941. doi:10.1037/a0012842

Whyte, G. (1986). Escalating commitment to a course of action: A reinterpretation. *Academy of Management Review, 11,* 311–321.

Willoughby, T., & Wood, E. (1994). Elaborative interrogation examined at encoding and retrieval. *Learning and Instruction, 4,* 139–149.

Woloshyn, V. E., Willoughby, J. T., Wood, I. E., & Pressley, M. (1990). Elaborative interrogation facilitates adult learning of factual paragraphs. *Journal of Educational Psychology, 82,* 513–524.

Wong, B. Y. L. (1985). Self-questioning instructional research: A review. *Review of Educational Research, 55*(2), 227–268. https://doi.org/10.3102/00346543055002227

Xu, Y., Hartman, S., Uribe, G., & Mencke, R. (2014). The effects of peer tutoring on undergraduate students' final examination scores in mathematics. *Journal of College Reading and Learning, 32,* 22–31.

Yeung, N., & Monsell, S. (2003). Switching between tasks of unequal familiarity: The role of stimulus-attribute and response-set selection. *Journal of Experimental Psychology: Human Perception and Performance, 29,* 455–469.

Index

College Reading and Learning Association International Peer Tutor Training Program Certification (ITTPC) topics appear in the index in **bold**.

Page numbers in *italics* refer to figures, tables and boxes.

memory: long-term, 22–31, 104; short-term, *111–12*; working, 22–31, 76, 77
message boards tutoring interactions, 157, 159, *160*
metacognition, 32
metacognitive knowledge, 140, *141*, 142–43
microaggressions, *120–21*
Miller, W. R., 82, 84
mindfulness, 77
Modelling problem-solving, 6, 37–41, 141–143
MOOC. *See* Massive Open Online Course (MOOC)
Motivational Interviewing, *82–84*
Mueller, Pam, *105, 106*
multitasking, *94–95*

neurodiversity, peer tutoring across, 127–29
neurons, 75, *76*
neurotransmitters, role in learning, 74–77
Nussbaum, E. M., 136

online collaborative learning theory, *159*
online tutoring, 151–70; direct messaging, 156–57, *158*; message boards, 157, 159, *160*; text chat, 160–62, *162*; video chat, 163–64, *165*; whiteboards, 164, 166, *166*
Oppenheimer, Daniel, *105, 106*
outcome bias, *145*
overconfidence effect, *145*

pedagogy, 54, 154; critical, *35–36*; definition of, 35; learning center, 35–51
peer observations, 173, 175; feedback form, *175–76*
peer review, 46
peer tutoring, x–xi, 1–13, 53; across linguistic and cultural diversity, 123–27; across neurodiversity, 127–29; and affective domain, 71–87;

benefits of, 3–4; definition of, 6–7; diverse student body, engaging, 118–22; long-term memory and, 24–31; and students' right to privacy, 9–10; working memory and, 24–41
Pentoney, C., 136
persistence, *80*
planning fallacy, *145*
post-racism, *122*
practice in pairs, 47
prefrontal cortex, 74–77
prioritization of time, *54–55*
procedural knowledge, 140, *141*
project creation, 176–77; sample ideas for, *177–78*
punctuations, *161–62*

Raichle, M. E., 75
Rausch, V., 103
reading, 108–9; basic framework for, *110*; and elaborative interrogation, *108–9*
Referral skills, 54, 68
Reinheimer, D., 4
repeated recall, *96, 98*
responding to questions, *63–66*
The role of learning centers in higher education, 8–11
Role modelling, 6, 37–41, 89–116, 141–143
Rose, D., 128
Round Robin, 46–47
rushes of students, *60*

sample weekly schedule, *99–100*
Sanz de Acedo Baquedano, M. T., 136
Sanz de Acedo Lizarraga, M. L., 136
scaffolding, 38, 40, 41, 140, 153; direct messaging, 157; in drop-in labs, 59, 62; in group learning, 63
schemas: and academic learning, 19–21; cognitive, 15–19; and tutoring, 19–21; and writing process, *111–12*
scholarship of peer-led learning, *180*
Self-regulated learning, brain learning, and/or memory, 15–33

About the Author

Daniel R. Sanford, PhD, is a cognitive linguist, composition scholar, and learning center administrator. He is the director of writing and of the Academic Resource Commons at Bates College in Lewiston, Maine; prior to this he was the director of the Center for Academic Program Support at the University of New Mexico. His research interests are learning centers, writing centers, linguistics, language rights, cognitive science, and faculty development. He holds a Level IV Learning Center Leadership Certification from the National College Learning Center Association.

CPSIA information can be obtained
at www.ICGtesting.com
Printed in the USA
BVHW030937130322
630955BV00003B/12